July 2000

THE LEYS SCHOOL
CAMBRIDGE
CB2 2AD

With Compliments

Geoff Houghton

PHONE 01223 508900 (exchange) - FAX 01223 505333

GW00481860

Well-regulated minds and improper moments

A history of The Leys School

by Geoff and Pat Houghton

Writing out the following line a varying number of times was a
punishment at The Leys for nearly a century:

"Few things are more distressing to a well-regulated mind than
to see a boy who ought to know better, desporting himself at
improper moments."

E.E. Kellett (Leys Staff 1889-1924)

ISBN 0 9501721 8 9

Published by The Governors of The Leys School, Cambridge.
Printed by Chris Godden Design
at Hart-Talbot Printers, Saffron Walden, Essex
2000

Contents

Preface

Several years before North B House reached its Centenary in 1983, I realised, as Housemaster, that stories about life in the House needed recording. I had also become interested in the life of James Hilton, which then led me to seek information about W.H. Balgarnie, the real "Mr. Chips". I was further stimulated by correspondence from Old Leysians and others wishing to know some specific thing about the school. Gradually, the idea of writing another history of the school emerged. Readers will find that, rather than covering the stages of the school through its 125 years, I have taken a 'thematic' approach. The book can therefore be used as a kind of reference source or something that, hopefully, provides interest for all. I hope that Chapter 1 will now correct anyone's ideas that Robert Sayle ever lived in The Leys house. He owned and lived in the house further along Trumpington Road, which is now the premises of the Preparatory department of the Perse School for Boys.

I am aware that I have not followed too closely the story of the enormous debt which the school got into, and the struggles of the Governors to find funds to clear that debt. A more complete picture can be found in Derek Baker's *Partnership in Excellence.* Nor have I shown the rise in fees or salaries, since the value of today's money is difficult to compare with that of the past. There have been epidemics and occasionally pupils have died whilst at school. These I have not dealt with either. There have been countless visits, lectures and demonstrations. Anyone wanting more information about these activities can find the material in issues of *The Fortnightly.*

I am particularly aware that there are few references to girls in this book. That is because this is essentially a history, and girls are only part of the very recent history of the school, so most of the events dealt with occurred before they came. They have already made a tremendous impact on the present life of the school, but there has not yet been a sufficient lapse of time for them to be listed as "famous women".

I cannot express how much I am indebted to my wife, Pat. She has spent hours, armed with a red pen, correcting the manuscript of this book. We have often discussed the meaning of a passage which she has expressed more clearly so that you, the reader, should understand what are sometimes complex issues. I therefore felt it appropriate that her name should be linked with mine as co-author.

Geoff Houghton

Acknowledgements and Sources

The documents of the early history of The Leys Estate are now lodged in the Cambridge Record Office at the Shire Hall. They consist of the Enclosure Act of 1811, the conveyances of the separate strips of land, copies of the will of Thomas Hovell, the marriage certificate of his nephew and his consequent change of name, by deed poll, to Morgan Treherne, together with the marriage certificate of Robert Sayle. The rate books of the parish of St. Mary the Less and the Census Returns for 1861, 1871 and 1881, also in the County Record Office, give an insight into the history of the house. My thanks go to John Durrant, who was at one time Mayor of Cambridge, for providing information about Thomas Hovell and for giving permission for his portrait in Cambridge Guildhall to be photographed by my wife, who also took the photographs of the Revd Dr. J.C.A. Barrett, Malcolm Lowry's house and gravestone, the Wesley artefacts and the one of the chapel on the dust jacket. I am similarly grateful to the Trustees of Wesley's Chapel, 49 City Road, London for permission to reproduce the portrait of John Wesley in Chapter 18. Many of the colour photographs were taken by Tim Rawle for two recent editions of the school prospectus and my thanks go to him for permission to use them in this book.

The 123 years of issues of *The Fortnightly*, together with the twenty one editions of *The Leys Handbook and Directory,* were an invaluable source of material. I have used the Governors' Minute Books from 1874 to 1958 and I am grateful for permission to use these. Derek Baker kindly gave his permission for me to quote from *Partnership in Excellence*. Priscilla Douglas and Pauline Humphries allowed me to use information about Caldicott School from their book *The House that Bartlett Built - the story of the Caldicott Site in Hitchin*. I am grateful to Old Leysians for their letters about their time at school. Many of them are now dead, including Gilbert Thomas who gave permission for me to use his *Autobiography* as long ago as 1977. E.O. Brieger (E.O. Blake) kindly gave permission for me to use his essay on his internment. As Leys archivist, I have provided information for the various publications about Malcolm Lowry which both Sherrill Grace in Canada, and Gordon Bowker in London have produced, and I have quoted from their books. I was fortunate to be allowed by his cousins, Rowland and Elizabeth Hill, both now deceased, to examine and copy the small archive of James Hilton which existed.

The section on Moulton was taken mainly from his biography, written by his sons, W.F. and J.H. Moulton, together with a small retrospective diary written by Moulton's sister, Elizabeth, describing the last five weeks of his life. This diary was kindly donated to the archives by Mrs Marjorie Moulton, widow of Harold, the grandson of the first Headmaster. I am grateful to Bertie Bellis and John Barrett for advice on their respective sections in the chapter on *The Headmasters* and also to Bill Humphrey for providing extra material about his father, Gerald. John Barrett also provided the last paragraph of Chapter 15. The small entry on The Leysian Mission was produced from the entries in *The Leys Handbook*. Many of the entries in the later editions had been written by Miss E.M. Pook, who has written a much fuller history of the Mission. Similarly, F.M. White's *A Short History of St. Faith's* was a valuable source, supplemented by help from the present Headmaster, Richard Dyson, and the Registrar, Mrs Sue Grice. Tony Lees and Peter Watson, both of whom were "exiled" in Scotland, have read the chapter on the school's time in Pitlochry. John Harding also read most of the book in manuscript, and made invaluable revisions, and where would I have been without Maurice Howard, who as ever, was on the end of a telephone and willing to answer my questions. The archivist of Addenbrooke's Hospital, Philip Rundle, kindly gave me access to papers relating to the hospital's wartime occupation of the school. I am grateful to Nigel Washbourn for assistance with the Old Leysian Golfing section and to Christopher Godden for his help with the section about the Old Leysian Lodge. I owe much to him for his assistance in getting this book printed, and I also thank David Mason of Hart-Talbot Printers Ltd and all members of their staff for their invaluable assistance in its production. I am also indebted to Margaret Bird, Marilyn Buck and Doreen Cawte for helping to publicise this book.

When Derek Baker listed his sources in *Partnership in Excellence,* he commented that there was a mass of material in the school archives which need to be sorted. Twenty five years later there is even more! I have attempted to sort and catalogue some of the papers and ephemera, but much work remains to be done. Perhaps the author of the next history of the school will be able to succeed where we have failed.

Geoff Houghton

The Leys, 2000

CHAPTER ONE

Early Days

To understand The Leys, its name and its foundation, it is first necessary to understand two Parliamentary Acts. The first was one of the Enclosure Acts. In the late 1700s, pieces of Common Land were being 'enclosed' by wealthy persons to make their use more efficient. The site where the school would later be established then consisted of several strips of land. A local businessman named Thomas Hovell, who owned both the site where Eaden Lilley's department store later stood in Market Street, and the site where Heffer's Bookshop in Trinity Street has been built, enclosed the various pieces of land on Coe Fen Leys into one estate by an Act of Parliament dated 1811. In some cases he purchased the strips of land; in others he exchanged for them land which he already owned elsewhere in the town.

In the words of the Act:

"And whereas the said Coe otherwise Cow Fen Leys, lie in an open State, intermixed and dispersed in small Parcels, and yield but little profit, and the same in their present State are incapable of any considerable Improvement, and it would be advantageous if the same were divided and inclosed [sic], and specific Shares thereof were allotted to the several Owners thereof and Persons interested therein, in proportion and according to their respective Estates, Rights and Interests: but in as much as such Division, Allottment and Inclosure cannot be effected without the Aid and Authority of Parliament."

Hovell built the house in 1815 that was later to become the residence of the Headmasters of The Leys. He was a well known figure in the town, becoming the first of the Mayors of Cambridge in the style still prevalent today, set up by the Metropolitan Corporation Act in 1835. A fine portrait of him hangs in the Cambridge Guildhall. The name of The Leys Estate was given to the enclosed land - a ley being a piece of meadowland. His nephew, Morgan Treherne, owned the house for a few years after Hovell's death, leasing it to various Cambridge businessmen to house them and their families. One of these was John Dennis, another draper, who had had a shop in Sidney Street. In 1861, a General Census return shows that the house was empty. It is probable that during this empty period some alterations were done to it, perhaps most notably the construction of an arched doorway complete with doors, between the sitting and dining rooms. When these doors were renovated during the Headmastership of Mr Bertie Bellis, the workmen discovered that brown wrapping paper addressed to John Dennis' shop with the date 1861 was glued to the inside of the planks used in making the doors.

The Trustees who eventually founded The Leys chose to keep the name of the estate for the new school. For a short while in the 1930s, the name was shortened to Leys School, with some of the Governors using the argument that other well known schools such as Eton College did not include the definite article in their titles. However, there was considerable pressure from Old Leysians and others for the return of 'The' in the title and so it was quickly reinstated.

The second Act of Parliament which was instrumental in the founding of The Leys was one of the so called Test Acts. The Test Acts had come into force in the 1600s when anyone wishing to hold public or military office had to profess his belief in the teachings of the Church of England, and to take communion according to its rites. Gradually the application of these Acts to various positions had been eased. By 1855 non-conformists could obtain BA and MA degrees at Cambridge and MA degrees at Oxford University. The final Test Act which had been a bar to holding University offices, including professorial chairs, lectureships and being Heads of Colleges, and also to proceeding to higher degrees, was repealed in 1871.

In the mid-1800s the whole question of improving secondary education in England was being addressed. Derek Baker in *Partnership in Excellence* (published in 1975) gives a full and scholarly account in his first two chapters of the background which led to the founding of The Leys. Although there were already several leading schools which offered an education for the sons of ministers, Methodists were asking for schools for sons of lay members of their church. Prior to 1871 there had been discussions over

2

founding a school at Twickenham. The removal of the final Test Act added impetus to the question of higher education for Methodist families. In 1871, the Revd William Arthur, who had been the first Principal of the Methodist College, Belfast, suggested at the annual Methodist Conference that a committee should investigate what steps could be taken to make use of the altered circumstances of the two Universities.

The committee was given two tasks. One was to consider improvements in the new Kingswood and Woodhouse Grove Schools, and the other to look at the situation in Oxford and Cambridge. Its convenor was Dr William Fiddian Moulton, who was Tutor at Richmond College, a Methodist theological college. Much of the committee's time was spent in inquiring into the management of the two schools. However, some of their findings would inevitably be reflected in the second part of their task. The special committee was reappointed at the Methodist Conference of 1872. Two of its specific tasks were those of deciding whether or not it was desirable to found a public school and an undergraduate hostel at Cambridge, and suggesting practical steps to advance the Methodist cause in Oxford. At first it had been thought that Oxford might be chosen as the site both of the school and the hostel, since this had been Wesley's own university and the roots of Methodism were there. However, one thing that seems to have influenced the committee not to choose Oxford was that John Wesley once commented that 'Oxford men had too much side'.

The committee sent a deputation of three to Oxford and to Cambridge to seek information from members of the University and teachers in the two cities. In Cambridge, as well as talking to representatives of the University, they questioned both the Headmaster of the Perse School and a master at the Perse who took some boarders into his home. Remarkably, both of these men were Wesleyan Methodists. As well as asking questions about what influence the undergraduates of the University might have on the school and whether the moral life of the pupils would be affected by them, the three wished to find out if it would be possible to get young graduate members to help with teaching and also whether Cambridge was a healthy town to live in. Following their visit, any misgivings that they may have had were removed.

It was felt that the temptations of Oxford or Cambridge were no worse than those of any large town or city and that in fact there could be a positive value in locating the school in either, since members of the school would be

Thomas Hovell

The Leys House circa 1865

better prepared for undergraduate life through their proximity to the University. However, it was strongly urged that contact with undergraduates should be restricted, and in fact the rule books of the 1970s still stated that undergraduates' rooms were out of bounds unless specific visits were permitted by the Housemaster.

Whilst the official committees had been meeting and producing their reports, there had been much discussion and negotiation about setting up a proposal for Cambridge to be the front runner as the site for the new school. As early as December 1871, Joseph Ryder had approached Robert Sayle and explained that a committee was investigating the possibility of founding a school in either Oxford or Cambridge.

Robert Sayle was a Cambridge businessman and a good Wesleyan, who owned a shop (which still carries his name but is a branch of the John Lewis Partnership) and who also rented a farm opposite to the Hills Road Methodist Chapel, from Jesus College. Ryder asked Sayle if he would be prepared to give up the farm so that it could be purchased as a site for a school. However, on the previous day Sayle had received a letter from Morgan Treherne, the owner of The Leys Estate, offering him this property for purchase. After more discussion with Ryder, Robert Sayle agreed to purchase the estate. At the time the house was occupied by a Dr George Humphrey, who was Professor of Surgery at the nearby Addenbrooke's Hospital and no relation at all to the fourth headmaster of The Leys. He had for some time used the house as a hostel for undergraduates, and this added weight to the suitability of the site for a new school. It had also been suggested that the far side of the grounds, where the Sports Hall now stands, would be an ideal situation for the undergraduate hostel. Eventually the idea of a twin development was ruled out by the committee in its final recommendations.

It is interesting that in the mid-1800s various sites were investigated in Cambridge for a railway station. One of the areas suggested was, in fact, the site where the Sports Hall now stands. Fortunately this area was not selected. Had it been, the estate would certainly not have been considered so suitable for a school. T.P. Walker, who had joined the staff in 1875, recalled in Early Recollections of The Leys:

"It is said that it was desired to rent the house as a residence for the Prince of Wales while he was keeping terms at the University

5

in 1861. But the idea, if ever entertained, came to nothing, and
the Prince lived at Madingley Hall, 4 miles away."

Sayle's shop ledger shows that on 27 September, 1872 he received
£14,275-1s-4d for the Leys Estate from the Wesleyan trustees. As well as
being prepared to help the cause of Methodism in Cambridge, he was a good
businessman, since he thus made about £1,000 profit in six months. He also
had a guarantee that if the site was not used for the proposed school he could
repurchase it at the same price. It was rumoured that a Cambridge builder
had offered him a higher price for the land to become a housing
development. The nine Trustees were the Revd William Arthur, J.S. Budgett,
John Chubb, R. Haworth, James Heald, Sir Francis Lycett, Alexander
McArthur, William McArthur, and William Mewburn.

Another architect of the Cambridge proposal was the Revd Thomas
Adams who was Superintendent of the Cambridge Circuit. His brother-in-
law, Henry French, had been strongly in favour of Oxford as the site for the
new school. Adams invited French to come to Cambridge and when he saw
the Estate and heard of the secret progress which had already been made, he
was convinced that Cambridge should be chosen. Although he strongly
supported Cambridge as the site at the next committee meeting in February
1873, the committee passed a resolution in favour of founding a school but
did not yet finalise its location.

A week later Sir Francis Lycett suggested to Sir William McArthur that
they should secure a site at Twickenham. As early as 1847, he and his wife
had been present at a meeting in London to consider a project of a Methodist
school for the sons of laymen. It would seem that somewhere between this
meeting and 1872, a site was proposed in Twickenham and that Sir Francis
had taken the committee's indecision as to where to site the school as an
opportunity for him to secure and offer the Twickenham one. However Sir
William said that he and his brother, Alexander, would not do anything about
that until the Cambridge proposal had been properly looked into. The next
day Sir Francis and Alexander McArthur went to Cambridge and visited The
Leys Estate. On seeing the house, Alexander said "Twickenham will not do
after this; the Committee will have to reverse its decision." Joseph Ryder
then invited T.P. Bunting, who had also been against Cambridge being
chosen as the site, to visit the town. After a few days Bunting also became
in favour of the scheme.

6

A comprehensive report was presented to the Methodist Higher Education Committee on 2 July, 1873. In stating 'that it is desirable to establish a good Public School upon the Leys Estate, Cambridge', it went on to say that the school should be under Methodist management but open to boys belonging to other churches. It also stipulated that if a Chaplain should be appointed he should be non-resident and be appointed by the Wesleyan Conference. It went on to suggest how money should be raised to fund the school and the construction of new buildings on the site. It laid out a scheme of Donors and Life Donors which had been used by other Public Schools to raise money. The Donors (who gave £50) and Life Donors (who gave £100) had the right to nominate pupils to be educated at the school.

The report suggested that during the period of attempting to raise £15,000, if the ordinary annual fee was eighty guineas, then pupils nominated by Donors would have their fees reduced to seventy-five guineas and those nominated by Life Donors reduced to seventy guineas. The requirement for becoming a Life Donor remained at £100 until 1983. It was then raised to £500 but subsequently, with the falling value of money, it was set at 20% of the annual boarding fees, so that in the late 1990s a donation in excess of £2000 was required to become a Life Donor. Life Donors are still to this day responsible for electing some of the Governors at their annual meeting, although they usually choose to confirm a list of names submitted by the existing Governing Body.

The sub-committee did not recommend the establishment of an undergraduate hostel either in the school grounds or elsewhere in Cambridge. Instead they suggested that should a Chaplain be appointed to the school, he might take undergraduates into his house. In this way Methodist parents would feel confident that if they sent their sons to Cambridge University they would be in the hands of someone they could trust.

The third matter dealt with by the report was what should happen in Oxford. The Superintendent of the Oxford Circuit, Revd F. Greeves, had suggested a scheme which involved enlargement and alterations to the Methodist Chapel in Oxford, the paying-off of an existing debt, and the erection of a vestry and a Minister's house. The estimated cost of this would be around £5,000. The proposals were endorsed by the sub-committee, who said they felt that the interests of Methodism would be greatly promoted by this scheme in the University and City of Oxford.

The report of the subcommittee was accepted unanimously by the Higher Education Committee. They, in turn, agreed to ask Conference to appoint two separate committees to implement the proposals for Oxford and Cambridge, to confirm Ebenezer Jenkins as fund-raiser and to provide for a full and favourable consideration of the scheme by Conference.

The committee had made enquiries of headmasters of other Public Schools all over the country about principles of management, fees and curriculum. Some of its members had visited Marlborough and Haileybury Colleges, and Charterhouse. Other information was received from Rossall, Cheltenham, Clifton and Bradfield. It was Marlborough which proved to have the greatest influence on the structure of the new school. At the time second only to Eton in numbers, Marlborough had a very successful record of winning open scholarships to Oxford and Cambridge.

Dr Moulton was asked to become Headmaster of the new school, a proposition which he had not anticipated. In the previous year, 1874, at the Newcastle Methodist Conference he had said:

"...the Headmaster made or marred a school, ... the post must be made attractive enough to secure the services of a first class man."

It was typical of him that he should have been quite unconscious that it might be upon him that the "making or marring" would depend. After a great struggle with his conscience as to whether he should accept the post or not, for he thought himself "incapable of such responsibilities", he finally decided that he should do so "as a matter of obedience" in January 1875. How far the scheme on which The Leys School was framed was of his own devising will never be known for certain, but the three fundamental principles seem to have their origin in him:-

"Everything was to be of the best quality"

"Religion should be the underlying principle of all elements of school life"

"Although Methodist, it must be free from a narrowly sectarian character"

The first pupils were all from English Methodist families. J.C. Isard, chosen to be the Prefect, transferred from Queen's College, Taunton. In all there were sixteen boys, including one of Dr Moulton's sons, James Hope Moulton. The estate consisted of undulating, wooded parkland surrounding the house which was to become the Headmaster's House and some "half-finished buildings" attached to it.

The first day was described in *The Fortnightly*:

"Tuesday, the 16th of February, 1875, brought to The Leys School its first small band of scholars. The true February day, with cloud above and mud beneath, did little to beautify the half-finished buildings and slough-like roads which were the first features presented to the gaze of the hardy explorers of that unknown region - the new school. But light hearts and sanguine hopes needed much to dampen them in the presence of a kind reception and novelty of scene: so doleful looks and words were at a discount from the beginning. The first on the ground was Jenks, who lost no time in forwarding the interests of the school by accompanying the Second Master (Mr Vinter) and one of the Governors in their search for a convenient site for a cricket pitch. When dinner-hour arrived some half-dozen boys, with such friends and masters as had put in an appearance, were entertained by Dr Moulton and his lady. This was a trying time for the youth of the party, who, strange to each other's faces, names and pursuits, awed by the august presence of their future Headmaster and other dignitaries of the place, did not find the conversation flow spontaneously among themselves, yet were ill-content to desert their fellows and borrow the topics or join the discussions of their elders. But the programme was admirably arranged to familiarise them with the locality and set them at ease with each other. Under Mr Vinter's friendly guidance the town was inspected, a fair idea of its general character and of the University and College buildings being obtained. The shadows would have lengthened had there been any sunshine to allow such an operation when the sightseers returned to join the late arrivals. "Tea came - and went," and then the young school began to realise its existence as we drew together and whiled the time away with anecdote or ever bolder mutual questioning.

The many classrooms, the spacious dining-hall existed then only in the brain or on paper of the architect. Walls indeed had risen, marking out the present schoolroom, No.1 classroom and dormitories Nos. 1 and 2; but none of these were tenable when "The Original XVI" took possession. The names of these adventurers should here be chronicled for the edification of those who have entered into their labours; they are H.G. Atkinson, H. Benson, R.A.H. Bickford-Smith, I. Blore, W.S. Ellis, J.L.B. Gedye, J.C. Isard, J.W. Jenks, R.G. Lindsay, J.P. McArthur, J.H. Matthews, J.H. Moulton, H.T. Parke, J.M. Richards, W.G. Richardson, R.M. Richardson."

Dr Moulton, before sending them to bed in rooms in his own house, announced that Isard was to be Prefect and McArthur and Bickford-Smith Dormitory Captains . The next morning all the pupils were tested in various subjects so that the programme for the term could be arranged. In the afternoon the Games Committee (at that time called the Football Committee) was inaugurated. Their first act was to order the purchase of an Association football and goal-posts. There were obviously not enough pupils to contemplate starting Rugby yet. They were also told that only one street was in bounds - the main one leading as far as the Round Church. However, on the Friday they were allowed to go to the river and watch the occupants of the University boat practising.

Only four weeks later, building work had sufficiently progressed for the formal Opening Day to take place. The boys had been able to move into No. 1 Dormitory the night before, which they decorated with flags and garlands to receive their guests. *The Fortnightly* continued its story:

> "When the next morning brought the visitors the labours of recent hours showed good results; sloughs had become neatly gravelled roads, and barren, brick-strewn earth was transformed into shrub-decked lawns and garden-beds. As the morning drew on towards midday guests flocked in, until the gaily arrayed upper-room was occupied by a goodly company."

A service was held in this room and during the address the objects and hopes of the School were set forth. After the closing prayers, the entire company, including the boys, moved along Trumpington Street to the Guildhall where a cold lunch was provided from the kitchens of St. John's College. There were over one hundred guests at the lunch, after which several speeches were made including eulogies about Dr Moulton and his wife.

That following Sunday was the birthday of the Headmaster and the next day the boys were given a Whole Holiday, a tradition which continued until his death. After such an exciting start to the life of their new school, it must have been quite difficult for the sixteen to settle down to a daily routine.

By the beginning of the second term the boys were accommodated in both of the dormitories, school-room and class-room which were now complete with the exception of some desks and other pieces of furniture. The adapted buildings also improved the quality of life for the boys. The gymnasium was sufficiently complete for use early in June. The building which had once served as the coach-house and harness-room for the original house was being rapidly transformed into a laboratory by the addition of benches, gas and water pipes and other appliances. Workshops for carpentry and engineering were being constructed and improvised Fives and Rackets courts provided. The bathing shed had been completed beside the river, and it was put to good use in fine weather.

The Leys School had been established on firm foundations in a remarkably short time.

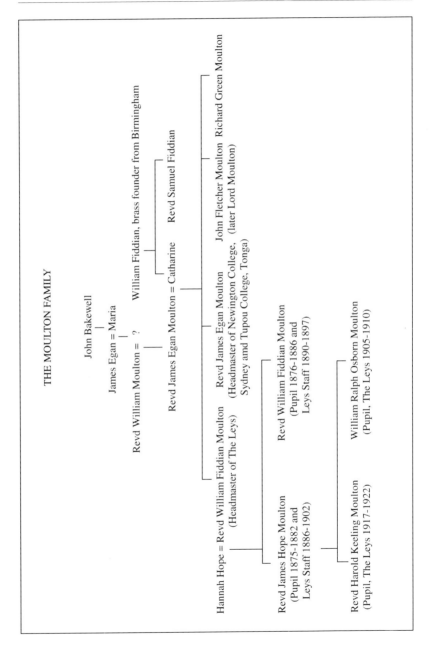

THE MOULTON FAMILY

John Bakewell

James Egan = Maria

Revd William Moulton = ?

William Fiddian, brass founder from Birmingham

Revd James Egan Moulton = Catharine   Revd Samuel Fiddian

Revd James Egan Moulton
(Headmaster of Newington College,
Sydney and Tupou College, Tonga)

John Fletcher Moulton Richard Green Moulton
(later Lord Moulton)

Hannah Hope = Revd William Fiddian Moulton
(Headmaster of The Leys)

Revd William Fiddian Moulton
(Pupil 1876-1886 and
Leys Staff 1890-1897)

William Ralph Osborn Moulton
(Pupil, The Leys 1905-1910)

Revd James Hope Moulton
(Pupil 1875-1882 and
Leys Staff 1886-1902)

Revd Harold Keeling Moulton
(Pupil, The Leys 1917-1922)

CHAPTER TWO

The Headmasters

The Leys was very fortunate to have such a eminent scholar and committed Methodist as its first Headmaster in William Fiddian Moulton. His life was so different from what it would have been today that it is worth including here some material from the biography published just after his death by his son. William Fiddian Moulton was descended from John Bakewell, an intimate friend of John Wesley. Bakewell's daughter, Maria, married James Egan and their daughter, in turn, married the Revd William Moulton. They had 15 children but only nine reached adulthood. One of them was destined to become a Methodist minister, James Egan Moulton and he was the father of William Fiddian Moulton, born 14 March 1835 and destined to become the first Headmaster of The Leys.

There are very few records of William's early life. However there was a story that when his father left the Wednesbury Circuit, the new Minister and his wife were greeted by the Stewards who apologised for the condition in which they feared they would find the crockery of the house. The previous minister, they said, had a little boy, only three or four years old who had a mischievous habit of smashing crockery. It was suggested that William had thus worked off his allotted portion of original sin before he went to school.

The pleasures of crockery smashing soon gave way to a passion for study. He showed little interest in sport and preferred to read a book whilst the other boys were in the playground. He said in later years that his non-involvement in games was due to poor eyesight - he was short-sighted enough to have to wear glasses from the age of eleven. He confessed to boys at school that he regretted not having been able to play cricket, which was a game he followed with great enthusiasm.

He was sent to Woodhouse Grove School, near Leeds, one of the two institutions founded by John Wesley for the education of the sons of

Methodist preachers. His time there must have helped to prepare him for the management of a boarding school in later life. He was to recall that four of his school friends died whilst he was there and he had no doubt that the small, ill-ventilated dormitories were responsible for their deaths. There were other privations. Breakfast consisted of a thick slice of dry bread and about half a pint of milk, slightly warmed in winter. Supper was an exact repetition of breakfast. They never saw butter, tea or coffee. During the Irish potato famine of 1848, badly cooked rice was served as a substitute.

The pupils were isolated from the world outside. The French Revolution of 1848, which led to the Second Republic, was little more than a rumour. However the cholera panic of 1849 did extend to the school, even in the absence of newspapers.

In 1850, at the age of fifteen, Moulton left Woodhouse Grove for Wesley College, Sheffield where he was to remain for the next three years. Here he qualified to matriculate at London University. Despite the College being better staffed in those days than any other school open to him, he was compelled to wait for the annual visit of the External Examiner in Mathematics to get assistance with the advanced problems that were causing him difficulties. Among the other subjects which interested him at this time were Hebrew, chemistry, practical mechanics and music both theoretical and practical. Whilst at Wesley College, he played the organ regularly.

In 1853, he became a master at a private school in Devonport for a year, before securing a post to teach Mathematics at Queen's College, Taunton. As a junior master, his duties took up long hours. With the exception of one hour, from 7 to 8, he was busy from 6 am to 9 pm. Since junior masters were not provided with a study of their own, he worked in his bedroom standing at his chest of drawers. When the gas was turned off at 10.30, he lit a candle and continued working at higher mathematics until midnight. He obtained his London University BA in 1854 with honours in Mathematics, and two years later his MA, being awarded the Gold Medal for Mathematics and Natural Philosophy.

For some time he had been contemplating entering the ministry. After the rigorous test by the authorities of his Circuit and District, he came before what was known as the "July Committee", which represented the Methodist Church as a whole. The marks he received on every test were the very highest possible, and the Conference accepted him for "Home, Immediate"

Revd Dr. W.F. Moulton, Headmaster 1875-1898

Tutor at Richmond College

Dr. Moulton in 1893

Dr. Moulton with his wife, Hannah

Standing at his desk

15

which meant work in Great Britain rather than abroad and without a preliminary three years at College, which was deemed unnecessary in his case. He now had to pass through four years of probation, prior to ordination. At first he was put down for Circuit work at Blackburn, but the Revd Benjamin Hellier strongly contended that his correct position should be as a teacher, and he was appointed Assistant Tutor at Richmond College. Here he stayed for ten years as Assistant Tutor and a further six years as Classical Tutor.

At one time, shortly after entering the ministry, William had strongly considered being a missionary. However, it was never his habit to choose his own path, and he accepted that if those in authority in his church had marked out a certain course for him, he should accept it. In conversation with a missionary who had returned on leave from China, William confided that he had often thought of an appointment in China. When it was reported to the Missionary Committee that Moulton would like to go to China, the secretaries replied that grateful as they were for his offer, they thought that he would do more for the mission cause by training men at Richmond for such service, rather than by going out to the foreign field himself.

During his period at Richmond, he became a close friend of Revd Hellier who had been responsible for his appointment. They would go for long walks together in Richmond, and William appreciated his advice. The friendship was to continue into the early days of Moulton's headship at The Leys, with Hellier becoming a Governor of the school. Hellier translated the school song from Latin into English. It had been originally composed by B. F. Westcott, later Bishop of Durham, who was another close friend of Moulton's through the work both of them had done on the revision of the New Testament.

A week's work for Moulton might involve teaching Hebrew to one year group, and Greek to another. He also took classes in Animal Physiology, Chemistry and Physics and assisted in playing the College organ. As well as being a formal teacher, Moulton was constantly accessible to give guidance. At first his rooms were in the tower at the College, and he would strike many of the newly invented matches before his fire could be persuaded to light on a winter's morning. One morning he counted eighty-three failures before success. Many students' troubles were lightened and difficulties relieved by confidential talks within those walls. When he married and moved out of

16

College, the counselling continued with Mrs Moulton's assistance.

During Moulton's time at Richmond College, his father had been stationed in Guernsey. On one holiday visit to see his parents, he met Hannah, daughter of the late Revd Samuel Hope. They became formally engaged in 1856, but the Wesleyan Church had a rule that no probationer could be married. He had to wait until ordination and that meant a long engagement of six years for William and Hannah. Soon after William's ordination at Conference in Camborne in 1862, he and Hannah were married on 14 August in Hanley Wesleyan Chapel.

In 1866, his father, who had retired to Cambridge, died and William set off from London for the funeral. His non-appearance at Cambridge caused some alarm. The King's Cross train reached Hitchin at 10.15 am, but about 30 minutes later the engine was derailed. Luckily the coupling broke in the accident and the carriages remained on the track, but the driver and fireman were killed. As it was now too late to attend the funeral, William hired a dog-cart to take him to Hitchin, a journey of fourteen miles, at a cost of £1. He then caught a train back and was safely home by 5p.m. However alarming the accident had been, it did not put him off travelling by train, but it did turn his hair grey. He was only thirty-one at the time.

E. E. Kellett who had taught at the school for 35 years wrote of Moulton:
"His influence was very great; and it was the more remarkable in that Dr Moulton was far from being a born master, as he was a born scholar. It was with reluctance that he accepted the headship of The Leys; and all his instincts drew him to the study rather than the classroom. He was forty years old when he came, practically for the first time, into contact with boys; and even sanguine observers might have hesitated to predict his success. Yet success he had."

"I was in a position to watch the Doctor somewhat closely for many years; and I can say positively that if he had not been a good and transparently sincere man, he must have utterly failed. He had peculiarities which would have destroyed the influence of almost anybody else; but his character carried him through. He was, of course, a scholar and a gentleman; but these qualities would have been quite useless, in the position he found himself, without the piety which impressed everyone with whom he came into contact."

"He was, indeed, an all-round scholar of great width and depth. But this, though useful to a master, is by no means indispensable; and some of the best teachers have been quite unlearned men. In one way, in fact, it worked against him. It made him one of the least exacting of examiners. He read his own knowledge into the answers of the boys. 'I have taken your form,' he said to me once, 'through the Greek contracted verbs; you will have no difficulty with them in the future.'   Two years later I was still engaged in teaching the same boys those elusive tenses. It is said that he once gave a boy an exhibition because the lad's French, though not good, was so much better than his other work as to deserve some mark of appreciation."

"His skill in turning boys inside out sometimes aroused admiration in its very victims. On one delicate occasion, where severity would have been out of place, and yet where it was necessary to make the boy feel himself in the hands of authority, his sudden twists and turns wrung from the youth an unwilling eulogy. "The Old Man's a genius," said he. "I tried all my tricks on him, but whenever I thought I had him, there was just a somersault and he had me."

"Omniscience, in fact, was his forte: but announcements were his foible. It was long remembered how he once addressed the school as follows: "I shall not announce it to-day, but I shall be announcing to-morrow that there will be a lecture instead of the usual preparation.""

Dr Moulton, while admitting that corporal punishment was occasionally necessary, wished it to be reduced to a minimum, and therefore retained it in his own hands. He wrote to each of the masters in 1897:

. "My convictions are stronger than they ever were as to the general undesirableness of corporal punishment and the necessity of retaining in my own hands the infliction of such punishment when it is required.

I am writing to every member of the staff, partly because I am (and wish to be) in ignorance as to what may have occurred in the past; but especially because any general communication would be less consistent with the intimate relations which I hold and trust always to hold with colleagues."

Such a liberal attitude was quite remarkable in a schoolmaster of his time. It is interesting that Alan Barker also wrote a similar letter during his Headship, stating that masters should not themselves subject boys to corporal punishment, but refer the necessity to him. In his case, however, it was partially as a result of a circular from the Department of Education.

Dr Moulton's concept of discipline was based upon the principal of completely trusting boys. He allowed a very large degree of freedom, and had sufficient faith to believe that the result would justify this course of action. The country was in bounds every afternoon and the boys were only debarred from the town on market days. Undergraduates' rooms were, however, out of bounds.

As well as in the exacting task of running the school, Dr Moulton's time was also taken up by his work as a member of the Committee for the Revision of the New Testament. His scholastic merit was soon recognised by Cambridge University and he was awarded an Honorary MA degree. Only eight others had received the award before him. When the Perse School for Girls was founded in 1881, he was invited to join its Board of Managers, partly because of his practical experience in school management, and partly, "because the presence on the Board of so well trusted a Nonconformist would allay any fears that might exist in case the school should be exclusively and aggressively Anglican". He was one of the most active members of the House Committee, watching carefully over every detail of management of the school.

In 1893, he had been appointed a Magistrate for the Borough of Cambridge - an unusual position for a Nonconformist minister to occupy - and he appeared on the bench every Wednesday morning. Later, when a personal friend of his, Mr. S. R. Ginn, became Mayor of Cambridge, he became his personal Chaplain.

On 8 October, 1895, he had had a particularly busy schedule starting with a meeting with the Bishop of Chester in Manchester. Immediately after the meeting he caught the train to London, but was taken ill at Crewe and found himself unable to speak. However he carried on and went to the St. Pancras Hotel where he had booked a room in anticipation of several meetings in London the next day. He thought that he was over-tired and so went to bed immediately. He could not sleep and feeling very ill sent for a doctor at 3 o'clock in the morning. The doctor diagnosed that a small blood-vessel had burst near the brain and although his speech was impaired, he was in no immediate danger, provided he rested.

When his wife, Hannah, was sent for, his first remarks were characteristic of his usual cheerfulness. "I was talking Temperance on Monday night [at a large meeting in Cambridge], I was talking Temperance all yesterday; and here I am to-day talking like a drunken man!" He stayed at the hotel for a week, until he was well enough to travel to Cambridge. After a short time he was sent to Herne Bay to convalesce. Gradually he returned to his usual busy life.

Just after Dr Moulton's death, his sister, Elizabeth, wrote a small retrospective diary which gives some insight into the life of this Christian, Victorian family. Starting with Christmas Day 1897, she recorded the walks that she and her brother frequently took together. For most of this period Mrs Moulton seems to have been indisposed with a very bad cold and therefore Dr Moulton looked to his sister for company. On Boxing Day they walked for nine miles inside the school grounds, but the next day he walked for a mile indoors, in the school hall. Again, two days later, as it was a very stormy day, he walked in the hall for three quarters of an hour. The entry for New Year's Eve contained an entry in Hannah's writing:

> "We spent the last minutes of the year - he kneeling in prayer at the end of the sofa (on which I sat) by the fire. As the clock struck he was thanking God for Willie's (their son) dedication to the work of the ministry."

On Saturday, 1 January 1898, now in Elizabeth's hand:

> "Dr Allbutt came about ten o'clock and was here for more than an hour. He thinks his (Dr Moulton's) cough and expectoration arise either from the remains of his former attacks of Asthma or from inherited Asthma and are not bronchial. He therefore advises him to go out as much as possible. He says his pulse is absolutely right now- that there is no <u>kicking</u> as formerly and all fear of the breaking of another blood vessel is over (!!)."

The daily entries continue with most of them concerned with church business around Cambridge. Thursday, 20 January 1898:

> "Beautiful day. William and I had a long walk in the Botanical Gardens. Hannah walked in the grounds and we joined her for tea

on our return. Temperance Committee in the Drawing room. Tea sent in. Just heard that the Fernley Trustees will give £1,000 towards the debt."

Because all the funds donated at the foundation of the school had been used to purchase the estate, the school had gone into debt. Term started the next day, 21 January and now there are more references to meeting parents and teaching. On Thursday, 3 February, Elizabeth, Hannah and Dr Moulton travelled to London for a reception to be held in connection with the Leys Committee for raising £30,000 for the Leys Debt:

"We had a very quiet journey up. William remarking how restful it was to be by ourselves and safe from interruption; he slept a good part of the way. I need give no particulars of the meeting - only remarking how well people thought William looked and how strong his voice was."

Inserted in pencil in Hannah's hand:

"After the meeting I said "Now you won't say people want a younger man at The Leys" - referring to the hearty welcome everyone had given him. (He had said a few days before "I suppose the Governors want a younger man in my place"). He answered "Everybody is <u>very</u> kind"."

Saturday, 5 February 1898:

"Very bright day. We had breakfast early as William wanted to go into School the first hour. As I came down stairs he stood at the bottom and as he kissed me, he said in answer to my question "How are you?" "I feel hurried". "Why?", I replied - "breakfast is ready and it is still quite early". "I know all that" he replied "but I have that feeling". He had four classes to take and also some new parents to see. It was a very busy morning for everyone and I hardly saw him till one o'clock. At Dinner he was very bright and seemed to have got over his feelings of hurry. He got the Old Leysian Directory to verify some statement about a boy. I laughingly said "I think it would be better to put the Directory on the Table at every meal." After Dinner he sat a little in the arm chair before going out to see Mr. Green. On Hannah's urging him to go upstairs and rest he said "I must go to Mr. Green's this afternoon even if I have a cab" He left the house about 3."

21

In Hannah's hand:

"after I had kissed him, I said "You will come back if you find it cold - won't you?" "Oh Yes" he answered, "I'll come back if it is cold" - his last words to me! (The wind was east and struck one as cold). I had entreated him not to go, or at any rate to have a cab if he felt he must go to Mr. Green's. But he was unusually resolute and said he should certainly go - and went alone, alas!"

In the penultimate passage above, Hannah had inserted the visiting parents' name: Mellor. The son, J.E. Mellor, joined the school in the September of that year and after a distinguished career at school and Cambridge University, he joined the staff, became a Housemaster and retired in 1947.

Unfortunately, Mr G.E. Green, one of his assistant masters, who had been unwell for some time, was still too ill to see Dr Moulton when he called. After talking to Green's brother and sister for about half an hour, he was seen walking firmly on his way back in Sidgwick Avenue. He crossed the portion of Coe Fen that lies between Newnham Mill and the footbridge and then climbed the steps of the footbridge over the main river. (There was no road bridge over the river at that time.) Here he was seen to sit down on one of the top steps The gardener of Clare College seeing him there, offered to help him. "No, th....." Unconsciousness seems to have occurred immediately on loss of speech. A London physician was passing at the time and had him removed to the gardener's cottage. His own doctors, Professor Allbutt and Dr Ingle were sent for, but he had died within half an hour of his seizure.

The funeral service was conducted in the school hall and the congregation included representatives of the Methodist Church, the Mayor and Corporation to whom he had been Chaplain, the Magistrates, Old Leysians and the Governors. Outside the hall, the quadrangle was lined with The Leys boys. The procession led by the horse drawn glass hearse which went to the Histon Road Cemetery was nearly half a mile long and included the Mayor and Corporation, a large number of Heads of Colleges, University Professors and others, past and present Leys Masters, a strong contingent of Old Leysians from all parts of the country, members of the School, and many private friends.

The grave is in the very centre of the cemetery and as well as being a fine

The Great Hall, prepared for Dr. Moulton's Funeral, 1898

memorial to Dr Moulton, the grave stone also carries the names of his wife and his granddaughter. The kerb stone bears the name of his son, James Hope Moulton, who perished in the Mediterranean in the First World War. Sadly, soon after a complete restoration in 1994 involving the re-leading of the letters, the stone was vandalised as were many other stones in the cemetery. However, it was possible to join the stone across the two fractures. A short service was held at the graveside on the 100th anniversary of Dr Moulton's death. Since then the stone has been vandalised again, and no decision has yet been made about its future.

Immediately after Moulton's death, the Governors asked J.C. Isard to act as Headmaster until they could select another suitable person. At the Governors' meeting on 19 February, 1898, several names were suggested for consideration as the next Headmaster. They included Mr T.G. Osborne, Mr Workman, Dr Vinter, Dr Dallinger, Mr Way, the Revd W.T.G. Barber and the Revd James Hope Moulton, who was Dr Moulton's son.

Three days later, the sub-committee which had been appointed to make the selection proposed that the Revd W.T.G. Barber should be recommended as the most suitable candidate for election. They also suggested "that if possible the Revd James Hope Moulton should be made the Headmaster's assistant and Miss Moulton offered the post of Matron". All three were interviewed by one of the Governors, Mr Bunting and after some discussion on 5th March 1898, the Governors appointed Dr Barber as the second Headmaster of The Leys. There is no further mention in the minutes concerning the posts of assistant to the Headmaster or Matron.

Dr Barber, the son of a Wesleyan missionary, was born in January 1858 in Ceylon. Later that year his family moved to Wynberg, in South Africa. In 1869 he came to England to be educated at Kingswood and in 1876 came up to Cambridge to Gonville and Caius College, having won a Open Scholarship in Mathematics. Whilst he was an undergraduate, he taught at The Leys for a short period between 1877 and 1878 and after his graduation he taught at Dunheved College, Launceston. In 1882, the year in which he was admitted to the Wesleyan ministry, he was appointed Assistant Tutor at Richmond College. He had had a interest in missionary work from his childhood days and he volunteered for service in China. In 1884 he was appointed to be the Wesleyan Minister in charge of Hankow Christian College in China. In 1892 he returned to England when his first wife's health was failing. He worked for some time in the Leeds District and then was appointed Missionary Secretary of the Methodist Church. Dr Barber was a less learned theologian than Dr Moulton, but he had spent some years teaching in schools, and he was a very sound all-round practical teacher, capable of taking forms, high or low, in almost any subject.

During his Headmastership, Dr Barber had to deal with the problems brought about by the First World War. Not least of them was the composition of the sad notices he had to read out in chapel recording the deaths of Old Leysians on active service. The complete collection was published in the 1920 edition of *The Leys School Handbook and Directory*. Barber's second wife was Emma Clapham, the sister of three Old Leysians, including Sir John Harold Clapham, the distinguished Professor of Economic History. She was an admirable supporter during his Headmastership, writing numerous letters to parents about their sons.

In 1919, Dr Barber was elected President of the Methodist Conference and the Governors, in accepting his resignation as Headmaster, created him Provost. This was to enable him to be given the same salary and allowances he had been receiving as Headmaster, whilst carrying out the onerous task of President.

Three names were then considered by the Governors to succeed as Headmaster:- the Revd C. Kingsley Williams, Dr Gurney and the Revd Harry Bisseker. They interviewed the first two but decided that Bisseker was well enough known to them already, as he had been on the staff of the school previously. Kingsley Williams was offered the post first, but he declined it, and so the Governors unanimously invited Bisseker to become the third Headmaster of The Leys.

Harry Bisseker was born in Handsworth, Birmingham in 1878 and was educated at King Edward's School, Birmingham. After graduating from Jesus College, Cambridge, he entered the Wesleyan ministry in 1901 and was Chaplain at The Leys until 1904. He then spent six years at the Leysian Mission, where his work had a profound influence and where his personal contributions were remembered for many years after he had left. His gifts as a scholar were recognised when he was appointed Tutor in New Testament Language and Literature at Richmond College. During the period 1914 to 1918, he was the Minister of Hinde Street Church in the West London Mission.

Revd H. Bisseker
Headmaster 1919-1934

Revd Dr. W.T. Barber
Headmaster 1898-1919

During the fifteen years of his Headmastership there were many notable additions to the school premises. East House opened in Brookside in 1919, a new pavilion was built as part of the War memorial in 1923, and the next year an Isolation Hospital was added to the Sanatorium in Brookside. The new Science Building was opened in 1927, and in 1929 Lord Stamp opened a new building on the campus, into which East House moved from Brookside. The Latham Road playing fields were purchased in 1930, and the main school field was levelled. Also during Bisseker's headship, the school was visited by Crown Prince Hirohito, the Duke of York and the Prince of Wales (see Chapter 10 - *Royal Visits*).

In 1929, the Governors were informed by his doctor that Bisseker must be given 'a year's complete rest from work' on the grounds of ill-health. They appointed W.H. Balgarnie, who had just retired from teaching at The Leys, to act as Headmaster for fifteen months, until the end of 1930.

Bisseker then returned to office, and in 1931 he explained to the Governors "that as a result of trade depression it was likely that some boys now entered would not be sent to The Leys and also that there was a tendency to remove boys at an earlier age than usual. This might result in a shortage of numbers in the future". He proposed that if this shortage materialised, the loss might be partially counteracted by taking Home Boarders in excess of the ten authorised, and at the same time extending the privilege to the 'sons of any Oxford and Cambridge graduate or Minister of Religion who resides in Cambridge'. Until then only the sons of teaching members of the university were permitted to be home-boarders. This qualification was gradually relaxed from the 1970s until 1997 when the new category 'Day Pupil' was introduced in conjunction with Home-Boarders and Boarders.

On 14 May, 1934, the Governors were informed that Harry Bisseker's doctor had given him 'explicit orders to resign on the grounds of ill-health' at the end of term. He retired at the end of the Summer term and moved to live in Harston, a village a few miles south of Cambridge, with his wife, Doris whom he had married in 1908. He died thirty-one years later at the age of 87. One of his daughters, Ray, was married to Keith Payne (Old Leysian) who devoted much of his life to the Leysian Mission.

In 1934, it was therefore necessary to select a successor to Bisseker. The process is documented in the school archives. There were 20 applicants with a Methodist background, 19 Anglicans and 7 others. The selection committee, which included Lord Hayter, Lord Marshall, Sir Josiah Stamp and Dr Barber balloted for those they thought should be interviewed. As a result, a list of twelve preferred candidates was produced in order of popularity. Second in the list of twelve was an Old Leysian, Hugo Caudwell, who was a Housemaster at Oundle School. Gerald Humphrey was just behind him in third place. A questionnaire, drawn up by the selection committee, was circulated to the referees of these twelve candidates. When their replies had been received, they were collated into a single document which was printed and sent to the individual members of the selection committee. The timetable drawn up for the preliminary interviews of the twelve candidates, who were to be seen in alphabetical order, allowed ten minutes for each. However, the record of how long they actually were seen for by the committee, shows a range from four minutes to fifteen. Another ballot was taken and the list reduced to three. These were seen for a longer period and Dr W.G. Humphrey was finally appointed.

At the time of his appointment he was unmarried, but within two years Gerald Humphrey was married to an American whom he had first met whilst he was at Harvard University as a Research Fellow in 1930. They did not meet again until 1935 when she visited England. He proposed to her on Mount Snowdon. She did not give him an immediate answer, but returned to America. She later sent a telegram which read "EVERYTHING YOURS ABSOLUTELY SURE STOP ALL PLANS MUST SUIT YOUR CONVENIENCE FIRST LETTER FOLLOWS LOVE PEGGY". Gerald Humphrey went to America during the Christmas holidays and married her on 2 January 1936. They suffered a very rough crossing back to England and Mrs Humphrey's first impression of the house was that it was extremely cold. She sought to warm up by having a hot bath. She discovered that the bathroom window would not close, and she threatened that unless the window was repaired immediately, she would not live in the house. Needless to say it was repaired. However, thirty years later, the author and his family moved into in North B Housemaster's house and after fourteen years had still failed to get their bathroom window repaired, which similarly would not close.

The first three Headmasters had all been Methodist ministers. Gerald Humphrey was the son of a Methodist minister, but a chemist by training.

Dr. W.G. Humphrey – Headmaster 1934-1958

J.C. Isard sent him a card at the time of his appointment, warning Humphrey that he had inherited a very precious trust and must continue to lead the school in a Christian manner. Any misgivings he might have had were unfounded.

One of the first problems Gerald had to deal with was that of school dress. He reported to the Governors "that not only was the school getting a bad name in Cambridge owing to the slovenliness of boys and their varied and often fancy dress but a not inconsiderable number of cases were known in which parents, after seeing the boys here, had decided to send their own boys elsewhere".

After discussion, the Governors agreed to new regulations to take effect from September 1935, requiring:

1. A dark blue serge suit for Sundays
2. For Weekdays a mid grey tweed jacket and mid grey trousers with a pullover, if worn, of a similar shade. (The grey tweed jacket was still part of the dress regulations in the mid-1950s.)
3. White soft or semi-stiff collars on week-days, stiff white collars on Sundays.
4. Special straw hats (dark blue and white) for wear by boys in the town. White straw for prefects.

Another ongoing problem was accommodation for married masters. When Norman Holloway became the Housemaster of North A House in 1921, his father, Sir Henry Holloway, offered to pay £2,800 for the construction of a house attached to the boys' accommodation, for his son and his family to live in. The Governors agreed to repay part of the cost (not exceeding £1,500) when Norman Holloway ceased to be Housemaster. It was by this means that North A House became the first of the Houses to provide accommodation for a married Housemaster.

Gerald Humphrey saw the need for more such accommodation and pressed the Governors to provide it. By 1937, a house for the Housemaster of North B House had been constructed. Robert Morris and his wife, Lucy, moved into it and had six children during their time there. However, plans for provision of a Housemaster's house for East House had to wait until after the war.

The political uncertainty in Europe brought a request from the Academic Assistance Council of the Society of Friends to "offer suitable education to refugees from Germany and the Saar owing to their destitute condition". It was pointed out to the Governors that The Leys had so many vacant beds that the school ought to offer some places. Gerald Humphrey was told by the Governors that he "could take two per house and that they must not be over 15 years old. There would be no fees and no publicity would be given to the arrangement, nor should it be held out that the School was offering 'Free Places'". Sadly some of these boys were to suffer internment and were held in a Prisoner of War Camp in Canada for a while. (See Chapter 16 - *From the Four Corners of the Earth*).

The fact that there were empty beds had been giving concern for some time. In July 1937, Gerald Humphrey presented a paper to the Governing Body showing the correlation during the years 1918 and 1937 between the number of pupils throughout the country taking the Common Entrance Examination which was used by all boarding schools in the Headmasters' Conference, and the number of pupils at The Leys. The greatest number of boys at The Leys during that period was 271 in 1930 and was occasioned by the opening of the new East House in 1929. However, whereas from 1918 onwards there was a close correlation between the number of boys in the school and the total number of candidates in the country taking Common Entrance, the number of boys at the school fell to 227 in 1935 although the national number of Common Entrance candidates had risen. Therefore Gerald Humphrey suggested that any proposal to rebuild West House should be shelved. It was another 25 years before a new West was built.

Another cause for concern was that there had been a considerable increase in the numbers in the upper school and a corresponding decrease in those in the lower school. Caldicott School, which had been a 'feeder' preparatory school for The Leys, had moved to Farnham. The Headmaster pointed out to the Governors that it was desirable for The Leys to start a preparatory department. A sub-committee was designated to examine the possibility of acquiring St. Faith's School. After favourable reports, the Governors purchased the school in 1938. (see Chapter 17 - *Towards One Foundation*)

One problem brought about by the falling numbers in this period of the school's history was that of playing games, particularly rugby, against larger schools. In 1937, Gerald Humphrey reported to the Governors that The Leys had played Bedford School on 31 occasions and had only won three times. It had suffered defeats in every match over the previous twenty years. The record against Oundle had been very nearly as bad, with The Leys winning only twice during the previous seventeen years. He suggested that it would be courteous to offer to drop the fixtures with those two schools. Later he had to report to the Governors that there had been a considerable difference of opinion between him and the Old Leysians on the Governing Body over the suggestion. The meeting of the Governors on 16 March, 1939 reaffirmed their support for the Headmaster in this matter.

Another problem facing Gerald Humphrey in 1939 was the number of staff requesting permission to get married, and the lack of nearby accommodation for married staff. He pointed out to the Governors that three masters lived at Harston (five miles away) and another at Stapleford (also five miles away). He said that this was most unfortunate because these masters and their families were bound to have less out-of-school contact with colleagues and boys. The coming of the war and the evacuation of the school to Scotland meant that this problem was shelved. Even in the year 2000, aggravated by soaring prices of housing in general in Cambridge and particularly near the school, it has not been solved.

The next few years under Gerald Humphrey during the war period are covered in Chapter 9 - *The Leys at War* and Chapter 11 - *Exile in Scotland*. He also maintained later that he really took over the functions of a Bursar whilst in Scotland, and that John Stirland acted as the day-to-day Headmaster.

The long-continued succession of duties and anxieties that Gerald Humphrey had to face during the war years, and the move back to Cambridge, took their toll. The school doctor, Dr Charles Budd, told the acting-chairman of Governors, Sir Henry Dale, without the Headmaster's knowledge, that in the doctor's opinion, Dr Humphrey was in need of a holiday. The Governors met and agreed, and Dale wrote to the Headmaster to tell him they had decided that he should take a term's leave.

However, their decision gave Gerald Humphrey even more sleepless nights as he wrestled with the problem of who should take over the running of the school. Many of his staff were older than himself and had also suffered the strain of the move to and from Scotland. From letters he wrote at that time, it is clear that he was not prepared to take a whole term off. He suggested that a fortnight might give him some relief and then the whole of the July and August holidays would put him back on his feet again. That was the longest period of time during which he was prepared to be away from the school. Although he eventually designated Jesse Mellor to be acting Head in his absence, he wrote to Sir Henry Dale saying "Mellor is an excellent schoolmaster, but he hates making decisions and dislikes detailed organisation".

In 1950, School Certificate and Higher School Certificate examinations throughout the country were replaced by the General Certificate of Education (G.C.E.) examinations at Ordinary and Advanced Level. Oxford and Cambridge Universities had until then used results in School Certificate as a qualification for matriculation. It was necessary to work out new criteria for matriculation in terms of the new examination system. A letter from the Vice-Chancellor of Cambridge University, Canon C.E. Raven, received by the Governors, acknowledged the debt that the University owed to Gerald Humphrey for formulating with Raven the new requirements which had been accepted by the Ministry of Education, the Headmasters' Conference and the two Universities.

Gerald reported to the Governors in March 1951 that an article in the magazine of the Lord's Day Observance Society had been circulated to the Headmasters of all Public Schools, containing the following statement:

"It is reported that in one of our University Towns the boys of a well-known Public School play their Football or their Cricket matches, as the case may be, on the Lord's Day in their School Playing Fields. It is not to be wondered that in the same town the Cinemas are now open on Sundays, and that the actions of the boys of this School were cited as a reason why these Cinemas should be opened on that day"

He went on to explain 'that this almost certainly referred to The Leys, for at a Public Meeting in Cambridge on the opening of Cinemas on Sundays in 1947, it was stated that if boys at The Leys were allowed to skate on Sundays, there was no reason why Cinemas should not be open'. The Governors agreed that no action should be taken.

In 1957 Gerald Humphrey informed all members of staff individually that, although he was not yet 60, he intended to resign his headship. He explained that he felt, since he had spent 23 years at The Leys, that the school would benefit from the leadership of a younger man. He said that he had been dissuaded by the Governors from applying for other Headships on previous occasions, notably at the time of the Munich crisis and again on the return from Pitlochry. He had now accepted a post as Chief Personnel

Officer to Fisons, an industrial chemical firm where he would not be required to retire at the age of 60.

Eventually he moved to the Cambridge University Appointments Board (now the Careers Service). Sadly, ill-health soon followed, requiring his resignation. He had painful hospital treatment for depression, but eventually enjoyed retirement with Peggy, living in Trumpington. When he was in his eighties, he and Peggy decided to move to Washington where their son, Bill, was working for the World Bank. Peggy died in 1989 and when Bill retired and returned to Cambridge, Gerald returned, and lived for a short while in the Hope Nursing Home where he died, aged 92.

The Governors chose W.A. Barker to be the next Headmaster, but only after opposition from some of them, because he was not a Methodist. He, like Humphrey, had received mixed reactions following his appointment. John Stirland had voiced his worry that Alan Barker was an Anglican, and might change the religious ethos of the school. Alan recalled at the time of his resignation from The Leys that before the final interview for the position of Headmaster, by which time the field had narrowed to three, they all waited outside the interview room for nearly two hours. None of the final three was a Methodist. When summoned to be offered the post, he was told that some of the Governors had wanted to re-advertise the job to get a Methodist Headmaster, and that the subsequent argument accounted for his long wait.

He was, at the time of his appointment in 1958, teaching at Eton, and his contract required him to stay until the end of the summer term. Consequently Maurice Howard, who was Second Master, was asked by the Governors to act as Headmaster for the Lent and Summer terms of 1958.

Alan Barker was to see the school grow in numbers, buildings and public image. There was an early disagreement with the Staff when, at his first Common Room meeting, the new Head announced that he would come and watch each master teaching. The suggestion was met with horror and the Senior Master, Geoff Green, was instructed to inform him that this was not acceptable. The Headmaster's response was to request a full Inspection by the Department of Education. It was a far more drastic measure, but it gave him stronger supporting evidence when he was asking the Governors to make the changes which he considered necessary.

Alan was a man with great charisma. Always elegantly dressed, with a fresh carnation in his button hole and carrying a silver topped walking stick, his inspiration brought into being many of the buildings on the campus of today. The new West House building (1961) was followed by the Theatre, Pavilion and Fen House (1966). In 1973 the classroom block, the Queen's building, was the last of his visions to come into being. During the same period many of the other buildings were re-furbished or took on a new function. The building programme was accompanied by an increase in numbers from 320 in 1958 to 422 in 1975. Alan gave all his attention to broad outlines of policy, so that he would often discuss changes of curriculum or pastoral care with the members of the Common Room and then delegate to them the task of working out the minutiae of the schemes.

Alan was always interested in public affairs. Soon after his arrival at The Leys, he became an Independent County Councillor for Newnham Ward (just across the river from the school). Eventually he became an Alderman, but when asked if he would like to stand for Parliament, he replied that the salary was not high enough. Meanwhile, his wife, Jean, had become Conservative City Councillor for the Trumpington Ward. In 1971, she became an extremely popular Mayor of Cambridge. Both Alan and Jean had close friends who were prominent in the Conservative Party. Many of them visited the school, including Reginald Maudling when he was Home Secretary, Selwyn Lloyd, a previous Chancellor of the Exchequer, whose father had been at The Leys, and Edward Heath. The last had been due to address a meeting in the Moulton Room when Harold Wilson called a General Election in 1970. The meeting turned into the first address of that particular election campaign, and a photograph of Edward Heath was displayed in the Moulton Room for several years to mark the event. He went on to win the election and become Prime Minister.

During the years that Heath had been Leader of the Opposition, Alan frequently visited him in his rooms in The Albany. They played Bridge into the early hours of the morning. It was rumoured that the reason for Chapel being moved forward from before Period 1 to after, at 9.30a.m., was to enable the Headmaster to return from London and attend the service. Although he never became a politician, he was very proud when Jean was given a Life Peerage. However, he grumbled about the fact that whilst the wife of a Life Peer would have received the title 'Lady', he, as the husband of a Peeress, was still only a plain Mister.

W.A. Barker – Headmaster 1958-1975

Both he and his wife were dog lovers and he could always be seen with a dog at his heels. One dog was called 'Bumble'. Whilst Alan was watching a Rugby match accompanied by his faithful Bumble, the dog wandered from him. 'Bumble, come here!', he shouted loudly across the field, to the amusement of the boys who expected the Housemaster of North B House to run across the field, since that was his nickname at the time.

In due course Alan felt that he had been at The Leys long enough, and moved to be Headmaster of University College School, Hampstead. Sadly, whilst he was there he suffered a stroke and was forced to retire. After several years of illness, he died in the Star and Garter Nursing Home at Kew.

The next Headmaster was Mr Bertie Bellis. The son of a Methodist Minister, he had been educated at Kingswood before winning an Exhibition to read Mathematics at St. John's College, Cambridge. He taught first at Rossall between 1951 and 1955 before moving to be Head of Mathematics at Highgate School, where he became a Housemaster in 1958. Whilst at Highgate, he founded the Mathematics in Education and Industry Schools Project, and the resulting MEI Mathematics syllabuses became popular at both Ordinary and Advanced Levels. The Leys joined the project at an early stage. In 1965 Bertie was appointed Headmaster of Daniel Stewart's College, Edinburgh, and when this school was amalgamated with Melville College in 1972, he became the first Principal of the combined schools.

Also during his time in Edinburgh, he had been Chairman of the Scottish Education Committee on 'Computers and the Schools' which resulted in the widespread introduction of Computer Education into Scottish schools. In recognition of his work in Education, particularly in Mathematics (he had been President of the Mathematical Association) and Computing, he had been elected a Fellow of the Royal Society of Edinburgh.

He was persuaded to apply for the Headship of The Leys by two leading Methodist educationalists when the vacancy was announced in 1975. Although he had some misgivings that he had not long been Principal of the Edinburgh school, he and his wife Joan were very impressed with what they saw when they came to Cambridge for the interview. The short list contained some very strong candidates, several of whom gained Headships later in the year. Bertie and his wife were returning to Edinburgh via the Great Northern Hotel at King's Cross Station, London, when he received a telephone call offering him the post.

Several major developments took place during his eleven years at The Leys. The Science department had been in the same building for fifty years. One of the Governors who had a scientific background suggested that the best people to consult on what was needed to improve the laboratories were the Science staff themselves. After discussions with his colleagues, the Senior Science Master, David Gardiner, presented plans for the refurbishment of the building which were largely followed. It was reopened in 1977 by Mrs. Charnock, the daughter of Sir J.J. Thomson who had originally opened it, using the silver and enamel decorated key which had been used in 1927, and which Thomson had retained. She very kindly donated the key to the school after the ceremony, and it now hangs on display in the foyer of the science building.

Bertie Bellis saw the upgrading of the accommodation for the Chaplain in 6 Brookside. Martin Ludlow (Old Leysian) was responsible for raising funds for the creation of a meeting room behind the new manse which was named the Bisseker Room in memory of the third headmaster.

In 1980, the large ground floor room between the Kelvin Building and the Swimming Bath was divided to provide a smaller classroom and a careers room where pupils could not only receive advice on their futures, but consult for themselves a large range of literature on Universities, Colleges of Further Education and vocational courses. Mrs Joan Bellis had completed a diploma course in Careers Counselling just before she and her husband left Edinburgh, and she was able to give valuable advice on the design and planning of the new room.

Having been instrumental in introducing computers into Scottish schools, Bertie encouraged computing at the start of his career at The Leys. This began as a punched tape system which was connected by telephone to a shared computer in London. When the BBC computers were developed for use in schools, he ensured that The Leys was one of the first in the country to have a computer laboratory. Patrick Jenkin (later Lord Jenkin), the Secretary of State for Industry, came in 1982 and formally opened the Computer Laboratory, which at that time was housed in the old West House building.

At a critical time for the school in 1983, Sir Arthur Armitage, the Chairman, actively supported the Headmaster in persuading the Governors to undertake a 10 year development plan. This was to include some major

B.T. Bellis – Headmaster 1975-1986 with Mrs. Bellis

constructional and refurbishment projects, and also involved the revolutionary decision to admit girls to the school.

There had been some dissatisfaction with school food for some time. To rectify the situation, the school kitchens were completely refitted and a new self-servery for the distribution of food was constructed. The Dining Hall itself was given a new layout which enabled everyone at the school, including teaching and support staff, to be fed. The previous formality of meals was sacrificed, but the quality of food and the reduction of waste more than compensated for this. Jean Barker, by now Lady Trumpington, returned to the school and performed the official re-opening ceremony.

This change in the kitchens and Dining Hall made available the area above the kitchens which was at one time where the maids lived. Only a small number of rooms was now occupied for this purpose, and so space was made available for girls, who were to be admitted to the Sixth Form. A great deal of the success of the design of the accommodation was due to the Headmaster's wife, Joan, who supervised the furnishing and decorating of the girls' rooms. The first girls moved into the new Granta House in 1984. The staff were prepared for the changes that would come about with girls both inside and outside the classroom, by a series of talks by guest speakers with relevant experience. One of these was the Chaplain of Kingswood and Headmaster elect of Kent College, Pembury (a girls' school), the Revd John Barrett. After a very stimulating talk, someone commented that it was a pity the speaker would not be available to apply for the Headmastership of The Leys after Bertie Bellis's retirement. It was remarkable that a few years later he was appointed to be the eighth Headmaster of the school.

For many years there had been discussions of the need for a Sports Hall and a Design Centre. Rival schools in the market for pupils were building such facilities. Members of the Common Room were divided as to whether priority should be given to the Sports Hall or the Design Centre. The decision had been made by the Governors to appeal for a Design Centre first, partly on the grounds of cost, because it might have been possible to convert the old West House. Plans were even drawn up to demolish the building and there is a model in the archives of a possible Design Centre on that site. Eventually it was decided that an area next to Fen House would be more suitable. An appeal was launched for the Design Centre, under the chairmanship of Sir Percy Rugg (Old Leysian), a former leader of the

Greater London Council. He was a member of the Bernard Sunley Trust, who generously donated the cost of the building and arranged for their own construction firm to build it, in honour of Sir Percy. Sir Percy himself laid the Foundation Stone in 1985, but sadly died just before the school started to use the building, which was opened by H.R.H. The Duke of Edinburgh in 1987.

An outstanding portrait of Bertie Bellis by the painter Ray Smith hangs in the Dining Hall. One remarkable feature is that the Rugg Centre, as the Design Centre is now called, can be seen in the background. At the time, the building had not been finished and the painter used the model of the Centre to link that building with Bertie. The artist has published a book on portrait painting. A whole chapter in it is devoted to the Headmaster's portrait, and it is interesting to follow in detail how the painting developed. When Bertie Bellis retired just before his 60th birthday, T.G. Beynon, Headmaster of Denstone College, became the seventh Headmaster of The Leys. At the start of his Headship, the Rugg Centre was opened by the Duke of Edinburgh (see Chapter 10 - *Royal Visits*). Encouraged by the rising number of applications, the Governors decided to open another girls' House. This was achieved by a clever refurbishment of the old West House building and re-housing the Medical Centre from there into the Tuck Shop. School House moved into the refurbished building. A new House for girls was created in the restyled former School House building, which was named Dale House after Sir Henry Dale.

Tim Beynon had been experiencing some dissatisfaction among the Staff over his lack of interest in the school. He had had considerable personal problems when his wife left him and his two teenage daughters stayed in his care. The Governors unfortunately had to ask him to resign in 1990. As mentioned above, the Revd Dr J.C.A. Barrett was selected to be his replacement.

John Barrett was educated at Culford School and Newcastle University where he read Economics. He became a member of Fitzwilliam College and Wesley House, Cambridge, where he read Theology. In 1968, he became Chaplain and Lecturer in Divinity at Westminster College, Oxford. The following year he became Assistant Tutor at Wesley College, Bristol. In 1971, he became Circuit Minister of Hanley Trinity, Stoke on Trent and at the same time he was acting Head of Religious Studies at Birches High

41

T.G. Beynon – Headmaster 1986-1990

School. In 1973, he became Chaplain and Head of Religious and General Studies at Kingswood School. Ten years later he was appointed to be Headmaster of Kent College, Pembury.

When he saw the position of the Headmaster of The Leys advertised, he felt that perhaps he had not been at Kent College long enough to apply for it. However he was persuaded to do so by Donald Tranter, Secretary of Methodist Schools and Colleges. He was placed on the final short list. After a preliminary interview with the then Chairman of Governors, who said that some people wondered whether a Methodist Minister would be suitable for the school, he thought he would be passed over. The selection panel of the Governors, however, did not consider this to be an insuperable problem and offered him the job.

It is worth mentioning his contribution to world Methodism before reviewing his first ten years at the school. He has been a member of the World Methodist Council Executive Committee since 1981 and was elected to the Praesidium in 1996. He was Secretary of the British Committee from 1986 until 1997 and in 1999 (following the death of Revd Donald English) was elected as Chairman. He campaigned for several years for formal recognition by the World Methodist Council of the work being done world wide in hundreds of Methodist Schools and Colleges. In the end, two bodies were set up in 1991: The World Methodist Council Education Committee of which he was elected to be the first Chairman, and the International Association of Methodist Schools, Colleges and Universities of which he is the Vice President. He was awarded an Honorary Doctorate of Divinity by the Florida Southern University, USA in 1992 "for his work in promoting Methodist education world wide". He was also a member of the Steering Committee of the Bloxham Project between 1986 and 1992. He, like Dr Charles Moseley, a member of The Leys teaching staff, was invited to become a Fellow of the Royal Society of Arts in 1996.

When John Barrett joined The Leys, there were girls at the school, but only in the sixth form, and his first impression of the school was one of a 'macho' society, where the pupils were not always civil to one another. Planning for the introduction of full co-education began almost immediately, and girls formally entered the lower school in 1994, though three brave pioneers entered the third form (Year 9) in 1993 in anticipation of this. His view is that the aim of co-education is not simply that the girls should

Revd Dr. J.C.A. Barrett – Headmaster 1990-

civilise the boys, but that the two sexes should civilise each other. The provision of accommodation for girls is covered in Chapter 5 - *The Buildings*.

Articles critical of the school appeared in the newspapers as a result of reports of pupils drinking in a Cambridge public house whilst under the age at which they could legally do so. The Headmaster was concerned also by the excessive drinking of those who were legally entitled to visit public houses. He felt that Sixth Formers should have their own club in the school, and that it should have its own bar, selling limited amounts of alcohol under specific conditions. He hoped thereby to encourage responsible drinking in an environment over which the school had control.

As a result, it was suggested that a licence should be obtained for the sale of alcohol in the Sixth Form Club. This gave rise to the publication of many letters in the *Methodist Recorder*, opposing such a move. The Editor finally declared "this correspondence is now closed". Despite a carefully argued response from the Headmaster which was also published, there were objectors living in the West Country who threatened to oppose the licence application when it came before the Magistrates. However, for their objections to be heard officially, they had to live in the vicinity of the place where the licence would be held, so they had to drop their protest. The bar was licensed and now runs very successfully.

The Headmaster felt, when he took up office, that the school had lost its sense of direction. The results of examinations were satisfactory but not excellent. There has been a concerted effort, supported by all teaching staff, to push up academic standards. One measure of achievement is the percentage of A and B grades obtained at A level, which has improved from 40% to 57% over the last ten years.

The numbers in the school were around 390 and there was an unplanned overdraft of £600,000. John Barrett persuaded the Governors that it was necessary to increase the size of each year group to 100 in order that there could be sufficient numbers to promote the range of courses and activities required by boys and girls. To ensure that this was the case, it was agreed that from 1998 there should be a small 11+ entry to The Leys to augment the usual entry at 13+. As a part of this, a junior co-educational boarding house was opened in 6, Brookside, capable of accommodating twenty boarders. This was quickly filled to capacity, and the group of 11 and 12 year olds as a whole has been named Moulton House.

The introduction of day-pupils is mentioned in Chapter 16 - *From the Four Corners of the Earth*. They are accommodated in North B House, which was converted in 1997 to provide changing facilities, common rooms and locker spaces for them, and the provision for boarding in that House disappeared. At the same time, boarders were concentrated in other houses thus strengthening the sense of the boarding community in the Boys' Houses. By the year 2000, the school numbers have reached 500, and the aim is that they should reach 540 by September 2002.

John Barrett and Richard Dyson, the Headmaster of St. Faith's (see Chapter 17 - *Towards One Foundation*), quickly developed a warm friendship and looked for ways to bring the two schools into a closer relationship, and in particular to encourage more Fidelians to move on to The Leys. On two occasions, the Governors set up sub-committees to try to redefine the relationship between the two schools, while maintaining their independence. The term "The Leys and St. Faith's Foundation" was eventually adopted to embrace the two schools, and the numbers of Fidelians applying to The Leys has grown to the point where not all of them can be accepted. This growth has led to the adaptation of some areas of The Leys to provide more classrooms. Further plans are being discussed either to alter existing buildings or possibly to build new facilities to cope with the increasing numbers. The Headmaster has set up a Senior Management team to assist with the running of both the academic and the pastoral side of school life.

The Leys has been very fortunate in having not only a succession of strong Headmasters, but in that each of them has had unstinting support from a wife of unusual calibre. The latest of them, Sally Barrett, has, like her predecessors, added her own particular contribution to the routine activities as hostess to gatherings of governors, staff, pupils and parents. In her case, as a former teacher of Physical Education, she was able to coach hockey and netball and organise the fixture list of these sports against other girls' teams.

All the Headmasters of The Leys have had Bursars to assist them. J.C. Isard was the first of these, and was succeeded by Col. A.J.V. Durrell, Paymaster-Captain R.G.T. Sennett, A.McM. Buchanan, J. Marnham, M.R. Marchant and E.P. Magill. They have all worked long hours for the good of the school. New legislation over 'Health and Safety at Work', security, lettings, development plans and building projects, add to the traditional problems of finance and the maintenance of existing buildings experienced by all Bursars. The present Bursar, Peter Magill, deserves special mention for his rôle in the successful growth of the school.

Together, John Barrett and Peter Magill have overseen a period in the 1990s of major expenditure on building and refurbishment. In addition to the changes to Fen and Dale Houses, North A, North B and East Houses have been substantially altered internally. The East House building has been renamed the Stamp Building, and encompasses the Modern Languages department, and the Bisseker Room. Moulton House has been established, the Library has been extended, and a new Sports Hall and all weather playing surface have been built. Many aspects of these changes are amplified in Chapter 5 - *The Buildings*.

Dr. and Mrs. Barrett

CHAPTER THREE

The Governors

Bertram Nelson, who was acting as Chairman of the Governors, at Speech Day in 1971 said that the duties of the Governors were to appoint the Headmaster and then not to disappoint him. Throughout the past 125 years of the school's history there have been many distinguished men and women who, as Governors, have helped successive Headmasters to guide the school through prosperous and also less prosperous times. It is only possible to describe the influence of a few of them in this chapter.

When the school was founded, the President of the Methodist Conference was listed as being the Chairman of the Governors. However, the minutes of Governors' meetings show various Presidents to have been present at only fourteen of the first two hundred meetings. In 1921 there was a subtle change whereby the President of Conference was made President of the Governors rather than Chairman. At the same time, the ex-President and Secretary of the Methodist Conference became ex-officio governors. It would have been difficult for someone appointed President for one year to take the chair at meetings of a body of which he had little or no knowledge. In 1999, the title was changed to Visitor. The President of the Conference attended the March 2000 Governors' Meeting in that capacity.

Derek Baker in *Partnership in Excellence*, in the chapter *Bricks without Straw* depicts the Governors calmly accepting year after year that the school was substantially in debt. The original purchase price of the estate was paid by a loan from the Star Life Assurance Society which was secured by guarantees of nine leading Methodists: Revd William Arthur, Sir Francis Lycett, Alexander McArthur, William (later Sir William) McArthur, J.S. Budgett, James Heald, R. Haworth, William Mewburn and John Chubb. Of these, Heald would have been considered a millionaire today, but he died before the foundation of the school. Although he left considerable legacies

George Hayter Chubb – 1st Baron Hayter of Chiselhurst
Vice-Chairman and Hon. Treasurer of the Governors 1891-1921

to several Wesleyan causes, The Leys was not one of them. It was his sister who subsequently gave The Leys £200. The other eight guarantors eventually contributed a total of about £6,100. It had been hoped that the Life-Donor Scheme would have initially raised much more. The Scheme was that "any person who, being approved by resolution of the Governing Body, shall subscribe £100 to the funds of the Foundation, shall become a Life-Donor of the Schools". A Life-Donor could nominate a pupil to attend the school who would receive a reduction of ten guineas (£10.50) from the school fees. The sum payable to become a Life-Donor stayed at £100 for over 100 years, and was then increased for a short while to £500. It is now 20% of the annual boarding fees. The Life-Donors also, in theory, elect most of the Governing Body, although it seems that in practice they have for most of the time simply endorsed the nominations of the existing Governing Body. Lady Trumpington seems to have been the only governor to have been directly elected by the Life-Donors in the twentieth century.

Of all the Governors, Sir George Hayter Chubb, first Baron Hayter of Chislehurst, was probably the person who was chiefly responsible for saving the school when it was faced with an enormous debt. He was the grandson of the founder of Chubb and Sons' Lock and Safe Company. While he was young, his health was delicate, and at the age of nineteen he was refused life insurance. He died 79 years later on 7 November 1946, aged 98. He later became a director of Star Life Assurance Society, which had originally refused him life insurance, and now they allowed him a life policy on which he paid premiums for over seventy-five years. The company became the Eagle Star Insurance Company and he was its deputy chairman from 1938 until his death. He was a Governor of The Leys for 60 years and Vice-Chairman and Treasurer of the Governing Body from 1891-1921. In fact, since he took the Chair in the absence of the President of Conference, and this was for most of the time, he was the real Chairman of the Governors. From its foundation in 1911 until his death, he was also Chairman of the Governors of Farringtons, often considered to be the sister school of The Leys.

Derek Baker in *Partnership in Excellence* puts some of the blame on the early Governors and Headmaster for mistakes which had led to the school's unfortunate position. He claims that "there was a fundamental failure in public relations: they displayed a striking inability to make friends."

The Minutes books show the Governors to have been completely oblivious of the impression they made on the wider Cambridge community. Time and time again there are reports of requests to use the school grounds for worthy causes being refused. They did allow the Cambridge Show to be held on the field in 1904 but, not surprisingly, they turned down the request for the sale of alcohol. The next year they refused permission for a German Pastor and also the Cambridge Methodist Circuit to use the school grounds. A similar request for the Leysian Mission Boys' Brigade to camp on the field in 1910 was turned down. Although the school chapel was registered in 1906 for marriages, the Governors only grudgingly allowed the marriage of one of the daughters of Revd Harry Bisseker to take place there after his retirement.

Nowadays, through a combination of good public relations and good business sense, the school buildings and grounds are used by many groups in Cambridge. Marriages of teaching and support staff frequently take place in the chapel, with receptions afterwards in the Dining Hall. Meetings of the local Methodist Synod are held at the school, as befits its foundation. The swimming bath, sports hall and astro-turf bring in useful revenue from hirings. During the summer holidays, most of the premises are used by a local language school.

When Chubb became treasurer and vice-chairman, he brought into these offices considerable skills from his business experience. He first appointed new auditors and with them an improved system of accounting was introduced. A sub-committee of the Governors reported on the financial position of the school. It called for all expenditure to be sanctioned by Chubb. He was assisted by J.H.S. McArthur, Secretary to the Governing Body, who was an Old Leysian and nephew of Sir William McArthur. Chubb and McArthur launched the 1896 appeal and successfully reduced the debt.

The early Governors closely controlled many aspects of the school which today would be solely the concern of the Bursar. It is amazing that at a meeting attended by two members of the House of Lords, two Knights of the Realm and several leading members of the Methodist Church, such matters as the repairs to a sewer pipe should be lengthily discussed. Their penny-pinching, impractical decision to encase the leak in concrete showed how ill-qualified they were to deal with minor repairs. At the next meeting

J.H.S. McArthur
Hon. Secretary of the Governing Body 1899-1943

they had to give permission for the pipe to be replaced. When electric light was introduced into the Houses, the Governors ruled that only one electric light bulb of 30 candle power was to be used in each study: this was equivalent to 20 watts, and no boy might replace it with one of higher power. Later they did allow the bulbs to be of 40 candle power. There are accounts of them giving the Headmaster, Dr Moulton, permission to purchase another cow. Another minute allows him to put a glass roof over the boys' outside urinals. They did, however, show some signs of compassion. They paid the funeral expenses of Dr Moulton's granddaughter, aged 7, in 1902. She is buried in the same grave as Dr Moulton and his wife.

Although there were many examples of their dealing with trivia, they also, of course, had to face far more important issues. The increasing debt was one obvious worry. In 1882 the debt was £44,000 which according to the values of the day was an enormous sum of money. An appeal for funds was made at a meeting in Manchester, but only £900 was raised. Six years later, the school accounts showed enough profit to pay the interest on the debt. The whole financial history of the school until after the Second World War is full of accounts of mortgaging the school premises, raising funds by debenture flotations and very severe budgeting. This did not deter the Governors from making ambitious plans for new buildings. No sooner was one major project finished, than another was undertaken. Much of this drive came from Chubb, who must surely be one of the most outstanding and generous Governors the school has ever had.

As mentioned earlier, overlapping the time that Chubb was Vice-Chairman and Treasurer, was J.H.S. McArthur (Old Leysian, 1877-1883), who was the Honorary Secretary to the Governors from 1899 to 1943. He lived in 1, Belvoir Terrace and later in 2, Brookside. He and his wife entertained the new boys to tea, starting a tradition carried on by Balgarnie during his retirement in 6 Brookside. Living so near, McArthur was able to devote a lot of his time to the school. It is reported that when he was due to be called to the Bar, the event coincided with an Old Leysian Rugby match and he preferred to play in the match. It is not certain whether he actually practised as a barrister, although he claimed it as his profession in his entry in *The Leys Directory*. The same entry showed that he was also the Director of a coal mine.

He was an outstanding sportsman at school, being in the Rugby, Lacrosse

Lord Chubb (left) with Lord Marshall, Chairman of the Governors 1921-1936

and Cricket teams. He was Swimming, Rackets, Fives and Tennis Champion. After graduating from Peterhouse, where he gained a Tennis Blue, he qualified for the Bar, both at the Inner Temple and in Sydney, Australia. He was the co-founder of the Leysian Mission. He played in the tennis championships at Wimbledon, and he represented both Surrey and Middlesex at Rugby. McArthur was on the Rugby Union General Committee and an England selector from 1889 to 1892. He paid for the portrait of Lord Hayter Chubb which now hangs in the Dining Hall. When it was proposed that The Leys should have a preparatory school at Hitchin, he jointly financed it with Jenkins, the first Headmaster of Caldicott.

The minute book for 1905 contains a seven page memorandum which Chubb, McArthur and Isard presented to the 20th Centenary Fund, Secondary Education Sub-Committee of the Methodist Conference. The school had applied to the 20th Century Fund for a substantial grant to help to pay off some of its debt. However they were disappointed when they received only £4,000, which furthermore had to be used to set up a scholarship fund. To add to their disappointment, a large grant was made for the purchase of Rydal Mount. The deputation pointed out that The Leys' Governors were especially concerned that a rival Methodist Public school in the North would undoubtedly divert potential pupils from The Leys. Their main worry was that The Leys had not yet achieved its very early target of 200 pupils. Since the wealthiest Methodists lived in the North, they might well choose to send their sons to Rydal rather than The Leys. The deputation also pointed out that since the Leysian Mission depended upon the generosity of Old Leysians, the flow of funds might be reduced by the establishment of a rival school.

Raising an interesting class distinction of the time, the deputation claimed that much of the money for the 20th Century Fund would have been given by 'middle class' Methodists. Therefore Rydal should only be seen as a middle class Public School whereas The Leys was for the wealthiest Methodist families. The deputation reported to the next Governors' meeting that 'they regretted having failed to elicit any undertaking to their pleas, and could only hope that the Conference might give some directions in that sense'. Nothing more was heard of their request for funds and perhaps the building programme which followed was an attempt to ensure that The Leys had outstanding facilities to combat the competition from Rydal. The rivalry

*Lord Renfrew (right), Chairman 1984-1992
with Lord Todd, also a Governor*

*Sir Arthur Armitage
Chairman 1971-1984*

later re-emerged when the Secretary of Rydal Mount wrote to the Leys Governors in 1910, complaining that the advertisement which had recently appeared in the *Methodist Times* stating that The Leys was the only first class Methodist High Grade School was incorrect.

Chubb and McArthur dominated the fortunes of the school in the early years of the 20th century, but, of course, many others were to guide the school to the end of the millennium. Following Chubb's resignation in 1921, Lord Marshall and Lord Stamp each held the office of Chairman of the Governors in turn until 1941 when the latter was killed in an air-raid in London. Sir Henry Dale was acting Chairman until 1955, when Sir Norman Birkett was elected Chairman. Birkett had been involved in the War Crimes trials in Nuremberg at the end of the Second World War. Four masters of Cambridge Colleges then followed one another as Chairman. Sir Henry Thirkill was Master of Clare, Sir Frank Lee, Master of Corpus Christi, Sir Arthur Armitage, President of Queens' and Lord Renfrew, Master of Jesus. Dr John Long (Old Leysian 1938-1942) was the next Chairman until Lord Lewis, Warden of Robinson College, Cambridge took over in 1996. These have been assisted on the Governing Body by men and women, many of whom have reached the top of their professions. The expertise they have brought to their task has enabled the two schools to survive difficult times and ultimately to flourish today.

If the early Governors were tied to trivia, the modern Governing Body still has very lengthy meetings which often consider matters better delegated to sub-committees. Although The Leys Governors had purchased St. Faith's in 1938, it was not until 1949 that the 'Scheme' used the term 'the Foundation'. The 'Scheme', it should be pointed out, is a document setting out the terms under which the school became registered as a charity. There had been much earlier versions, and even now the Scheme is adapted from time to time, to encompass changes in the running of the two schools.

Changes in the 'Scheme' have to be approved by the Governing Body, the Life Donors and the President of the Methodist Conference. The 1949 document states that: "The object of the Foundation is the establishment and conduct of a School and a Preparatory School to provide high-class education. The religious teaching in the school shall be in accordance with that of the Methodist Conference, which Conference is a Body established pursuant to the Methodist Church Union Act, 1929."

Lord Lewis
Chairman of Governors 1996-

Dr. F.J. Long
Chairman of Governors 1992-1996

In 1996, a sub-committee was set up to bring about closer ties between The Leys and St. Faith's. The comments of the committee on the arrangements at the time were:

1. The Executive Committee of the Foundation dealt largely with Leys business, but some items were included which affected both schools.

2. The Fabric Committee, which included members of Leys staff, reviewed the need for various works and was able to rank their urgency in terms of deterioration of the fabric, but could not make judgement about priorities for development driven projects.

3. The Audit Committee had three separate functions; investment strategy, reviewing the accounts for the previous year and noting the auditors' comments. These were all done at one meeting and it was suggested that the review of the investments should be separated from the audit.

There was a St. Faith's Committee which reported to the main Governors' meetings but sometimes it was attempting to run the school without full knowledge of the Foundation's financial position.

After discussions in the Governors' meetings it was agreed to restructure the committees. A Leys Committee and a St. Faith's Committee would prepare proposals for the Governing Body, always bearing in mind and stating the effect a proposal would have on the other school. Both Headmasters and Bursars were to serve on each committee, helping to see that such effects are acceptable. The committees would also cover proposals about projects and maintenance work, which in the past had been reviewed at the Leys by the Fabric Committee. There had always been a representative on the Governing Body elected by the staff of The Leys. The 'Scheme' was altered recently to provide a representative for the St. Faith's staff. These two Governors are ex-officio on their respective committees.

The Foundation Executive took on the rôle of the former Executive Committee, and is responsible also for the Support Staff Pension Fund and The Leys Enterprises. There is also a small Audit committee. These committees prepare reports for the main Governors' Meetings which now take place only once a term. To enable the Governors to have an overall picture of the Foundation, membership of each committee rotates every three years.

CHAPTER FOUR

They served them all their days

Any successful school needs continuity of staff. On the other hand those who have been in post for many years may resist change when it is needed and new, recently graduated staff can bring fresh ideas, outlooks and energy into the school.

The Leys has been fortunate in having had many staff who dedicated their lives to the school and the aim of this chapter is to highlight some of them. The longest serving master was T. P. Walker who joined the staff in the Christmas term of 1875 and finally retired in 1919. His total of 44 years service now that the normal retiring age is sixty can never be exceeded. Walker was a scholar of St. Catharine's College, Cambridge and taught Mathematics and Greek at The Leys. He was also responsible for the school time-table, organising the life both of boys and masters. Twice he acted as Vice-master when Dr Moulton was ill or had outside engagements, but he declined to hold the office again when the Headmaster's sudden death created an emergency.

Members of staff in the year 2000 will be amazed to hear that he did not find his first term hard, and he had enough leisure to read nine Waverley novels. At his retirement in 1919, colleagues wrote in *The Fortnightly* that his discipline was strict; but he used to say he ruled by kindness. Towards the end of his career he was often unwell and this is thought to be the reason for his outbursts of temper. On at least two different occasions when his class was having difficulty with work, he said that he was not surprised, as they were all sons of tradesmen. The insult was conveyed back to some of the parents who wrote to the Headmaster. Walker was reprimanded by Dr Barber and had to apologise to his classes.

H.R.P. Boorman (North B 1915-1919) remembered that Walker had a little black book in which he kept his notes about each lesson during the

J.C.Isard
Staff 1880-1918 – (note the cantilever bicycle - see p.64)

Dr. A.H. Mann
Staff 1894-1922

year, together with a fund of stories which he would tell at intervals during each lesson. The boys laughed heartily, of course, whether they understood the story or not. He appreciated this and would say, "I told that story five, ten, twenty and forty years ago," with a satisfied chuckle. By that time in his life, he was sporting "mutton-chop" whiskers which had earned him the nick-name of "Chops" Walker. James Hilton (School 1915-1919) was to write many years later that he thought that this was what suggested the name "Mr. Chips" for his novel.

Although Walker's long service as a member of staff could not be equalled, J.C. Isard's life-time connection with the school constituted another record. Isard had spent more than five years at what is now Queen's College, Taunton. When The Leys opened in 1875, he was one of the "Original XVI" and was made Senior Prefect. Although only at the school for five terms, he was the inspiration for many of the Leysian institutions that exist today.

He played in the first Cricket and Rugby matches, scoring the first goal at Rugby. He was the Gymnastics champion, secretary of the Games Committee, played the organ and sang in the choir. As a pianist and flautist he played a useful part in the early days of the Musical Society, started the Literary and Debating Society, and the Leys Christian Union and was the Editor of *The Fortnightly*. It seems that the only blot on his name in those five terms was an appearance in the police court for cycling on the public footpath.

Entering Trinity College, Cambridge in 1876, he studied Classics and then English for four years before returning to The Leys as Assistant Housemaster in School House. Three years later, in 1883, he became the first Housemaster of the newly opened North B House. In 1897 the school was crippled by a debt of £60,000 and numbers had fallen. Dr Moulton's health was declining, and a debt-relief fund had to be organised at once. Isard was offered the post of Bursar. He was responsible for making sweeping economies, and assisted by J.H.S. McArthur as treasurer of the fund, he managed to reduce the debt by £30,000 and the school weathered the storm.

By now he had moved into North A House to be nearer the school office and to become the Housemaster there. For a short time following Dr Moulton's death, he was acting Headmaster until the arrival of Dr Barber. A colleague, H.H. Dale (later Sir Henry) wrote of him:

"It was common gossip in the Masters' Room that, however late any of us might find occasion to cross the Quad, the light in the Bursary would always be burning. We had difficulty, indeed, in finding direct evidence that he went to bed at all. He seemed to welcome interruption for hospitality, however late the caller, returning then cheerfully to his office, and arriving punctually next day at school breakfast with an air of a man who had already done a good morning's work."

He was a dedicated sportsman. Whilst at Trinity, he and E.S. Whelpton had led the formation of the Old Leysian Football Club. For many years he was a playing member and also played for the school sides at Rugby and Lacrosse. He founded the Bicycle Club and cycling remained his favourite pastime for the rest of his life. Indeed, a 50-mile run meant little to him even when he was close to eighty. His "Cantilever" bicycle, with its slung saddle and peculiar frame, had long been a byword for speed on school cycle runs. The original machine had to be replaced in his later years but the replacement was still of the same design. When he was 75, following a cycling tour in Brittany, he cycled from Southampton to Reigate. It was an extremely warm day and his undue haste brought on a slight stroke. He took warning from this and the problem did not recur. He also enjoyed walking and had walked from Cambridge to London (55-60 miles) on at least three occasions, covering the distance in sixteen hours.

He took a prominent part in Chapel services. He had been a local preacher in his teens, and was still active in the Methodist circuit in Tonbridge when he was eighty. He had suffered an injury to his throat whilst playing lacrosse and that had left him with a weak voice. The manager of the Tuck Shop, Freddy Brett, once said, "I think that if one could hear better what he said, and understand better what he meant, Mr Isard would be an excellent preacher".

His last four years at the school and as Bursar were those of the First World War. War was declared on 4 August, 1914 and during the holidays The Leys was converted into a military hospital, which served its purpose until the required beds could be made ready elsewhere in mid-September, when the school returned. The six weeks of turmoil brought him great satisfaction. There was plenty of work which he loved and did well. As the war dragged on there were signs of weariness in the school and impatience for the end. Isard especially, as the economist, had a difficult task, which he tackled resolutely and successfully. He retired in July 1918 before the end of the war came in November.

He was elected to the Governing Body and remained active on this until his death. After retirement he took up residence at The Leysian Mission where he was Warden. It was here that he edited the last edition of *The Leys Handbook and Directory* having been associated with eight editions in total. He finally settled at the age of 64 in Tonbridge, the town where he had been born. He became the Chairman of the Queen Victoria Cottage Hospital and took an active part in the management of the town library, in the Ratepayers' Association, in social service and in Methodist and Free Church activities. Towards the end of his life he spent some time in a nursing-home but returned to his house, Kentleys, to die on 27 August 1941 at the age of 83.

E.E. Kellett joined The Leys staff in 1889, having been a boy at Kingswood and a scholar of Wadham College, Oxford. He was to spend the next 35 years of his career at the school. He became Housemaster of North B House in 1890. Perhaps the thing for which he was most remembered was his introduction of the school line which read as follows:

"Few things are more distressing to a well-regulated mind than to see a
boy who ought to know better, disporting himself at improper moments."

There are countless Old Leysians who can repeat the line without realising who initiated it. Kellett was a composer of copious verses. He published two volumes of *Musa Leysiana,* which varied from a mixture of House and sporting songs, to elegies on the death of Tennyson and Dr Moulton. He gave up the Housemastership of North B in 1907 in order to get married. At that time there was no married accommodation in the school. He had a larger sphere of influence than just the school. Kellett attained widespread recognition as an author and as a critic. He published 35 books on varying topics, ranging from *Religion and Life in the Early Victorian Age* to *A History of the Pianoforte and Pianoforte Players.*

Another member of staff who dedicated much of his life to the school was W.H. Balgarnie. He was the son of a Presbyterian Minister at Woolwich. He first attended the Roan School and then Gravesend School where he passed his London Matriculation exams. He then moved to Elmfield School, York (now closed), a Primitive Methodist foundation where he was an usher (student teacher) and whilst there he studied for his external London BA, which he obtained in 1889. After a short period teaching at Fowey School,

W.H. Balgarnie
Staff 1900-1930, 1940-1946

in Cornwall, he moved to the School for Sons of Missionaries, now Eltham College in London, where he continued his studies and obtained his London MA in 1893. He had, during the whole of his employment, been saving up to pay his own way through Cambridge University. His brother, Eric, had done a similar thing three years earlier. William came up to Trinity in 1894 at the age of 26, which made him much older than most of his contemporaries. He obtained a First in the Classics Tripos and joined Professor Gilbert Murray in the Department of Classics at Glasgow University. After only a short time, he left the Department to teach at Woodbridge School. Eventually in 1900 his career began at The Leys, although he did have a short leave of absence to be acting Headmaster at Woodbridge until the appointment of a new Head there. During the next 29 years he was to dedicate his life to the school and was beloved by most of his pupils. Old Leysians whom he taught and influenced wrote after his death expressing their thanks for what he had done for them. Contemporaries of Hilton remember how Balgarnie encouraged him in his writing, and the enjoyment they all got from hearing James read out his essays in class. Balgarnie, in his retirement, lived just across the Trumpington Road in Brookside and would entertain the new boys to tea - just as Hilton's fictional character did. A colleague later described how Balgarnie was often to be seen in the evening, with a devoted cat on his lap, his mouth puckered as he happily puffed at a pipe filled with Boer tobacco, pen in hand, rejecting, annotating and amending scripts for the next issue of *The Fortnightly.*

Although retired from the staff, Balgarnie spent much of his time in the school. One member of staff recalled that when he was first at the school, Balgarnie would join them most evenings for dinner. Jessie Mellor presided and Balgarnie sat beside him. Those present had to listen to Balgarnie repeating stories time and time again. Mellor would kindly laugh, but the others were not so respectful.

Immediately following his retirement at the age of 60, he was recalled to act as Headmaster during the year's leave of absence granted to the Headmaster, the Revd Harry Bisseker, for reasons of health. He had previously been Acting Headmaster after the retirement of the Revd Barber and before the arrival of Bisseker, and he must have felt a certain irony in the situation which had arisen once again.

Once Bisseker had returned, Balgarnie was able to retire again to his Brookside accommodation. This was where he was living when he was visited by his old pupil, James Hilton, who like many others, would call upon him when he visited Cambridge. Hilton wrote these words later in *Good-Bye, Mr. Chips:*

> "Across the road, behind a rampart of ancient elms was Brookfield, russet under its autumn mantle of creeper".

Sadly, the tall elms have now disappeared through Dutch Elm Disease and the creeper has been torn down, as it was damaging the mortar in the brickwork. The view Balgarnie would have had across the school field is now dominated by a skyline of modern buildings. Whether he would have approved of the relative luxury in the new boarding house which replaced the West House of which he had been Housemaster, is doubtful. The Design and Technology building with its aluminium, geometrically sloping roofs, housing computers and cookers, lathes and kilns, would have been an object of fantasy to such a scholarly classicist.

Good-bye, Mr. Chips was turned into a play and when, on the first night in London, Hilton was called onto the stage for a curtain call, he had a spotlight turned onto the box where Balgarnie was sitting. Balgarnie told colleagues when he returned to Cambridge that he was very embarrassed, but some of them thought that he had quite enjoyed it. Later in his life he did say that it was not much of a reputation being half of a fictional character. When Balgarnie died in 1951, Hilton wrote to Dr Humphrey, who was still Head of The Leys and said:

> "Balgarnie was, I suppose, the chief model for my story, so far as I had one: certainly in my school life his was a personality I have never forgotten. When I read so many other stories about public school life I am struck by the fact that I myself suffered no such purgatory as their authors apparently did, and much of this miracle (if indeed it was one) was due to Balgarnie. He not only realised that I was not a typical schoolboy, but I suspect he had discovered that deeper truth that no such animal exists."

Although Balgarnie never married, unlike the character of Mr. Chipping, it was reported that someone he had wanted to marry, but who had rejected him, eventually sent her son to The Leys and into his House. The boy later became a journalist and moved to Canada. The story cannot be confirmed because he is now dead, having never married. Balgarnie's brother, who had taught at Barnard Castle School, was reported to be terrified of the company of women. Balgarnie, later in life, was almost a flirt. A series of letters which he wrote to Miss Muriel de Vinny, the School Secretary, are in the school archives and show an interesting side of the man. The first few letters address her as "O fairest of women". In later letters he writes this in Latin and even in Greek. In one of the final letters it is turned into a symbol, a Greek capital Ω with the letters f o w written vertically inside the symbol, the whole making a M for Muriel.

Although St.J. B. Wynne Willson was only on the staff for a few years between 1891 and 1898, his distinguished career deserves mention here. He was the son of an Anglican priest who later became ordained himself. Whilst at his prep school he failed to win a scholarship to Marlborough. He must have enjoyed a particular sense of satisfaction when, thirty years later, he did get there as Head. At the age of 13, he instead won a scholarship to Cheltenham College and then later one to St. John's College, Cambridge.

On graduating in 1892, he joined the staff of The Leys. Although he was an Anglican, he found the Wesleyan Methodist atmosphere was not aggressive and he soon made himself at home. When he first arrived at the school, he looked so young that a boy asked him what form he had been put into. Whilst on the staff, he produced the first of many books, a school edition of *Prometheus Vinctus* with the help of E. E. Kellett. He wrote some reminiscences of his years on the staff in *The Fortnightly* in 1915:

> "At my first assembly for dinner, after giving out an announcement, I heard a boy echo some word. In the direction from which the sound came I saw one of the very few boys whose names I knew, and happening to have heard of his fame for villainy, I drew a bow at venture and asked if it was he who spoke. It was; and he got 1000 lines. I have always been thankful for that lucky accident."

> "I have never enjoyed teaching boys more than I did in my days at The Leys. I was master in West House which was the home of little boys in those days, but with great enthusiasm they worked hard and at last won the shield for lacrosse. It was a memorable occasion. Since that time West House have never looked back."

After leaving The Leys, Wynne Willson taught at Rugby, and there he

R. Morris – Staff 1921-1957

G.F. Green – Staff 1923-1960

was ordained into the Church of England. After six years, he was appointed Headmaster of Haileybury and then in 1911 became Head of Marlborough. After a short spell as Dean of Bristol Cathedral, he became Bishop of Bath and Wells in 1921, a position he held until 1937.

F.H. Marseille taught French and German at the school for 29 years from 1889 to 1918. He and his wife came from Alsace, a region which changed hands between Germany and France several times. Members of their families fought and were killed on both sides during World War I. This had led to the breakdown of his wife's health and her eventual death. Sadly, he committed suicide in January 1919. Several Old Leysians who had been taught by Marseille convinced themselves that the character of Herr Staefel, the German who was on the staff of Brookfield in Hilton's *Good-bye, Mr. Chips,* and left to fight on the German side, was based on Marseille. There is no evidence that pupils of The Leys at the time ever knew of his background, and he certainly did not leave the school to go to Germany.

A.H. (Daddy) Mann taught music at the school between 1894 and 1922. As well as being the organist at the school, he played in the chapel of King's College and was organist to the University. He was often to be seen cycling hurriedly from The Leys to King's, dressed in his academic gown. He had been involved as Director of Music in the first Festival of Nine Lessons and Carols held on Christmas Eve 1918. The internationally famed service has been held annually ever since, even during the Second World War, although it was not broadcast until 1928, which was Mann's last year at King's. There is a plaque in the choir robing room in King's College Chapel and a mosaic panel by the organ in the school chapel, both in his memory. The Mann Memorial Music prize also commemorates him.

J.E. (Jessie) Mellor had been a boy at the school between 1898 and 1903. He had had a distinguished career at school both on the sports field and in other aspects of school life. He was Senior Prefect, editor of *The Fortnightly,* secretary of the Leys Christian Union and a member of the Rugby, Lacrosse and Cricket first teams. He passed with five subjects in his Higher School Certificate and won an Exhibition to Jesus College, Cambridge. During his last year at university, he was chosen to play for Cambridge against the Old Leysians XV. He had the audacity to go to the captain and asked to be excused so that he might play for the Old Leysians. Despite this, he gained a place in the University side and was awarded a Blue for Rugby. On graduating, he joined the staff at The Leys in 1906 and became Housemaster of School House in 1913, an appointment he held until his retirement in 1947.

His obituary described him as terse and forthright. Once, when replying to a scribbled note asking if he would like to play fives on a certain afternoon, he returned it with a simple "No", without excuse or explanation. He said exactly what he meant, and no more. His major hobby was photography. Many of his negatives are in the school archives and some were enlarged for a centenary exhibition in 1975. The collection of portraits of his colleagues on the staff show them at work, in the laboratory or in the classroom. His Geography classroom was fitted with ingenious gadgetry of pulleys and strings for the concealment, revelation or transposition of maps and charts. He was responsible for the production of three editions of *The Leys Directory*, two in co-operation with Balgarnie. He enjoyed playing golf and always played to win.

John Stirland joined the school in 1919 immediately following his demobilisation from the army. He remembered that one day he was in the army and the next in front of a class, teaching French. He was to serve the school for the next 36 years as a member of staff and then in retirement until the age of 92 as Editor of Leysian News in *The Fortnightly* and editor of four editions of *The Leys Directory*. He was the first Housemaster of East House when it opened in 1919 in Brookside. He was the Commanding Officer of the Cadet Corps for many years and arranged the Guard of Honour for the visit of the Crown Prince of Japan, later Emperor Hirohito.

As second master, he was responsible for the time-table and day to day running of the school, advising on careers and assisting with university placements. Gerald Humphrey, the Headmaster during the period when The Leys was in Pitlochry, said that Stirland was really Headmaster during that time and he, Humphrey, acted as Bursar more than as Head.

Alan Buchanan was another member of staff who devoted his adult life to serving the school. 'Buck', as he was known, was one of a group of bachelor Housemasters, the others being Isard, Balgarnie and Mellor. He was born in Southern Ireland, and educated at Portora Royal School, where he was captain of Rugby, Cricket and Boxing. In 1925 he went to Trinity College, Dublin, where he became captain of the University Rugby side and also played for Ireland in the seasons 1926-7 and 1927-8. During that period

J.E. Mellor
Staff 1906-1947

J. Stirland
Staff 1919-1955

he was regarded as the best hooker in the games against England, Scotland, Wales and France. He came straight from University to The Leys in 1928 and the next year took over the new East House as Housemaster. When the school moved to Pitlochry, he became acting Bursar, where he had the task of fitting the school into a luxury hotel too small for it. He had the responsibility for the domestic arrangements, whereas Gerald Humphrey dealt with the Governors and the relevant Ministries which affected the school.

When The Leys returned to Cambridge in 1946, he became Bursar, and he was faced with repairing much of the neglect to the buildings of former years, and making plans for more efficient and regular maintenance in the future. Then followed an astonishing series of major additions and repairs to buildings directed almost entirely from inside and carried out with the minimum of outside help, thus saving the school thousands of pounds. The onerous task of being Bursar had started to take its toll in his later years when he was subject to nerve-strain and ill health.

The writer of his obituary in *The Fortnightly* said of him:

"He had also the defects of his virtues. He knew so much and was so often right that he could not bear to be wrong. He cared so much for the fabric and furnishings and grounds of The Leys that he could not bear that others should care less - which of course they nearly always did. His immense forbearance towards the foibles and anxieties of boys was offset by his intolerance of the follies of adults, who he thought should know better; it was always better to approach him in a spirit of inquiry rather than one giving instruction. He was so much aware of his responsibilities that he felt himself indispensable; and in the Pitlochry days, at least, he was very nearly right."

As well as being Bursar, he taught in the classroom and coached the 1st XV until 1954. He had also coached the Cambridge University side for a period. It was following his support of Cambridge against the Harlequins that he died in a road accident on the return journey.

W.N. White made a huge contribution to The Leys in post-war years. He had been a boy at the school from 1933 to 1939. During this time he was very much influenced by Buchanan. Neil was an outstanding sportsman who played for the 1st XV for three seasons, being captain for two, for the 1st

A.McM Buchanan – Staff 1928-1956, Bursar 1946-1956

Hockey XI for four seasons and captain for three and for the 1st Cricket XI for four seasons and captain for two. In 1938 he played for the Scottish Public Schools XV and in the next season captained the British Public Schools Cricket tour of Canada.

In 1939 he went up to Trinity Hall to read History, but the interruption of the war meant that he had to wait until peace-time to complete his studies there. He joined the Queen's Own Cameron Highlanders in 1940 and served for most of the war in India and Burma. He was involved in the action at the crossing of the Irrawaddy river. The place designated for the first crossing was well defended by the Japanese on the opposite bank of the river. As the first wave of inflatable boats began crossing, most of them were hit by machine gun fire and sunk with heavy casualties. Neil sent a company some 500 yards upstream to reconnoitre, and as little opposition was found, a small bridgehead was established and the rest of the battalion were signalled to reinforce it. For his part in this fighting, Neil was awarded the Military Cross.

When the Japanese surrendered in 1945, he became one of Lord Mountbatten's aides-de-camp in Singapore. When Neil was demobilised from the Army, he had reached the rank of Major. He returned to Trinity Hall in October 1945. In 1947, he added another Rugby Blue to the one he had won in 1939 and gained a Hockey Blue in 1948. He played occasionally for Cambridge University at cricket, but was not selected for the Varsity match. From 1947 to 1950 he played Hockey for Scotland, and won a silver medal with the British Olympic Hockey side in 1948.

In 1948, Neil was recruited by the Headmaster, Gerald Humphrey, to teach History and Geography and to coach games. His history teaching included that of the American Mid-West and enthusiasm for this subject earned him the nick name of 'Tex'. He was master in charge of Hockey from 1948 to 1962 and master in charge of Rugby from 1954 to 1966. For many years he was also President of the Cambridge University Hockey Club. In 1954 he became Housemaster of North B House and then in 1966 until 1973 he was Housemaster of the newly opened Fen House.

During his career, he suffered two devastating losses. In 1956 his close friend and colleague, Alan Buchanan, was killed in a car crash which Neil miraculously survived. Soon after moving into Fen House his wife, Phyl, died after a prolonged illness. He later married Celia Burrell, Sister in the

Schooldays

Great Britain Olympic Hockey XI 1948

Receiving the Military Cross

Presentation at Old Leysian Dinner

W.N. White – Staff 1948-1962

School Sanatorium, who was a tower of strength to him during his latter days in Fen and then later nursed him to recovery following a major operation.

Among the many other responsibilities he had during his teaching career was the Presidency of the Games Committee. He was secretary of the Old Leysian Union from 1962 to 1986 and President from 1976 to 1977. When he retired in 1982, he became Secretary of the Royal Worlington and Newmarket Golf Club. Neil died in 1990.

During the period between the wars many staff were appointed, each of whom were to serve the school for well over thirty years. They were: Robert Morris, Classics, Housemaster of B House and swimming coach, Harold Rose, Chemistry and Mathematics, cricket and hockey coach, Sidney Gillard, English, Housemaster of A House and director of many drama productions, Reg Ayres, Chemistry, Senior Science master and Scoutmaster, Geoff Green, Biology and hockey coach, Wilfred Sandbach, German and tennis coach, Ronnie Brown, Physics and Senior Science master, John Marnham, French and later Bursar.

Special mention in this list must be made of Maurice Howard. Appointed in 1936 to teach classics, his career was interrupted by war service. On returning to the school, he became second master, inheriting the post which John Stirland had held. On the resignation of Gerald Humphrey, he was acting Headmaster until the appointment of Alan Barker. After a short term as Bursar of St. Faith's, he still maintained his connection with The Leys, producing the Old Leysian section of *The Fortnightly* and editing three editions of *The Leys Directory*.

Since the war there has again been a number of staff who served for over thirty years. These include Sherard Allison (Housemaster of Fen), Richard Armstrong (Master i/c Rowing), Peter Chamberlain (Housemaster of West), David Gardiner (Housemaster of North A), John Harding (Housemaster of School), Geoff Houghton (Housemaster of North B), Stephen Siddall (English Department), Stan Whitehead (Deputy Headmaster) and Harold Wiseman (Housemaster of North A). Dick Bennett (Housemaster of West), John Dillistone (Art), Sam Grice (Music), Peter Marshall (Biology), Ken Naylor (Housemaster of School) and Eric Southern (Housemaster of West and then East) served for nearly thirty years. In all cases their main responsibility during their career at the school is shown in brackets.

78

Trevor Moore, Ronnie Bown, Peggy Humphrey, Donald Hughes

W.E. Sandbach – Staff 1930-1968

The Masters' Common Room – circa 1910

However during their long service to the school they were also involved in many of the extra-curricular activities of the school.

Many members of staff were for a shorter time at the school before moving on to become Headmasters. With the name of the school to the Headship of which they departed, they were:

A. Vinter (Woodhouse Grove School), W.T. Greenup (Mount House School, Ryde), L.W. Posnett (Pierremount School, Broadstairs and Kent College, Canterbury), J.L.A. Paton (Manchester Grammar School), St.J. B. Wynne Willson (Haileybury and Marlborough Colleges), J.H. Jenkins (Caldicott School), Revd A.J. Costain (Rydal School), J.T. Lancaster (Ashville College), Revd A.R. Wooley (Scarborough College and Wellingborough School), D.W. Hughes (Rydal School), C.H. Lewis (Kimbolton School), S.V. Peskett (The Royal Academical Institute, Belfast), H.J.C. Bashford (Wellingborough School), A.N. Pattinson (Sunnymede Preparatory School), L.G.D. Baker (Christ's Hospital), J.W. Horn (Aireborough Grammar School and Ossett School), R.P. Heazel (The Hall, Hampstead), G.B. Bean (Prince Alfred College, Adelaide), M.A. Lang (Durham School), T.M. Ham (Sherardswood School) and P.R. Lacey (King's School, Gloucester).

One former master became Master of St. John's College, Cambridge (Revd C.H.W. Johns) and another, the Recorder of Launceston, Tasmania (G.W. Waterhouse)

A school not only requires teaching staff, but a variety of support staff. In the early 1960s, a member of the teaching staff took his class into the bath for an unscheduled swimming lesson. This particular period was set aside weekly for the cleaning of the bath surround. A heated discussion between the member of staff and the cleaner led to blows being exchanged. The cleaner was dismissed but eventually rose to a very responsible position at a Cambridge College. The master left at the end of the year. Following the incident, the other bath attendant said that in his opinion the support staff were not appreciated and the most important member of staff at The Leys was not the Headmaster but the dustman. In those days, the dustman removed the accumulation of rubbish from all the buildings using a hand-cart and not a flat-back lorry as is used today. Perhaps his colleague was slightly exaggerating his importance, but certainly his function was vital to the life of the school.

From the foundation of The Leys in 1875, social attitudes of the past have meant that many people have helped to ensure its smooth running without perhaps being sufficiently recognised. The first school carpenter and handyman was called George Jacob. When he retired, his son succeeded him. The next school carpenter was Gus Leader who had an apprentice in 1956, called Peter Barker. Peter has been the Head Carpenter for many years, so he is only the fourth since the school opened. Of course, the buildings have grown in number over that time so he has been joined by other carpenters, plumbers and electricians.

After the return from Scotland, Ian Laing, who had had a short term of employment with the school in Pitlochry before he left to enter the RAF, joined the maintenance staff at the school in Cambridge. In 1958, he became senior engineer with the responsibility for maintaining the plant. He was a resourceful man who often made replacement parts for worn out machinery. One memorable night when the pump in the school well failed and there was no water supply anywhere in the school, he descended the well to the water level about 26 feet below. Here he was able to diagnose the fault, which was due to a broken flange just below the water level. He climbed out of the well, made a new flange in the school metal workshop, and climbed down the well again to replace the broken one. Since the Science department has had laboratory stewards, there have only been three; William Underwood, Leslie Wallis and Roger Wright although the last two were joined by assistants in Physics and Biology after the Second World War.

An elderly gentleman, George Rogers, visited the school one day and described how he had been assistant secretary to the Headmaster in 1920. He had used a 100 key typewriter, since the modern compact keyboard had not been invented. He also said he had walked home in his one hour lunch break to Grantchester, to eat there because he found the school food so unappetising. His pay was £1 a week and for this he worked six days a week and pumped the school organ on Sundays.

Muriel de Vinny was appointed by Gerald Humphrey to be his secretary in 1935. He wrote at the time of her retirement from the school after 37 years service "Her arrival marked a change in tradition, for formerly all members of the staff of the Headmaster's office and the Bursary had been men. Initially her position was not easy, but her tact, charm and efficiency soon established her as a welcome and popular member of the school

Muriel de Vinny
School Secretary 1935-1972

George Jacob
School Carpenter 1875-1903

community". She accompanied the school to Pitlochry and it was here that she probably got to know the boys well. She herself wrote, "We adults were allowed fires in our rooms and in this room (in the middle of 'A' House) many boys came to my tea parties. Unwittingly, I once invited rival factions in 'A' for cocoa and biscuits. The Housemaster told me afterwards that when he looked in and saw them looking so happy, he was most surprised."

When Muriel died in 1991, a memorial service was held for her in the school chapel. The choir of St. Faith's sang an anthem and Professor David Miller (Old Leysian) gave an address which included personal memories from her friends as well as his own reminiscences of her. The full account appears in *The Fortnightly* Volume CXVI, page 149. Her cousin, John Ellis (Old Leysian), established an endowment fund in her memory to support the study and enjoyment of music, which was one of Muriel's great interests.

The record for long service to the school must surely be held by Alf Haggis. He joined the ground staff in October 1908 and finally retired in October 1969. He had worked at The Leys for 58 years, the other 3 having been spent in the Army during the First World War. He wrote of his memories of the school over those years in *The Fortnightly* Volume XCV, page 295. He described how, as Garden Boy, his first job was sweeping up leaves and how his last job in 1969 was sweeping up leaves. He finished his article "May there always be leaves at The Leys and always someone to sweep them up".

Tom Hayward was groundsman at the school for 40 years and his son followed him in that position for a short time. Sergeant-Major Scott was swimming instructor for 42 years. Sergeant-Major Withers had served in the Scots Guards during the First World War. Towards the end of the war he was instructor of the Officer Training Cadet Company at Pembroke College, Cambridge, one of whose officers was Jesse Mellor. In 1919 Withers joined the school to assist John Stirland in running the school O.T.C. and the shooting. He introduced the system of Muller's exercises in which the whole school did P.T. on the upper quad during morning break between 1919 and 1939. He retired from the Corps in 1945 and took charge of the Book Room from which text books and stationery were issued, where he continued to work until 1957. From 1945 to 1971, Withers was the clerk to the Old Leysian Union. Every year he was to be seen at the Cambridge O.L.U. Dinner, standing at the Dining Room door checking tickets, until his ninetieth birthday, when the Old Leysians marked the occasion of his fifty years' service with a presentation. He died aged 96. His daughter, Mrs. Jean Heesom, was in charge of the Stationery Office for many years after his retirement and she also succeeded him in looking after Old Leysian affairs.

Among those whose names will not be remembered by former pupils were the resident maids who were responsible for the cleaning of the Houses and other buildings and serving food. They were the responsibility of the Lady Superintendent who ensured that they attended chapel, morning and evening, sitting in the gallery. They were nick-named 'Bombs' by some of the boys, a shortened form for Abominations. This is an unfortunate example of the social division between the pupils of those days and those who looked after them. The records of some of the maids are preserved in the archives. Many were aged 14 or 15 and against their names are remarks about their work and time keeping. Their records include in some cases where they were later employed. Their leisure time was organised and they had a club, which even entered folk dancing competitions. Despite the strict supervision of these girls, Leslie Wallis, the Chemistry steward mentioned above, did manage to talk to one of them on a number of occasions whilst he was collecting milk from the kitchens for the Science department. She later became his wife.

These are just some of the people who served the school loyally over the years. There were many others, including caretakers, cricket professionals, maintenance and ground staff, butlers and chefs, and secretaries, and the wives and husbands of resident staff. They all contributed to the life of The Leys during its 125 years' history.

The Headmaster's House, 1878

The Headmaster's House, 1990

CHAPTER FIVE

The Buildings

Visitors to the school often say how surprised they are to find so many buildings on the school site. As the school grew in numbers more accommodation was required. All of them have received refurbishment during their history and many have changed their use.

THE HEADMASTER'S HOUSE

This was the main building on the estate when the school opened in February 1875. Originally the house had a walled kitchen garden and stabling, with several outbuildings. These gradually disappeared as school buildings were constructed. A room was added to the north of the house when the school first opened which served as a classroom, library and reading room. It was still a classroom in 1958 when Alan Barker suggested that it should be refurbished as a meeting-room and called the Moulton Room. Since then it has been used for sixth-form lessons, serving tea to groups of pensioners as part of the school's community service activities, society meetings, and as a small examination room. The Governing Body meet there although the full number cannot all sit round the large table. From time to time, art exhibitions were held there.

Plans are being discussed at this time to change the function of the room. It could provide a larger and more attractive waiting area for visitors than the present small waiting room. One link with the past can be seen on the outside north wall. Deliveries would have been made to the school by horse and cart in the early days. An iron ring hangs from the wall to which the horse would have been tethered.

SCHOOL HOUSE, LATER DALE, AND PART OF GRANTA HOUSES

This building was not ready for occupation until a few weeks after the school opened. Described at the time as 'a plain house' it consisted of classrooms, dormitories and a small dining room. Gradually, additions were made to the original structure to provide more accommodation. One of the effects of adding rooms piecemeal was that there were different levels inside requiring short flights of stairs to join areas which should have been on the same level. Another was that a small area in the middle of these additions was left uncovered and created a funnel by way of which rain water accumulated in the bottom. With the lack of damp-proof courses in the early building and the large amount of match-board facing to the inside walls, dry rot flourished unseen for many years. In the 1960s some of the building was discovered to be in a dangerous state and all the wood on the walls and floors was stripped out in the Christmas holidays. Bare brick walls were treated to prevent the return of the fungus, plastered and the whole building decorated ready for the return of boys at the beginning of the Lent term.

The building had housed the main school dining room until just before the Second World War. Fortunately the school kitchens lay between the Great Hall and the old dining room, making the switch to the Hall for dining relatively simple. The old dining room became the school theatre. A permanent stage was constructed at one end and wooden benches provided the seating for the audience.

Much of the stage equipment was home-made. The curtain winder was made from the fly wheel of an old bacon slicer. This worked far more efficiently than a commercially built one installed later. The first dimmer system consisted of lead plates which were raised and lowered into salt water housed in drain pipes. This was subsequently replaced by old rheostats from the Physics department before a final upgrading in 1960 with slide dimmers purchased from Strand Electric.

The wooden benches were replaced by tip-up theatre seats from a redundant Rank cinema. These were a gift from Lord Rank, who was an Old Leysian. The main problem encountered in the auditorium was that there were two columns in the centre of the room supporting the floors above. Vital parts of the construction of the building, they did nevertheless impede the view of the stage from many seats. Eventually when the school theatre was opened in 1966, the room was converted, first into two classrooms and then into small dormitories and common rooms for School House.

In 1989, when the need for more accommodation for girls arose, the boys

The Dining Hall, 1996

of School House moved into their present quarters. An extensive refurbishment of the old building prepared the interior for the arrival of Dale House. The final addition was the building of a house for the Housemistress which released space for more bedroom-studies for the girls.

OLD WEST HOUSE, NOW SCHOOL HOUSE

In 1880 the school numbers grew to 100 and the Governors sanctioned the construction of what was intended to be a temporary building to contain West House. On the ground floor of this simple bulding, the entrance hall housed the trunks and tuck boxes. There was a single gas stove for the boys to heat food. To the left of the doorway was the 'boot room' with storage for shoes and boots which the House caretaker cleaned. This caretaker had a small flat on the ground floor where there was also a common room, four studies and baths. On the two floors above there were four dormitories, each for sixteen boys, and accommodation for a Housemaster and assistant.

With the opening of North B House, West House closed for a time, and the building was used as extra studies for the staff between 1883 and 1890. When the school numbers again grew, West House was once more occupied by boys until 1914. The school numbers dropped at the beginning of the First World War, the House was closed and boys distributed amongst the other houses. However numbers increased, and West House was able to re-open in1916.

By 1958 the building had fallen well below the standard of the other Houses and an appeal was launched to finance the building of a new West House. The eventual vacating of the old building by West House made a number of changes possible. The Medical Centre moved into the bottom two floors and the old Sanatorium in 5 Brookside was sold to the Perse School for Girls who converted the old Isolation Hospital into their Junior School and used the main building for music and sixth form rooms.

The top floor of the old West House then became the Art department. This released the old Art room which had been on the floor above the Masters' Common Room (no female staff at that time), to be absorbed into the Common Room. It was not until 1982 that the Computer Department moved into part of the first floor.

Another re-organisation of the building occurred in 1987 with the opening of the Rugg Centre. The Art and Computer departments moved to

The Rt. Hon. Patrick Jenkin (later Lord Jenkin)
Secretary of State for Industry opening the Computer Laboratory, 1982
(from l. to r. John Bower, B.T. Bellis, Patrick Jenkin, Sir Arthur Armitage, Dr. R.D. Gidden)

Photo by courtesy of Times Newspapers Ltd.

Some of the first girls in September, 1984
with some of the school prefects
(girls from l. to r. Sarah Seward, Claire Ang, Antonia Beamish, Helen Pring, Gillian Beardon)

the Design Technology Centre. Meanwhile the tuck shop was relocated to part of the space under the Dining Hall, making room for the Medical Centre to move into the two floors previously used by the tuck shop.

This left the old West House building empty again. An ingenious redesign of the interior provided junior dormitories, bed-room studies, common room and classroom as well as flats for a married Housemaster and an assistant.

In 1989 School House boys moved into the refurbished building leaving their old home which became Dale House. For a building which had been conceived as being temporary, it has stood the test of time remarkably well.

THE GREAT HALL, NOW THE DINING HALL

In 1877 the Governors invited several architects to submit designs for a number of new buildings. From a distinguished field, they selected Robert Curwen who designed not only the Great Hall but also the North block, the first Science building, the swimming bath and the Chapel.

The Hall, at the time of building, was larger than many of the Cambridge College Halls. Its splendid roof beams resembled those of Westminster Hall. The north end had a large dais which was used for assemblies, with room for desk, lectern, ornate chairs and a small organ in the north-east corner. This was later replaced in 1889 by a much larger instrument in the gallery. This permitted the construction of the spiral staircase which is still a feature of the exterior of the Hall.

As well as doubling as an assembly hall and chapel, the Hall was the place where the boys did their 'prep' (work set at the end of lessons to consolidate what had been learnt) seated in individual desks. Until the numbers grew too large to be accommodated, Speech Days were held here and H.M. King George V received loyal addresses here when he opened the library block in 1914. When the Moulton Memorial Chapel was opened in 1906, the Hall was no longer required for worship. The walls were covered by honours boards listing civil and military awards, first class degrees and other academic achievements by Old Leysians. In the early 1960s, the hall was refurbished. The honours boards were replaced by portraits of past headmasters, governors and even King George V.

Meals were served by juniors, some of whom became adept at carrying six plates at a time. However on some days it could take as long as forty minutes for everyone to be served. Boys had to accept what was put on their

The Great Hall, 1880 – (note the small organ on the right of the platform)

The Great Hall, 1910 – (the enlarged organ is now in the gallery)

The Dining Hall - pre 1939 – now part of Dale House

The Dining Hall - 1946-1966

plates and wastage was enormous. Pressure was put upon the junior waiters at supper, when staff were rarely present, to get the seniors second, third and even fourth helpings of popular meals such as egg and chips. Following decades of complaints about school food, the Governors decided to make radical reforms.

In 1983 the kitchens were completely overhauled and the dining room itself was adapted to become a self-service cafeteria. This enabled a greater choice of food to be offered and, at the same time, considerably reduced the waste of uneaten food. The post of Lady Superintendent was abolished and an outside firm was given the contract to produce the school food. Compass Catering, under the management of Howard Dickinson, produces extensive, interesting menus and can serve formal lunches and dinners as well as day to day meals. They also produce all the food for the School Ball, a bi-annual occurrence at the end of alternate school years.

THE NORTH BLOCK - A and B HOUSES

The next of Curwen's designs was that for boarding. A long, tall building went up on the north side of the site. This provided accommodation for two separate Houses of forty boys each. On the ground floor was a common room and six day-time studies for the prefects. On the two floors above were long dormitories with twenty beds in each. Each boy had a small partitioned area behind his bed, the so-called 'horse-box', which gave some privacy whilst changing and washing. Each boy had a wash-bowl, soap dish and chamber pot. Since there was no running hot-water and only one cold tap on each floor, the caretaker and house-maids had to fetch all the water, carry it up to the dormitories from the basement of the house, and clear away everything later in the day. This included emptying all the chamber pots.

The Housemaster had a flat and there was some accommodation for the caretaker and his wife. North A House opened first in 1881 and, on completion of the building in 1883, B House was filled with boys by closing West House. The School Office was in A House.

There was no provision for a married Housemaster until the 1920s when N.J. Holloway was Housemaster of North A. Much of the cost of the Housemaster's dwelling was initially paid by the Holloway family. The Governors recognised the value of having a married Housemaster, and provided a rather more modest house at the other end of the North block in

B House Common Room, 1914

The Reading Room, 1886 – (now the Moulton Room)

1937. This released the space previously taken up by bachelor Housemasters, for an extra smaller dormitory in each House. The Houses were occupied by hospital staff and patients during the 1940-46 exile in Pitlochry. Apart from some minor alterations, the two Houses remained unchanged until 1958 when four studies in both A and B were added at the back of the Common Rooms, with changing rooms underneath.

The next major change occurred when it was found how successful bed-room studies were in Fen House. In 1974 the first floor dormitories were divided into ten rooms for Lower and Upper Sixth Formers to have bedroom studies, and the large room above was divided into two smaller dormitories. In 1997, when the new category of Day Pupils was introduced, work was started to convert North B House, floor by floor, into a day House, with new separate changing facilities in the basement for boys and for girls.

SCIENCE BUILDING, LATER THE KELVIN (BURSARY) BUILDING

On 28 October 1893, Lord Kelvin, the President of the Royal Society, opened the first science building at the school. Among the distinguished guests were nine Heads of Cambridge Colleges, the University Orator, sixteen Professors and twenty eight lecturers from University Science departments. Lord Kelvin described the building as probably containing the finest science laboratories that any Public School had at that time.

As well as the usual biology, chemistry and physics departments, there was a large amphitheatre lecture room. It was fitted with the latest technology for projecting slides - a single-ray gas lantern which had only just come on the market that year. Perhaps the most striking feature of the department was the Museum. This is described in detail in Chapter 18.

When the new Science building (Thomson building) was opened in 1927, only the Physics and Chemistry departments moved out of the Kelvin into the new accommodation. Part of the old building was used for offices and the Biology department expanded into the remaining space. Following the end of the Second World War, the Government, together with sections of industry, set up a fund to improve the science facilities in schools, but only Physics and Chemistry. When The Leys was inspected to see if it would qualify for funds, the 1927 building was reported to be too good to warrant a grant. The Biology department needed more space but did not qualify for assistance. However, the Headmaster, Dr Humphrey, persuaded the Fund

Kelvin Lecture Theatre, 1900

Kelvin Chemistry Laboratory, 1900

Biology Department

Chemistry Lecture Room
(now flattened to make an extra laboratory)

executives to give the school a small grant for a small extension to be built between the west end of the Kelvin building and the swimming bath. His grounds were that moving the Geography department out of the Thomson building where it was at the time, and into the lower floor of the proposed extension, would make room for Physics to expand.

Sir Henry Dale opened the extension in 1958. The ground floor consisted of a large classroom for Geography and above it there was a spacious Biology laboratory. By now the amphitheatre lecture room had been flattened and turned into another large laboratory. In 1988 this room, which was very high, was converted into four classrooms by inserting a new floor. During the previous year, the Biology department had moved out to join the Physics and Chemistry departments. This enabled the Geography and Economics classrooms to be together in one building. A little earlier, in 1980, the large Geography classroom on the ground floor, which had been paid for by the Industrial Fund, was sub-divided and became the classics department and the careers room.

THE GYM BLOCK AND SWIMMING BATH

Following the plan to build a chapel, which is described in another chapter, the Governors decided that an indoor swimming bath and a gymnasium would meet the needs of the school at the beginning of the 20th century. The swimming bath was for many years the only indoor heated pool in Cambridge. No large-scale expense was needed to excavate the ground. The actual pool is above ground level, the bath being approached by steps at both entrances. The pipe work runs in large ducts under the walkway round the bath and there are storage areas under the changing rooms. The pool was thirty yards long, requiring races of 50 or 100 yards to finish on a rope held across the water. The base and walls of the pool itself had been constructed by Italian craftsmen.

The bath was extensively used, not only by the school itself, but also by other schools and clubs who hired it throughout the year. Even when a public indoor bath at Parkside in Cambridge was built in the early 1960s, clubs continued to hire the school pool because it was available for exclusive use for a limited period, which the public one was not. During the First World War, the bath was ceded to troops training in the area. This was also true in the Second World War, when there were very large numbers of Royal Air

Bathing Sheds, pre-1900

Swimming Bath, pre-1958

Force personnel in Cambridge. Even in the 1950s and 60s both the RAF and the USAAF hired the bath to practice emergency dinghy drill on a regular basis.

Chlorine used to purify the bath water is very corrosive and in 1958 it was found that the walkways were getting weak and other parts of the bath needed replacing or upgrading. It was closed for a year whilst the work was carried out. New brickwork on the exterior disguises the fact that it originally matched the other of Curwen's buildings. A new non-slip floor was installed throughout, and a ladies' changing room fitted into what had been the open gallery. The high diving boards were removed for safety reasons.

In 1986, the main girders and the roof had to be replaced because of corrosion. The work was carried out by the school maintenance staff which caused the least disruption to the use of the bath. Much work had been done on the building housing the bath since the Second World War, but little to the actual pool itself. A lot of water was being lost from seepage through the walls. The pool was closed, lined with a plastic membrane and shortened to twenty-five metres in length. It is once again used extensively throughout the day by the school and other clubs. There are plans to upgrade the changing rooms in the near future.

An artesian well was incorporated into the pool building. This is described in more detail in Chapter 18.

The Gymnasium Block contained, as well as a large Gymnasium, a Common Room for the staff, an Art Department and an Armoury. The foundation stone of the building had been laid in 1907 by the Prime Minister of the day, Sir Henry Campbell-Bannerman. By the time the school returned from Pitlochry, the necessity for wall-bars and ropes declined and they were removed, although the hooks from which the ropes hung can still be seen in the roof beams. The viewing gallery was removed and a new floor laid. This coincided with the move of the Art Department to the old West House building. A staircase was constructed inside the Common Room to give access to the old Art School which now became an extension of the Common Room. This doubled the space for the staff, whose numbers were to increase significantly in the next thirty years.

Art Department, 1910

Gymnasium, 1910

THE KING'S BUILDING

The final building of the scheme the Governors had planned with the Architect, Robert Curwen was a library and classroom block. Before any basic outline could be approved, Curwen died. The Governors appointed Sir Aston Webb to complete the task. Webb was well thought of as the architect for the main entrance to the Victoria and Albert Museum. He kept to a similar style, but with a slightly different red brick, and with bands of stone running round the building. The opening by H.M. King George V is described in Chapter 10 - *Royal Visits*.

The ground floor consisted of four classrooms, and there was one large classroom above, adjacent to the library itself. In the basement were storage rooms and a small flat for a porter with a separate staircase into a Porter's Lodge. At that time, the King's Building gateway was the main entrance to the school. There was a still a school night watchman, who used the basement facilities until the 1960s. The ground floor classrooms are much as they were in 1914 and the Porter's Lodge is now an office for the Mathematics department. The Library itself has been made a very welcoming room by the first full-time professional librarian, Mrs. Mary O'Keeffe.

The large classroom, which had been used as a supervised day prep. room had been fitted with curtains, carpeted and decorated for the Centenary opening by H.R.H. the Duchess of Kent. This was still used for private study by the Lower Sixth, and also for examinations until 1998. Part of the ongoing Development Campaign raised funds to convert this room into a satellite of the main library, with sixteen computer stations linked to the Internet and specialist information software packages. This was opened by the author, P.D. James (Baroness James), on Speech Day 1998. Very generous support for the funding of this part of the Library was given by Old Leysians who spent their schooldays in Pitlochry. This is acknowledged in the room, by a plaque which was unveiled by Gordon Cook, President of the Old Leysian Union, in September 1999.

EAST HOUSE, LATER THE STAMP BUILDING

In 1919, the Governors acquired 5 and 6 Brookside for £5,000. 5 Brookside became the School Sanatorium, which until then had been in Edinburgh House, Bateman Street. Later, in 1924, Sir Henry Dale opened an

The School Library
The Headmaster and Mrs Barrett with Baroness James - Speech Day 1998

The Information Technology satellite in the Kent Room

isolation hospital which had been constructed in the garden of 5 Brookside. 6 Brookside became East House. In 1929, East House transferred to a purpose-built boarding house, which was opened by Lord Stamp, 1st Baron Stamp of Shortlands, the Chairman of the Governors.

Built in the same vernacular as the previous houses, there were dormitories with horse-boxes, studies and a Housemaster's flat. The basement provided better changing facilities than there were in North A and B, but there was no provision for a married Housemaster.

During the Second World War this building contained the Operating Theatre for the Addenbrooke's Hospital annexe. To get the patients up and down the building, a lift was constructed on the end of the House and was still there when the school moved back into the Cambridge buildings in 1946. After some discussion with the hospital authorities, they were persuaded to remove the lift. The Governors decided not to proceed with the original plan to build West House, attached to East as a mirror-image, and a Housemaster's House with a flat above was constructed instead.

When the school numbers increased in the 1970s, the extensive loft space in the House was converted into bedroom-studies. In 1991, a sixth-form bar was created in the basement. In Autumn 1997, the House was re-opened by Peter Lacey, a former Housemaster, following refurbishment of the top floors into a boys' sixth form boarding house, with a Housemaster's flat.

The former Housemaster's house became the Manse, with a smaller replacement for the Bisseker Room within it. This room, named after the third Headmaster, was a large meeting room which had been incorporated into the Manse when it had been in 6 Brookside. It was used by some school societies, especially the Leys Christian Union. Much of the funding for the room had come from various Methodist trusts. Other parts of basement and ground floor of the East House building were converted into the Modern Languages department and common room accommodation for the new Junior House, Moulton. The sixth form bar was moved to the basement of King's Building in 1999. The building encompassing all these varied functions has the overall title of the Stamp Building. It incorporates East House, the Modern Languages department and the day-time facilities for Moulton House. Appropriately, the present Lord Stamp, the 4th Baron (Old Leysian, East 1948-53), re-opened the building in 1998.

Baroness James is shown the new technology

The Junior Library, also in the Kent Room

THE THOMSON BUILDING, THE NEW SCIENCE DEPARTMENT

In 1927, Sir J. J. Thomson opened the new Science Building. Its high tower dominates the school skyline. The tower housed water tanks to store pumped water and to produce a good pressure to drive water round the site. Below the tanks were two small rooms which housed the science library. The physics department was on the ground floor, with the chemistry department above it. In the semi-basement there were large engineering and carpentry workshops which were used for hobbies classes as well as by the maintenance staff. There were also two or three storage rooms, one large room for chemicals, a smaller one for concentrated acids and alkalis and another for storage of physics apparatus.

After fifty years of use, some of the services in the building needed replacing. Chemicals had attacked the drain linings, and blockages and overflows into the rooms were common occurrences. The wiring of the building needed replacing and the bench tops were showing signs of attack by chemical spillage. An extensive refurbishment of both departments took place, including the reversing of the teak surfaces and refitting them. The fire services would not permit the continued use of the rooms in the tower as a library, so these became storage rooms. Sir J. J. Thomson's daughter reopened the building in 1977, using the same key which he had used fifty years previously to open it. She kindly donated the silver and enamelled key to the school, and it is on display in the foyer of the building.

The opening of the Rugg Centre meant that workshop facilities in this building were no longer needed for the pupils. The maintenance department moved into the space vacated by the large boilers attached to the swimming bath, when the heating of buildings devolved to a number of smaller boilers dispersed around the school site. This left the bottom floor of the Thomson building available for the Biology department to move into. At last all the three sciences are in the same building. With the change in curriculum requiring more practical work, and more pupils in the school, the raked floors of the two chemistry lecture rooms have been flattened and the rooms converted into extra laboratories.

Kelvin Biology Laboratory, 1958

Physics Laboratory, 1958

Chemistry Laboratory, 1958

THE NEW WEST HOUSE

Perhaps the planning of this new building happened just a little too soon. It was based on the concept of four equal sized dormitories with a few day studies for the senior boys, and it was opened in 1961. In Fen House, opened in 1967, the provision of study bedrooms for senior boys set the new trend for all the boarding houses. Although there has been some success in converting the new West House to provide study bedrooms, it would have been easier if the fenestration had been more adaptable.

In its day, the building had a high quality finish. Outside, the walls were of small bricks with deep raked joints. Inside, expensive teak hand rails on the staircases with granite terrazzo stair treads and landing floors made an almost luxurious impression. Twenty-two razor points were available in the wash rooms, although less than half the members of the house had electric razors or even shaved. It was ironic that the morning the Housemaster moved into his new premises, he discovered that no provision had been made in his bathroom to plug in an electric shaver.

The opening of the building by H.M. Queen Elizabeth, the Queen Mother on 6 October, 1961 is covered in Chapter 10 - *Royal Visits.*

THE RUGG CENTRE

The building brought together many aspects of design and technology which were being provided in other buildings of the school, though in less well-equipped rooms. The background planning and opening are covered in other chapters - *The Headmasters* (under Bertie Bellis's headship) and *Royal Visits* (Duke of Edinburgh's second visit).

The architect, Harding of Lister, Harding and Grillett, had designed what are basically two cubes, of different sizes, linked by a central staircase at mezzanine levels. The two cubes have large sloping aluminium roofs. The layout of the floors attempts to provide inter-reacting disciplines near to each other and internal windows enable an interest to be taken in what everyone is doing. The pottery has external windows which allow passers-by to see the colourful, fascinating modelling. The main workshop with facilities for working with wood, metal and plastics is now too small for the increased numbers in the school, and an extension has been completed recently.

West House, 1961

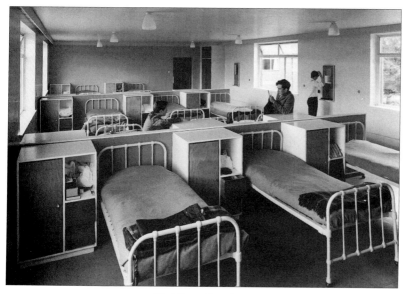

West House Dormitory

West House Study, 1961

The Bathroom

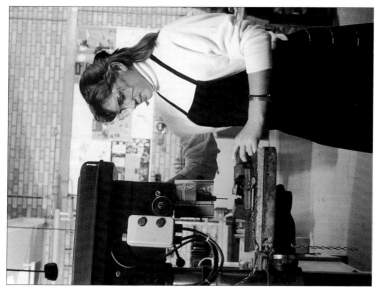

Rugg Centre Workshops

The computer room has been extended and the Camfield Press, which was housed near the Art Room, has been moved to behind the Sports Hall, to enable the room it occupied to be used as a classroom.

THE SPORTS HALL AND ASTRO TURF
(All weather playing surface)

When, in 1995, the Sports Hall was opened by H.R.H. the Duchess of Kent, the school acquired a facility which had been long awaited by many of the staff and pupils. The floor of the main hall is marked out for indoor hockey, tennis, badminton and basketball. Included in the building are three glass-backed squash-courts and a weights-room. Upstairs, there is provision for two cricket nets and an open area suitable for aerobics, trampolining and table tennis. Not only is the building extensively used by pupils of The Leys, but other schools and clubs hire various parts of it to such an extent that it is in use for almost seven days each week from 9am to 9pm. The building had been funded by an appeal to governors, staff, parents and Old Leysians, together with a very generous grant from the Foundation for Arts and Sports. Two neighbouring girls' schools, the Perse School for Girls and St. Mary's, also assisted the Development Campaign to reach the required target.

Once the Sports Hall was in use, a smaller appeal was made for funds for an all-weather hockey pitch. This facility was already available at leading hockey playing schools and some threatened to drop their fixture with The Leys if we could not also provide such a surface, because the game played on it is very different from that played on grass. Named in memory of Neil White, one of the greatest Leysian sportsmen and holder of an Olympic silver medal for hockey, the new pitch, like the Sports Hall, is used by many outside clubs. The floodlights allow evening use up to 9.30 pm. In the summer, the surface can be used for tennis. Although an application to the Lottery Fund for help with financing this project was successful, the terms under which the school would have received the money would have taken control of the pitch away from the school. In the end the project was financed by an appeal to those with close links to the school.

Pottery Class

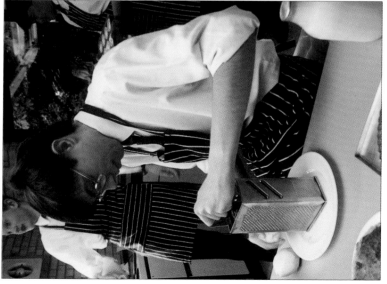

Rugg Centre Kitchen

Photo by courtesy of Cambridge News

Lady Trumpington cuts the first sod for the Sports Hall

CHAPTER SIX

The Chapel

In a school which is a Christian foundation, it is usual to provide a special place for worship. When the school first opened, the numbers were not sufficient to warrant a separate chapel. The Hills Road Methodist Chapel was only about a quarter of a mile away, so the pupils and staff attended Sunday morning and evening services there.

The Governors soon had plans for further buildings. Robert Curwen was appointed architect in 1877 and work soon started on these with the first of them, the Great Hall, being opened in 1879. The basement contained music rooms until the building of the new theatre in 1966 incorporated new ones, and it also housed the museum until the Science Block was built in 1893. The main room upstairs, with a roof structure modelled on Westminster Hall, had a large dais at one end from which assemblies and services were led. Below the dais were rows of individual school desks where the boys did preparation.

At first there was a modest organ on the dais on the east side, but this was replaced in 1899 by a larger organ situated in a purpose-built gallery at the south end of the hall. At the beginning of 1948, this organ was dismantled to provide extra space in the gallery for eating. The organ builders, Norman and Beard, extended the scope of the Chapel organ, using parts of the Hall organ, and paid the school £55 for the remaining parts.

The hall was the setting for early Speech Day gatherings as well as for concerts and plays. When Doctor Moulton died in 1898, his funeral service was conducted in the Hall and there is a photograph of his coffin in the centre of the dais, with the hall draped in mourning. It is reported that nearly a thousand people attended the funeral service. Following his death, the staff and boys presented oak chairs and canopied benches to be placed on the dais, and oak panels for honours lists were fixed to the walls.

The Governors felt that the school was now large enough to warrant having its own chapel, and that such a building would be a fitting memorial to Dr Moulton. They decided that they would not need to launch an appeal for funds, but that the total cost might be forthcoming from about half a dozen leading Methodists. This proved to be the case, and building commenced in 1905. The Duchess of Albany, a daughter-in-law of Queen Victoria, laid the foundation stone. The chapel was completed the next year, a remarkable feat, especially as there was a problem with the walls at the south-east end of the building. The architect had required a certain amount of rebuilding because of early settlement. In the resulting dispute over liability, the builder claimed that there were strata of soft sand running under the building at that point.

Once the shell had been completed, money was raised to pay for the stained glass windows which had been designed by H. Salisbury. Sir George Hayter Chubb paid for the East window, which depicts the Ascension. The ten windows in the main body of the Chapel represent the life of Jesus from the Nativity to the Resurrection and again were donated by individuals with the exception of one which was the gift of Scottish and Welsh Old Leysians. The West window depicts Old Testament subjects which forecast the coming of the Messiah. This was the last window to be installed and was dedicated on Speech Day, 1908. One of the two remaining windows in the chancel, opposite the organ, is remarkable in that it was the gift of Japanese Old Leysians who were at the school before 1900. They also presented the vestry furniture. A board in the vestry records their names, which include Viscount Yamanouchi, Count Hirosawa, Count Kawamura and Count Ogasawara.

One small window which is passed by anyone using the South door to enter or leave the chapel, is in the lobby. It is a sad memorial to Harold Pickup. He had joined the school in September 1897, only to have to leave the next term through ill health. He returned in September 1903 when he seemed stronger, but died at school of pneumonia in November of that term. There are three small stained glass windows in the vestry which are not generally visible. These were the gifts of parents whose children had been baptised in the chapel.

The building was opened by Mrs. Moulton on 27 October, 1906 in the presence of the Duchess of Albany, who had laid the foundation stone (see Chapter 10 - *Royal Visits*). At the end of the service, at which the Revd Dr

Lady Chubb unlocking the Vestry entrance

The Chapel, 1906

Barber, the Headmaster, preached the sermon, the congregation followed the choir during the singing of the penultimate verse, and gathered round the memorial stone outside the main entrance. Sir George Hayter Chubb then invited Mrs. Moulton to unveil the stone. Following this unveiling, Lady Chubb formally unlocked the south door to the vestry. Recently the author had occasion to write to the present Lord Hayter (grandson of the first Baron) and commented that the keys to the Chubb locks on the chapel doors still worked. In his letter of reply, Lord Hayter mentioned that the keys to the Chubb locks at Broadmoor Prison are turned in excess of 600 times, twice a day and have to be replaced every three years.

An important feature of the interior of the chapel is the wood-carving, nearly all of which was done by amateurs. The pulpit had been the first task, and this took two years to complete. The flat top edge bears an inlaid brass inscription which states: "To the Glory of God and for the Preaching of His Holy Word this Pulpit was carved by Anne Hobson, Helen Mary Chubb, and George Hayter Chubb, and presented by the latter to The Leys Chapel, October 1906". The chapel at first used the benches from the Great Hall. They were soon replaced by the present pews with their beautifully carved ends. The designs, by Mrs Baines (née Anne Hobson), who carved most of the panels, together with Sir George Hayter Chubb, are of plants and animals from the Book of Psalms. There are also panels representing the Coat of Arms of The Leys School and that of H.R.H. The Duchess of Albany. As the school grew in numbers, the pews have been extended at both ends which prevents the panels at the ends nearest the walls from being seen. They are, however, duplicates of the carving on the aisle ends.

The very back seats were designated for use by the Headmaster and Governors, and the fourteen individual seats immediately in front of these were for the masters. The masters' seats lift up to become misericords, most commonly found in ancient cathedrals, where the small projection on the under side serves to support a person standing for long periods. The underneath of the first ones on each side are richly carved and have presentation plates. The remainder await donors to pay for their carving to be done.

A later chaplain was the Revd Gordon Bennett, whose family presented a silver altar cross in his memory. Quite recently, a member of the family visiting the chapel asked why the spot lights which illuminated the cross no

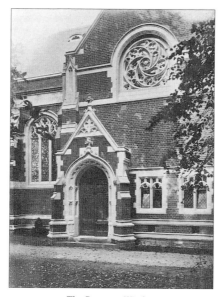

The Bayonne Window

The masters' seats showing the misericords

longer functioned. In fact it is a feature of the chapel that, if the cross is placed in exactly the right position on the altar, natural lighting from the open West door lights it up. There never were spot lights. When the visitor complained, the matter was remedied very simply by moving the cross back to its original position.

To begin with, electric light pendants resembling large crowns, tinted old gold like the other visible metal fittings in the building, illuminated the chapel. By the 1950s, they had been replaced by vertical fluorescent tubes mounted on the east side of each roof truss. These were in their turn replaced in the 1990s by a series of spot lights, but in the opinion of the author these still do not adequately illuminate the interior of the Chapel, although there are plans to try to improve the lighting as part of the school's plan to celebrate the Millennium.

There are two external features of the building which are not often appreciated. One is the rose window above the vestry, in which the tracery is adapted from the design of the famous window in Bayonne Cathedral. Originally it was visible inside the chapel, but subsequent additions to the organ have completely obscured it. The other is the weather-vane on top of the bell tower. It is in the form of crossed bicycle wheels. The Bursar at the time of the chapel construction was also President of the Cycle Club, which paid ten and a half guineas (just over eleven pounds) for the cost of this unusual weather-vane.

Originally there had been accommodation in the Chapel for 360 boys, and there were also 55 seats in the gallery for the use of the domestic staff. In the early years of the school, there was a considerable number of resident maids who were required to attend both morning and evening prayer. They paraded under the watchful eye of the Lady Superintendent. There were still a few of the support staff living above the kitchens until the area was converted into part of Granta House for the girls who joined the Sixth Form in 1984. Compulsory attendance at Chapel by the support staff was discontinued long before the Second World War.

At their meeting on 1 February, 1907, the Governors passed the following resolution:

> "It was decided that the Chapel should be reserved for the religious services of the School such as Daily prayers and Sunday worship, and that it should not be used for outside purposes. No

variation shall take place without special leave of the Governors".

For years this was the case. However, in more recent times, concerts, plays and secular assemblies have been held in the building and the Governors were certainly not consulted. One such notable occasion was in 1960, when members of North B House performed *A Sleep of Prisoners* by Christopher Fry. It was one of the entries for the house drama competition, and was set in a church, so the chapel was the obvious venue. The direction and acting were awarded the House cup that year.

There have been at least two radio broadcasts from the chapel by the BBC. The first was on Sunday, 23 May, 1937. It provoked a letter of criticism from an Old Leysian who was a Choirmaster and former organ pupil of Dr A.H. Mann and J. F. Shepherdson. The gist of his complaint was that there was no introit, no anthem, the hymns were not suitable for the boys, and that the sermon was directed at adults and therefore was not suitable for a school service. The Headmaster, Dr Humphrey, in his letter of reply had explained that the B.B.C. had invited his predecessor to conduct the early morning service for them and had asked if he would prefer any particular chapel or the studio for the broadcast. The Revd Harry Bisseker asked whether he might use The Leys Chapel, and whether the choir might sing the hymns. He pointed out at the time that his sermon was not intended for the school, but for a wider audience throughout the country. At the very last minute, however, it was found that the Chapel was acoustically difficult without an audience, so most of the boys were brought into the Chapel but did not sing. Dr Humphrey finished his letter by saying:

"You had better write and complain to Mr Bisseker, as it would be rather presumptuous for a young layman like myself to instruct Mr. Bisseker about the arrangements for a Methodist service."

The second occasion was at the time of the outbreak of the Gulf War, when a service was needed which dealt with the issues of war. The scheduled Radio 4 service for 3 February, 1991 was to have been a recording of a normal morning service at a parish church. It was felt that the President of the Methodist Conference, Revd Dr Donald English, would be the right person to lead the service at this particular time. It so happened that on that particular Sunday he was due to preach at The Leys. Hasty preparations were therefore made, and it was this service from The Leys Chapel that was broadcast.

The chapel has also been the setting for television broadcasts. The first was the screening of a Sunday morning service. The interior of the building was scaffolded, and lights and cables festooned the sides of the chapel. Due to the skill of the cameramen, none of this equipment was visible during the actual broadcast.

Between 1968 and 1972, the Chaplain of Jesus College, the Revd Peter Allen, was on the staff as a part-time member of the English Department. He was an accomplished singer, and he hosted an ITV series on Sunday evenings in which members of the school were often featured singing well known hymns alongside himself and a group of professional singers.

Naturally, sermons played an important part in worship. *The Fortnightly* records that a Leysian, writing under the pseudonym of Tempus, had kept statistics of the length of sermons and published the preachers' averages for 1947 to 1950. The shortest was attributed to the Revd Norman Dawson at 11 minutes, 7 seconds, whereas the longest was 34 minutes, 50 seconds, given by the Revd Dr Whitehorn. The article prompted an Old Leysian to write to the magazine as follows:

"In my time, the late twenties, a number of Leysians were concerned about the sermon lengths and the inverse ratio of their interest. A scheme was devised by which each member of a select Society in "B' House drew the name of a preacher out of a cap, and invested his pocket money. We were not concerned with averages. The longest sermon won. In this little flutter, I was fortunate or unfortunate to draw the field, a surprise preacher who lasted a mere forty-five minutes. Seconds seemed unimportant. While some Leysians found this sermon tedious, to me every minute was valuable".

The sufferings of these Leysians were nothing compared with those of the first pupils. The average length of a sermon at Hills Road Chapel was fifty minutes. On the evening of the first use of the new organ in that building, the preacher took as his text Hebrews ix, 14 ("How much more . . .") and as he preached for seventy-three minutes and frequently repeated the words "How much more"), the younger members of his congregation were amused rather than educated.

Preachers for services have to be arranged well ahead of the term. It so happened that the person who had agreed to take a service in May 1940 found himself scheduled to conduct a "Service of Prayer for Victory' which had been called for by the King, for that Sunday. The preacher announced at the start that he was a conscientious objector. Some of the ideas he presented in his address caused an outburst from an Old Leysian who happened to attend chapel that day. The Old Leysian wrote to the Chairman of Governors, Lord Stamp, to protest about the preacher. Lord Stamp, who was not at the service, wrote to the Headmaster, Dr Humphrey, asking for material for his response. Several long-serving members of staff had attended, including W.H. Balgarnie, J.E. Mellor, C.A. Skinner and A. McM. Buchanan. They all wrote letters to Lord Stamp explaining that the content of the service was well balanced and far from "perfect Fifth Column propaganda" as was alleged. The Chairman's letter to the Old Leysian, pointing out that the content of the service had had a negligible effect on the boys, seems to have calmed the situation.

In recent years, the chapel has been used more often than in the past for the marriages of members of the teaching and support staff and for baptisms. One memorable occasion in 1994 was the marriage of the first Old Leysian couple - Helen Sherwood and Robert Bleehen, with parts of the service in Hebrew.

The school carol service had been held in Great St. Mary's Church in Cambridge for a number of years. However in order to make it a more domestic affair, it was moved back in 1992 to the Chapel, but had to be split into two services on the same afternoon, in order to accommodate everyone.

It was decided to celebrate the 125th anniversary of the founding of the school, and incidentally the Millennium, in Great St. Mary's Church, which gives good visibility whilst still holding large numbers. When King's College Chapel was used for the Centenary celebrations on 16 February 1975, most of the parents had to sit in the ante-chapel, and felt cut off from the service as they could not see what was happening.

With the school numbers reaching 500 and forecast possibly to become 550 in a few years time, how to seat everyone is causing concern. In future it will not be possible for the whole school to worship together, if these numbers are maintained and increased.

The Weather Vane

The Chapel, 1956

CHAPTER SEVEN

Leysian Sport

The 1956 edition of *The Leys Handbook* devotes over 25% of its content to sporting records. Lord Moulton, brother of the first Headmaster, once said that if one wanted to hear any news of The Leys, it was necessary to read the Sports Section of *The Daily Telegraph*. The main leisure activity in a Victorian boys' boarding school took place on the sports field. Indeed sport was considered to be almost as important in the curriculum as academic work.

Dr W.G. Humphrey, in an article about the school which he wrote in the late 30s felt that the balance had improved:

> "The emphasis which public schools have in the past laid on games has often been excessive and it is a cause for congratulation that a saner and more restrained attitude to them is now being adopted; it is perhaps more generally realised to-day than ever that games are a means and not an end, that they exist for the enjoyment and benefit of the boys rather than for the prestige of the school, and that if a game is worth playing it is worth playing even if badly. But it is still gratifying to notice that The Leys has produced its share of distinguished athletes."

RUGBY FOOTBALL

On 17 February, 1875, Harry Benson, the youngest of the original sixteen, wrote home to his sister, recording the activities of the first day at school:

"We had a game of football this afternoon".

Since they were only sixteen boys, widely ranging in age, Rugby Football was not a possible activity. However, by the next year, through the energies of J.C. Isard and his friends in the first terms, Rugby had been adopted as the official game, although some Association Football was also played. In 1877 the first XV were unbeaten and only a dropped goal had been scored against them. The tactics in those days were very different from those of the modern game. There were usually ten forwards, whose chief duty was to keep the ball in the scrum and work it by main force steadily down the field. The remaining team consisted of two halves, one or two three-quarters and a back. Punting was much less common than now, and the drop-kick was normally used for finding touch.

In 1880, the teams entered a period of sustained success. In 1880, 1881 and 1882, they were unbeaten. Masters were for many years eligible to play for school teams, so team photographs for all sports in the early days included several mature members sporting moustaches. This probably gave rise to the later myth that the captain was allowed to grow a moustache.

It is not surprising that over a period of 125 years the names of schools in the fixture list have changed. However, the first school to play against The Leys in 1880, Mill Hill, was still doing so in 1998. Felsted has played against The Leys since 1919. Schools such as Oundle, Bedford, Bedford Modern, St. Paul's, Merchant Taylors' and Cranleigh have also regularly appeared in the fixture list.

The war years at Pitlochry naturally introduced some new opponents, namely Trinity College, Glenalmond, Glasgow Academy, Strathallan, Dollar Academy, Merchiston, and Perth Academy. Out of 27 matches against these schools, The Leys won 17. In 1946, on the return of the school to Cambridge, the fixture list of 1939 was renewed. More recently, overseas tours have taken place. The school first XV went to Australia in 1985 and 1992 and to South Africa in 1996. On this last tour, the school hockey XI accompanied them.

As early as 1877, two years after the foundation of the school, an Old Leysian Football Club was started by J.C. Isard and E.S. Whelpton. There were, of course, few rugby playing Old Boys in the next few years. However, in the 1881-2 season, out of twenty matches played, fifteen were won (including Old Millhillians, Old Marlburians and Gonville and Caius College) and three drawn.

The next year brought fame to the club. A short tour of Wales had been organised. The press were dismissive of the chances of this small, unknown club. However, they defeated Cardiff by a goal and two tries to a goal and a try. The Cardiff try was disputed. Rugby games at that time were controlled by two umpires and a referee. One umpire had tried to disallow the try. The next day the Old Leysians played a South of Wales team containing ten Welsh Internationals and another who had been a reserve for Wales. The Old Leysians lost by the narrow margin of a goal to a goal and a try.

The same team beat Cambridge University by two goals and two tries to nil. Three of the tries were scored by a member of the School XV, J.H.S. McArthur. Following that victory, a match was played annually against the University until 1954. By then the standard of University Rugby was so high that matches were played against the XL Club (the University reserve side) instead. However the matches were still very one-sided in favour of the University, and the fixture was abandoned after the 1957 match which the Old Leysians lost 53 - nil.

As a London club, the team had successful seasons and those which were less so. They played no matches during the Second World War, and during the season 1945-46, when the club was reforming, most Old Leysians of playing age were still overseas awaiting demobilisation from the forces. The XV was only completed for some matches by persuading those on the verge of retirement to postpone it, and by bringing in friends who were not actually Old Leysians. National Service and the post-war changes in University life made the team secretary's task of raising sides more difficult and the club discontinued its London fixture list after the 1949-50 season.. Until then no other Old Boys' Club had maintained for so long a continuous playing record in London, excluding the war years; and at the time it was the only Club of former pupils of a school outside the Home Counties with a London fixture list.

From 1957 until 1996, the Old Leysians played the School XV. Then the Rugby Football Union imposed new safety regulations under which only those under 21 years of age were permitted to play against school sides. The difficulty of finding young players who were available for the September match has meant that the fixture has been abandoned.

It is surprising that a club with such a distinguished record has produced so few full Internationals. In 1891, A.R. Richards played for South Africa. Contemporary reports about him described Richards as being the only person in the South African side who looked liked a first class club player and he was presented with a Distinction Cap for being the best player in the country. In the same year J.H.P. Strang was selected for England and J.H. Gould and E. Mayfield took part in the England tour of South Africa

A.B. Flett played for Scotland between 1900 and 1902 against England, Wales and Ireland. His international cap has been presented to the school archives. He later became the President of the Scottish Rugby Union. G. Llewellyn-Lloyd played for Wales in 1896 when he was only 19 and then between 1899 and 1903, becoming captain in 1903.

Perhaps the most unusual story of an International is that of J.T. Tulloch. In 1899, thirteen months after leaving school, he was selected to play for Scotland against Wales. Frost caused the game to be postponed, and Tulloch then sprained his ankle whilst skating and was unable to play for the rest of the season, including, of course, the rearranged match against Wales. The selectors were so concerned over his bad luck that they awarded him an International Cap although he had not played in the match. However, two years later, in 1901 he was able to represent his country. Like Flett before him, he was also President of the Scottish Rugby Union.

F.G. Handford (1909) and W.M. Lowry (1919) played for England and D.N. Rocyn-Jones (1925) and G. Windsor-Lewis (1960) represented Wales. In more recent years, with the introduction of junior national teams, J.W. Hooker has played for the England under-18 side.

The number of Old Leysians playing in Trial matches and for County sides as well as in the Oxford v. Cambridge matches are too numerous to mention. Whilst at Cambridge, T. Linder played Association Football for his College and the University. He then played for the England team between 1886 and 1891, and was its captain in 1888.

LACROSSE

Lacrosse was introduced into the school by boys who came from Manchester in 1881, and for the next thirty years it was the principal school game in the Lent term. During this time the school achieved marked success. Meeting only the best clubs from the South, The Leys on several occasions headed the First Division of the South of England League and twice won the South of England Flags. In several other years they were runners-up. The school second team were at one period regular winners of the corresponding Junior Flags, which they eventually won outright.

The 1900 Lacrosse Team – Winners of the England Senior Challenge Cup

Lacrosse was introduced into Cambridge University by Old Leysians and Oxford University followed suit. For many years Old Leysians formed a large proportion of the Cambridge team and in 1908, nine of the team of twelve were Old Leysians. Before the school gave up lacrosse in 1912, Cambridge University had only been beaten twice in the inter-university match, but following 1912 Cambridge were more often the losers.

J. Southall (1884), A.B. Whitehead (1885) and E.P. Jones (1901) played for England and several Old Leysians played for the South of England in the annual match against the North. C.H. Scott was chosen to play in goal for England whilst he was still at school in 1900 and later in 1903. He and B.H. Holloway represented the United Kingdom in the Olympic Games of 1908.

The reason for abandoning lacrosse as the school Lent term sport was the almost complete lack of other schools playing the game. Nearly all matches were against men, except the ones against Manchester Grammar School. Occasional matches were played between the two schools but this meant long journeys. The last match between them in 1898, resulted in a win for The Leys by 26 goals to nil.

HOCKEY

Hockey replaced lacrosse in 1912 and immediately became very popular. When the change happened, there was one boy who had been awarded his colours in rugby, lacrosse, hockey and cricket. This was John Ross Robertson, who sadly was killed in action on 12 May, 1917. His parents gave in his memory, a magnificent silver shield to be presented each year to the House which won the most points in inter-house competitions.

The shield was stolen from East House Common Room in 1987. Although the loss was covered by insurance, the Governors decided that it would not be possible to ensure that a replacement trophy of equivalent value could safely be displayed in the winning house each year. The championship was discontinued, and a fund set up with the insurance money to create a prize to be awarded by the Games Committee to pupils whose talent merits special coaching, or to assist with the costs of a team tour, either in this country or overseas.

The change to Hockey as the Lent term game did little at first to increase the fixture list with other schools. The outbreak of war meant that only five inter-school matches were played. After the war the standard of hockey soon rose, and in the first two years the school won 26 matches and lost only 8. Under the coaching of Mr G. F. Green, a former England International, the results continued to improve and between 1928 and 1933 all matches were won except for one which was drawn. The unbeaten team of 1926 toured the North of France at Easter, and won all six matches that were played. Perhaps of more note in that tour was the reporting of the matches for *The Fortnightly* by Malcolm Lowry, who was to become an internationally recognised author after leaving school. However, his humorous, irreverent reporting was not appreciated by the hockey players and he was sacked as a reporter.

The move to Pitlochry affected the Hockey much more than the Rugby. Because of the difficulty in preparing enough pitches for the whole school to play on, it was decided that only the First and Second teams, plus the First and Second Colts' teams should play hockey in 1941, whilst the rest of the school played rugby. Three matches were played and won. When the Lent term began in 1942, the countryside was under deep snow and this continued in Scotland for the rest of the term. Although it was possible to play in 1943, the majority of the team had played no hockey before. However the team won three of its four matches. Snow and frost again interfered with the season in 1945. Even on the return to Cambridge in 1946, the weather was so bad that no school matches were played in that year or the next. It took some time for the teams to regain some semblance of the pre-war form. The seasons of 1952, '53, '54, '55 and '56 saw some excellent results, with only two matches being lost against other schools during that period.

Hockey is the game which has proved to be the most successful in terms of international recognition for Old Leysians. Those who have represented their respective countries are listed below:

SCOTLAND
G.T.M. Mitchell (1931)
W.N. White (1947-50)
A.N. McPherson (1960-62)

ENGLAND
F.R. Fifoot (1921)
C.D. Terry (1924)
C.A.F. Fiddian-Green (1928-30)

IRELAND
G.H. McCormick (1906)

WALES
T.E. Morel (1919-1925)
H.A. Rocyn-Jones (1928)
O. Rocyn-Jones (1937)

135

ENGLAND (contd)	WALES (contd)
B.M. Schofield (1929)	T.G.J. Mathias (1938)
G.L. Slack (1938-39)	N.C. Pallôt (1952-54)
J.B. Aitken (1947)	D.S. Andrews (1963)
D.H.R. Fairey (1963)	N.C.D. Lloyd (1975-81)
P.J.T. Svehlik (1968-1972)	P.G. Spiers (1976-77)
D.J. Woods (1993-)	A.N. Palmer (Indoor 1983)

R.J. Chapman (U-21, 1970), T.A.J. Brookes (U-21, 1981), J.P. Swann (U-21, 1983), played for England junior teams.

Four of these deserve particular mention. Neil White played for Great Britain in the 1948 Olympics in London. He received a Silver medal when the British team was beaten 4-1 by India in the final at Wembley. He was to pass on his love and skill in the game to countless Leysians during his time on the staff of The Leys when he coached the Hockey sides. Paul Svehlik won 66 caps playing for England (a record) and captained the side in 1971-72. He also played for Great Britain, winning 33 caps and played in the Munich Olympic Games. Nick Lloyd, having won a record 173 caps for the Cambridgeshire side, played for Wales U-22 XI (4 caps), Wales Indoor XI (13 caps) and the senior Wales side (9 caps). He passed on his expertise by coaching pupils at St. Faith's School. Duncan Woods, who played for England U18 and U21 whilst at school, now has over 20 full England caps, and in 2000 received his first cap for Great Britain.

Girls' Hockey is now well established throughout the school, but there has not yet been a Leys name in an international women's team.

CRICKET

Records of the earlier years of cricket at the school reveal nothing very notable. The batting averages were distinctly poor, the bowling figures extraordinarily good, and reports of bad fielding appear again and again in reviews of the seasons. For the first fifteen years, the highest batting average had been 24.7 per innings and the amazing bowling average was 4.28 runs per wicket. These were all obviously due in a great measure to the rough nature of the pitch and the bad condition of the outfield. Improvement in cricket gradually came as the numbers in the school increased, but the enthusiasm for football was plainly far greater.

N.C.D. Lloyd (Fen 1967-1971), won 26 caps for Wales between 1973 and 1980, and represented Cambridgeshire 173 times between 1971 and 1990

The advent of a cricket professional, Tom Merriman, in 1890, led to greatly improved pitches. Bowling averages were no longer so low. In 1896, S. Brown, the school captain, finished the season with an aggregate of 1,032 runs and an average of 86 per innings, whilst the team won ten of the matches they played and lost only one. It was in that year that the annual matches against the M.C.C. were started. In 1908, N.J. Holloway scored 220 not out against the M.C.C.

Following the First World War, as with the other Leys' teams, results fluctuated from year to year. In 1923 the XI beat St. Paul's, Bedford, Felsted and Mill Hill, losing only to Oundle, while in 1924 a victory over University College School gave the team their only victory against another school side. Two more professionals were employed between the wars. They were Iremonger, followed by Cuthbertson. The services of both of them were paid for by the Holloway family. The new pavilion was formally opened in 1923 and a number of cement wickets for practice nets were laid down on the far side of the field. By now the wickets were pitched north and south instead of east and west. This pavilion had to be demolished in 1965 for Fen House to be built.

1929 was an outstanding season - the first time the school team had gone through the season without a defeat. The XI was captained by F.R. Brown who was to have a distinguished career in cricket on leaving school. During that season he scored an average of 65.4 runs per innings, and took 60 wickets at an average cost of 11.2 runs per wicket. For the second time, war intervened at a stage when school cricket was beginning to improve. The move to Pitlochry saw a pitch carved out of the golf course, which in the first season was composed of concrete slabs covered by matting and later by felt and matting. In 1943 a new substance was tried under the matting which made stroke play less risky and partially tamed the fast bowlers. The standard of fielding was hampered when the ball bounced from tussock to tussock and thence to knee-cap or nose. If the outfielding deteriorated, it was compensated for by excellent slip and gully fielding.

Unlike other sports, few Old Leysians have reached international standing at Cricket. A.R. Richards captained South Africa in 1891, the same year that he distinguished himself on the Rugby field. In 1911, B.H. Holloway went on the M.C.C. tour of the West Indies. A.E. Mallalieu represented Wales at cricket from 1924 to 1928. F.R. Brown was the one

Freddie Brown lays the Foundation Stone for the new pavilion, 1965

outstanding Old Leysian cricketer. He toured Australia in 1933 with the M.C.C. This was the infamous 'body-line bowling' tour. Later he played against New Zealand and India, and captained England against Australia in the 1950-51 season. Following his playing days, he managed the M.C.C. tour of South Africa in 1956 and Australia and New Zealand in 1958.

ROWING

It is not surprising, since the school was founded in a University town with such a tradition of rowing, that the boys wanted to start a Boat Club. However they were faced with two problems. Boats and a boathouse are necessary but very expensive. Furthermore the University had stringent rules which severely curtailed the opportunity for others to get on the river, with a total ban on all but Cambridge College and University boats during University term-time. The last recorded activity of the first boat club at The Leys seems to have been in 1886, when two members of staff offered their experience in rowing, and a professional waterman was hired to coach. Although races were suggested, the school authorities had not sanctioned activity on the river and there is no further mention of it in the records until 1960. It is interesting to note however, that until the early 1900s, it was compulsory for the whole school to turn out to watch the rowing on the last day of the University May Bumps.

A few senior boys had tried some rowing with the City of Cambridge Rowing Club during the summer holidays of 1960. In the following autumn they asked a member of staff, Richard Armstrong, to start a Boat Club in the school. Using the facilities of the City of Cambridge Rowing Club, enough experience was gained for two fours to compete at the Huntingdon Regatta. It was an encouraging start, although no trophies were won.

The following Lent Term, an appeal was launched to buy a set of oars for the school, so that when the racing season started the school could row under its own colours. Two eights were rowing regularly by this time. Successes of the season included reaching the final of the Maiden Eights at Peterborough Regatta, and winning the closed Maiden Eights at Cambridge and Bedford Regattas. After the end of term, the crew competed in the Cambridge Rowing Association Bumps and went up seven places in four days.

Following a very successful appeal at Speech Day 1962, a new racing

The Leys Boathouse

clinker eight was ordered from Banham's. At the same time a parent presented a four to the school. Success continued in the following seasons. In 1965, the school appeared at Henley competing for the Princess Elizabeth Cup. They won their first race but were then eliminated by the eventual winners. They also appeared in the 1967 and 1968 Henley Regattas. They also entered the Schools' Head of the River event each year,. The highest position reached has been 13th in 1965. Many regatta successes followed.

In 1968 a new boathouse was built in conjunction with Churchill, Selwyn and King's Colleges. Each club has its own bay and changing rooms, whilst all other facilities are shared. In the same year a new Donoratico eight was presented to the school by a parent.

The first girl member of the Boat Club was Caroline Young. She coxed the 1985 eight which competed at Henley in the Special Race for Schools. A girls' four was formed in 1986 and an eight in the next year.

The decreasing number of boys within the School has meant a similar fall in the number of those rowing competitively. However, the corresponding increase in the number of girls at the School has seen a large number of girls rowing competitively, so that the overall number within the Boat Club has begun to stabilise at around 35, boys and girls combined, near to the average number in the last ten years.

To accommodate the changing clientele there is a more flexible attitude, with pupils being involved for one, two or three terms a year. It is required that all junior rowers start in sculls, so there is now a great deal more sculling within the Club. The equipment provided has changed accordingly, and most of the boats are now rigged as sculling boats. The Club owns one VIII and one octuple, three coxed IVs and one coxless IV. There are four double sculls and we have recently augmented the single scull fleet.

Probably the most successful Leysian oarsmen have been D.L. Cruttenden, who rowed in two University Boat races, in winning Cambridge crews, and was President of the Cambridge University Boat Club, 1969-70 and A.N. Christie who stroked the winning Cambridge crew in 1975. He represented Great Britain in the coxed pairs in the Montreal Olympic Games in 1976. The success of the School Boat Club and Lysander (see Chapter 8 - *Leysian Institutions*) is largely due to the effort and enthusiasm of Richard Armstrong, who taught at The Leys from 1959-1990.

142

LAWN TENNIS

Although tennis had been played socially, and internal senior and junior championship competitions were held, it was not until 1931, under the direction of a member of staff, W.E. Sandbach, that it became an organised sport. From time to time it was allowed as an alternative to cricket as the compulsory summer game. However H.K. Lester represented England in the Davis Cup in 1926.

It was not until after the Second World War that tennis began to emerge from its Cinderella status. A number of matches against Colleges and other schools were played, and the first VI competed in the Glanville and Youll Cups for Public Schools. The best performance came when The Leys was runner-up in the Glanville Cup in 1953. J.H. Yong has represented Malaysia in the Davis Cup and the Asian Games between 1980 and 1990.

In September 1998 the School entered a scheme with the Lawn Tennis Association and Rover Cars to enable tennis players of outstanding potential to board at The Leys, whilst undergoing an intensive training programme in Cambridge. The effect of this on school tennis has yet to be felt and since some of the first entrants under this scheme are junior internationals, it will be some time before they may emerge as Old Leysian full Tennis internationals.

SHOOTING

With the founding of a Cadet Corps in 1900, rifle shooting became one of the school activities. The Handbook for 1912 reported that high places at Bisley were notoriously difficult to attain and small schools like The Leys hardly ever achieved them, unless they sacrificed other sports to shooting. Until then, the school had been about half way up in the Ashburton Shield Competition. With the advent of the First World War, ammunition became scarce and the competition was suspended until after the war was over. In 1932 the miniature range was constructed, and the arrival of C.H. Lewis on the staff brought about an improvement in results. In 1937, the school VIII was 10th in the Ashburton Shield competition and 5th in the Cadet Pair event. However it was not until 1950 and again in 1953 that the school won the Shield. The Leys last competed at Bisley in 1992. By then the numbers in the C.C.F. had dropped significantly, and only members of Cadet Forces

Winners of the Ashburton Shield, Bisley, 1950

are permitted to shoot at Bisley. There was also a problem in arranging full-bore practice firing on open ranges.

Some Old Leysians have competed at international level. W. Clemence shot for England in 1895, 1897 and 1902, G.M. Guinness represented Ireland in 1923 and 1924, Stuart Collings represented Great Britain against Canada in 1984, the West Indies in 1986, Africa in 1989 and South Africa in 1998. R.J. Cade was in the Great Britain team in 1964-67, 1969, 1970 and 1975 and represented Great Britain in the 1966 Commonwealth Games. P.J.A. Gaskell has represented both England and Scotland at full bore shooting and R.K. Hawley shot for the Irish National team between 1991 and 1997. J.H. Yong represented Malaysia in the Asian Games, the South East Asian Games and the Olympics.

CLAY PIGEON SHOOTING

The Club, founded in 1976 by S. D. Grice (staff), A. M. Hamilton and N. G. Darby (Old Leysians) with about a dozen enthusiastic boys, expanded rapidly in numbers and strength, and the School enjoyed unrivalled success and achievement in competitive clay shooting.

In 1978, the Eastern Area Championship, set up by S. D. Grice, R.T. Gallyon (Old Leysian) and Eley, the manufacturers of clay targets, generated a growth of clayshooting in East Anglian Schools: some 14 now compete annually in the event. The School, after an inaugural hat trick of wins, included yet another in their ten wins over twenty years and never finished lower than fourth place.

The National Championships were set up in 1979, again by Messrs. Grice and Gallyon and sponsored by Eley. First staged near Norwich, they moved to Kibworth and then to Shugborough, Staffs. Eley's generous sponsorship was complemented in 1986 by land agents, Smiths-Gore. The competition rapidly expanded from twelve schools to forty-five in 1990, and has become the largest one day event of its kind in Europe, with over 500 individual competitors.

The Leys holds a unique record of seven wins in fourteen years, including a hat trick in the mid-80s and yet another in the early 90s. Our girls' teams regularly won their sections in both the Eastern Area and National Championships. J. C. Fairey, an outstanding shot, was selected for the 1986 winning A team – the only girl ever to be included. She also

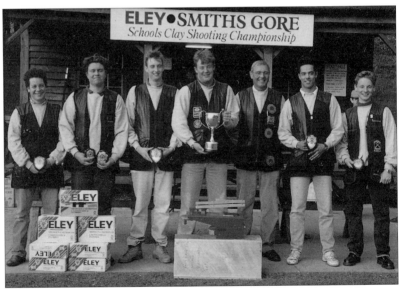

Clay Pigeon Shooting

returned the fourth highest individual score of the Championship.

In 1990, under the captaincy of C. N. Cryer, the team achieved the "Grand Slam" by winning all four major competitions: The British Championship, the Eastern Area, the Framlingham Invitation and the Warwick Challenge.

SWIMMING AND WATER POLO

In 1875, the embryo school was fortunate in being so near to the river. As soon as the weather became warm enough, the boys swam from a small island immediately opposite the school. In due course, a bathing shed was built with the City Council's permission and annual races held.

At first there were only three races. The course for the Championship was 332 yards long- upstream to the Town Sheds and back. The time was not often recorded, as the varying speed of the current made comparison difficult. Despite the lack of indoor facilities, one boy, P.S. Beves, won the Public Schools' Championship in 1884 and 1885, and was runner-up in the All-England Championships whilst still at school in 1885.

In 1905 the swimming pool was opened, and all races were then held indoors. Gradually, the number of events in the sports day competitions were increased, and an inter-house relay race introduced. The finals of this event were a feature of Speech Day entertainment until fairly recently. A fixture list of matches against Cambridge colleges and against other schools grew, and matches are still held in the Summer term. The school took part in the Bath Club Cup Race for Public Schools, which they won in 1939. Later they started competing in the Medley Invitation Race for Schools. The school still enters these events, which have been restructured to take into account the varying sizes of school numbers. The most notable swimmer of recent years was D. L. Walden, who swam in the Olympic and European Games trials.

The bath was also suitable for playing Water-Polo, although the difference in depth at the two ends sometimes gave one side an advantage. It was usual to include a water-polo match at the end of an inter-school swimming event, but the game was also played in its own right, with matches against college sides. It is, however, in the 1990s that the school team has reached the highest standard. In 1993, the side reached the final of the University Cup Competition and was promoted from the second to the first division of the University League. In 1995, the side was runner-up in

Division One, and then it came first in the 1996 and 1998 seasons. In 1998 they reached the semi-finals of the Schools' Knockout Competition, losing by a single goal to the eventual winners. One member of the side, C. Ashton, became an under 20 Scottish International.

OTHER SPORTS

During the school's 125 years' history, some sports have been played and then had to be abandoned for various reasons. Eton Fives was played for many years, first in open courts on the site where the Medical Centre now stands, and then in the squash and fives courts and miniature range complex at the far side of the school. W.H. Balgarnie was a very enthusiastic player, and it is claimed that he often played without gloves. However, lack of enthusiasm for the sport meant that the courts became store rooms. Recently, the University Courts in Portugal Place were demolished and replaced by housing. The University club provided funds to refurbish the school fives courts on condition that they could play there. There has been some interest from pupils at The Leys, who receive coaching from members of the University Club.

Boxing, Fencing and Gymnastics flourished for some time, but all eventually died out, as did the Bicycle Club even earlier. In the 1960s, the school competed against other schools in Athletics. For two decades, several matches a season involving three teams, Senior, Colts and Junior were staged. Several boys reached the finals of the English Schools Athletic Association Championships in the 1970s. R.E. Owen won the 400 metres event in 1971. However, the large numbers required to take part in track and field events together with the number of staff required to coach or judge the events, became difficult to recruit, so that this, too, ceased to be a school team sport, although some individuals have competed in athletic events.

Sailing has proved to be a very popular and successful activity, with several races against other schools in the summer. Squash has also been a very popular sport, both with pupils and staff. With the building of the Sports Hall, and the provision in it of three glass-backed courts, many members of the school have taken it up.

The Sports Hall has also enabled Badminton, Basketball, Volleyball and Trampolining to flourish. The weights room allows pupils to train for all sports. Judo continues to be an activity for many, with Martial Arts recently being offered as an alternative. New Netball courts have been constructed next to the Sports Hall, since it is necessary to offer this game now that The Leys is fully co-educational. Horseriding and Three-day eventing are available for the same reason, but boys also take part and compete in the teams with the girls. Although not an available sport in his school days, J.B. Sebire represented Great Britain in the Three-day event Championships in 1975. Golf is now played by a number of boys and there are matches against the Old Leysian Golfing Society. A recent sport, Canoe Polo has proved to be very popular in the swimming bath.

The Camfield Press – (basement of King's Building, 1980)

CHAPTER EIGHT

Leysian Institutions and Societies

At all Old Leysian Dinners, the toast "The Leys and Leysian Institutions" is proposed. Those Institutions are many and varied. Some exist today; many have long disappeared. There was a rule in the Blue Book at one time which said "no boy may start a society without the permission of the Headmaster and a master must be responsible for that society."

The entry for the 1963 *Directory* on clubs and societies demonstrates admirably the vast range of interests catered for in the period 1956 to 1963. There was an Essay Club and also an Historical Essay Club. Modern linguists were served by the Polyglots and there was a club for mathematicians. Scientists had several clubs. They were the Field Club, the Kelvin Club, the Senior and Junior Science Societies, and the Geological Society

There was an Exploring Society and a Climbing Club. Those seeking a less physically strenuous pastime could attend the Poetry or the Political Societies, or play Chess. Bridge was only available in later years. The Clapham Society offered a study of local and social history. As well as listening to talks by distinguished visitors, its members rubbed brasses, carried out a survey of local industries, and published an intensive survey of a nearby village. The Literary and Debating Society continued its long history with debates, literary evenings and visits to the theatre.

The article then described the activities of the Young Farmers Club, the Fantasticks, the Stage Club, the Radio Club and the Camfield Press. Musical interests were catered for by the Choral Society, the Glee Club, the Orpheus Society, the Gramophone Club and the Jazz Club. By now the Puppet Club was defunct, but those wishing for a practical hobby could join the Railway Club, the Aeromodelling Club, the Steam Model and Engineering Society, the Aeronautical Society and the Motor Club. Activities now covered by the

151

sports department of the school, but which were then hobbies, were sailing and canoeing. Finally, social life was covered by the Société Anonyme which practised Scottish country dancing with the assistance of members of the Perse School for Girls.

The author of the article in the Directory went on to say;

"Certainly no new entrant to The Leys need feel a lack of leisure-hour activities. In fact, in some instances it was found that there was too much pressure on post-preparation time with the result that boys may now use up to six preps. each week on the three half-days, for recreational pursuits."

An account of some of the Clubs and Societies which have spanned the 125 years of the school's history is given below.

THE GAMES COMMITTEE

The Games Committee was the first committee formed, on the first day of the school's existence, to be responsible for its sporting activities. The Governors paid for a plot on the field to be turfed for cricket. To preserve this, rugby was moved to the ridged and sloping area on the south of the field. Through a per capita grant from the school fees, the Committee purchased games equipment. An iron fence was erected to keep grazing cattle off the pitch, and a cinder track was constructed round the field. The Games Committee ran the tuckshop and the profits were added to the Games Fund. When the field was raised and banked to add approximately one third to the level area of the field, the tuckshop profit of £350 went a long way to covering the cost.

The Games Committee has always been involved in the provision of new buildings for sport, including the erection of the prefabricated pavilion on the Latham Ground, constructed in 1958 in memory of A. McM. Buchanan, the former Bursar who had been killed in a car accident. It controlled the award of colours for the school teams and the rules for inter-House competitions. The composition of the Committee has changed over the years. It still performs the rôle of monitoring sport in the school today, but with perhaps less pupil participation than sometimes in the past.

THE LEYS FORTNIGHTLY

On the 31 May 1876, *The Fortnightly* appeared for the first time. It is still the official school magazine, although it now only appears four times a year. It had been published, as its name suggests, every fortnight during term until the 1960s, although there was an experiment in April 1894 to make it a monthly. This idea proved very unpopular and in September it resumed its fortnightly appearance. Like many of the early societies, it had been initiated by J.C. Isard. At first it consisted of ten pages, but these soon increased to sixteen, which printers will know constituted a more efficient use of paper. J.C. Isard was the first Editor, and more recent Editors have included James Hilton, Alastair Burnet and Martin Bell.

To produce copy for a magazine every fourteen days must have been a immense task for the Editors, and often resulted in dull contents. Long articles on 'How to Scrummage' were to be found alongside 'A Few Conjectures as to the Pre-Historic Inhabitants of Our Country'. Heated discussions on the value of compulsory rugby continued through many issues. The third edition (1892) of the Directory contains a short article about the magazine which argued that because it felt itself "official', it had erred on the side of dignity, and this brought with it dullness. For this reason two so-called comic papers, *Comic Occasional* in 1880 and *Ate* in 1886 were started, but they ceased after only two issues each.

During the years of the school's existence, a number of alternative magazines have appeared. Sometimes a light- hearted dormitory magazine lasted for only six to eight issues. During the 1970s and 80s, several publications appeared, often with an anti-establishment approach. *Broadsheet, Comment, Illustrator, Phoenix, Splintur* (sic) and *Zapitty* have come and gone.

Due to the influence of W.H. Balgarnie as President, *The Fortnightly* started to include short stories in its pages. The contributions which he encouraged both from James Hilton and from Malcolm Lowry have aroused international interest. Lowry's irreverent articles on hockey matches caused him to be sacked as sports reporter in the 1920s. His stories from *The Fortnightly* are still analysed by biographers who seek deep meaning in words and passages which turn out simply to contain esoteric references to life at The Leys.

What probably made *The Fortnightly* uninspiring to many of its readers was the detailed reporting of every sports fixture down to the third and fourth school teams. Yet some of these details are important to archivists. Many people write to the school hoping to find some information about their relatives, long since dead. The present issues of *The Fortnightly* can perhaps be criticised for not providing enough detail about matches, especially school first sides and who played in them.

However, the breadth and quality of what it does include in its issues of sixty-four or more pages is very commendable. The ability to include colour photographs as well as having a coloured cover make it very attractive to read. The editorial staff now type up their copy on computers, cutting the cost of producing the magazine considerably.

Behind the pupil editorial staff, there has always been a President from the Common Room to guide them. There have been too many to give a complete list here, but during the past forty years Messrs. E.T. Moore, W.E. Sandbach, P.R. Chamberlain, N.A. Wilde, M.L. Wilcockson and J.C. Harding have provided invaluable leadership.

THE LEYS LITERARY AND DEBATING SOCIETY

In the school's first term, a debating society was formed with J.C. Isard as its first President. It called itself 'The Leys Literary Association'. It was not to last for long and was dissolved in July 1876. From its ashes arose 'The Leys Literary Union' and this carried out its objects admirably for the next three years; debates were well attended and membership of the society was much sought after. However, it was eventually found that evenings were too often being wasted in frivolous discussion. It was decided to close down the society and a new body 'The Leys Literary Society' took its place. In 1884 'The Parliamentary Society' was formed and debates were held with a Speaker and a Mace. In 1891 the two societies were amalgamated into 'The Leys Literary and Debating Society'.

The programmes included play readings, readings from set authors, short essays by members on subjects of their own choice and, of course, debates. The society flourished for many years under the title 'The Lit' and *The Fortnightly* contains many reports of its meetings. With the advent of more drama and essay societies, the literary side disappeared in more recent years. Debating has continued with various degrees of enthusiasm and has become more popular again in recent years, with both inter-house and inter-school

154

debates taking place. The institution of *The Rugg Prize* has brought new incentives into public speaking. A London dining club offers a substantial monetary prize (in memory of Sir Percy Rugg, Old Leysian - a former member of their club) which is competed for annually by members of the school. It is most interesting that since the admission of girls to The Leys they have come to dominate the list of prizewinners.

THE LEYS CHRISTIAN UNION (now THE ICHTHUS SOCIETY)

The Union was founded in 1882 with the intention of promoting Christian fellowship between the school and Old Leysians. From its inception, daily Scripture readings were sent out every month with explanatory notes, and members were exhorted to pray for one another at one of two fixed times every day. There were three general meetings held at the school when the Old Leysians were likely to be at The Leys for the Rugby and Cricket matches against the school, and for Sports Day.

The direction of the society had changed slightly by 1920, when in the school there were addresses after tea on half-holidays and sometimes in the mid-morning break, and after supper on Sundays. These meetings were conducted by boys, masters, or visitors. This practice continued until the move to Pitlochry, where it was difficult to find speakers. To remedy this, visiting Sunday speakers stayed until Tuesday morning, speaking to the members of the society on Monday evenings.

The pattern of meetings had changed by 1956. They were then held on Wednesday evenings once a fortnight. In 1994 the name was changed to the Ichthus Society, with weekly meetings for Juniors after tea, and Seniors later.

THE LEYS TEMPERANCE SOCIETY

This society was founded in 1881 for the purpose of providing "means by which the members may be made familiar with the efforts which are made in this country to reduce the gigantic evil of intemperance, and be encouraged in making a definite stand against those social habits which are calculated to lead to intemperance". The Headmaster, Dr Moulton, was its President, and members "took the pledge" by signing a document to say that they would not touch alcohol until they were at least 25. In 1888 there were forty-seven members, including eight masters and eight Old Leysians.

However, in the 1912 edition of The Directory, it was reported that "the number of separate special societies at one time or another promoted in the school has been felt excessive to sustain; and this is one which has lapsed again in recent as in earlier years".

THE LEYS WESLEYAN FOREIGN MISSIONARY SOCIETY

The first Missionary meeting at The Leys was held on 12 February, 1881 in connection with a visit from the Revd David Hill, who had been a missionary in China for eighteen years. Another speaker at that meeting was Sidney Hodge (Old Leysian) who was shortly to become a medical missionary in China. Members of the Society attended lectures in the school from visiting speakers, raised money for funding mission work, and maintained a specialist library and a collection of relics and curiosities concerning mission fields. Some of the relics were eventually housed in the School Museum (see Chapter 17 - *Odds and Ends*).

Partially as a result of membership of this society, several Old Leysians became missionaries: J.K. and P.K. Hill, E.F. Gedye, G.W. Guinness, D.B. Mellis-Smith, B.R. Vickers and G. Osborn followed Hodge to China; D.A. Hunter, A.P. Moore-Anderson, J.H. Parker and M. Gamble went to Africa; R. Smailes, W. Owston Smith, J.G. Bennett, W. Machin, M.D. Mawe, G.H. McCormick and E. Forrester Paton went to India. Much later Old Leysians, such as L.M. Ingle (China) and M.M. Temple (Zambia) continued this Christian service overseas.

Eventually this society was merged with the Leys Christian Union.

SCOUTING

In response to an appeal made to the Public Schools by Lord Baden-Powell, the Chief Scout, a course for boys in their last year at the school was started in 1933, under the leadership of Reg Ayres, to train them as Scoutmasters or other useful members of the Scout Movement. By 1935, the troop was growing rapidly and a scout hut, with a camp-fire circle, fireplaces and wooden shelters was constructed on the far side of the school field near Belvoir Terrace.

In 1936, a Junior Troop was formed, with Maurice Howard as Scoutmaster, and they were given a scout hut of their own by an Old Leysian. In 1939, a Rover Crew was formed. Investitures of Rovers, at the age of seventeen, took place in the School Chapel in the presence of members of the crew. Before the war, treks and camps abroad contributed to international scouting. Some notable visits were made to Luxembourg (1933), Switzerland (1936), Holland (1937) and Germany (1938).

The move to Scotland during the war provided perfect country for scouting. Sunday afternoon hikes became popular. The ice and snow of the first two winters (1940 and 1941) provided excellent scouting tests and members of the troop even assisted farmers by digging sheep out of the snow. One off-shoot of the school's stay in Pitlochry was that the school Rovers restarted the local scout group which was the oldest in Scotland, the 1st Perthshire Troop.

After the war, the overseas visits began again. Some of the highlights were the Paris Jamboree, camps in the Ardennes and the Forest of Fontainebleau and a ski camp in Norway. A Senior Sea Scout section was formed in 1947, under the leadership of D.E.S. Hayward (Old Leysian). They had regular cruises on the Broads at Easter and on one of the East coast rivers in September.

By 1963, the number of scouts exceeded 100. By now, Maurice Howard (1955) and Reg Ayres (1959) had resigned their positions as Troop Leaders and a succession of Leys staff continued to run the troops. During this period there were considerable changes in the programme and in the way things were organised. In many respects these anticipated and pioneered the suggestions of the Chief Scout's Working Party. The changes took Leysian scouting away from patrols and badges and, abolishing the distinction between the Troop and the various Senior Scout sections, achieved a coherent programme for the whole organisation. After the first year in the scouts, boys went on to Venture Scout training and, if they wished, attempted to gain the highest scouting award: that of the Queen's Scout.

During this period, the Scout Huts were restored, a mini-bus purchased, three sailing dinghies acquired and canoes built. Two car engines were bought for the mechanics course. Camping continued, with some trips travelling abroad, and others in Scotland and England. The cost of overseas camps had become prohibitive by 1970, so most camping activities were restricted to the Lake or Peak Districts or to Sutherland or Snowdonia. Richard Armstrong led camps at Easter in Scotland which were attended by a number of Old Leysians as well as current pupils.

In 1977 the national Scout Organisation felt that it could no longer accept The Leys scouting movement in the form it had tolerated for the previous ten years, and therefore it ceased to exist. The Duke of Edinburgh's Award Scheme provided a substitute activity.

THE SPITSBERGEN EXPEDITION

Possibly the enthusiasm for and success of adventure camps, which had been experienced by members of the scouts, led to the idea of an expedition to Spitsbergen, a large island in the Arctic Circle. In July 1976, a party left to take part in the expedition which had been carefully planned for two years. It was under the leadership of Ray Ward, assisted by two other members of staff, Charles Moseley and Edward Llewellyn-Jones. Eight Old Leysians and fifteen members of the school, plus Sister Helen Gowan of the school nursing staff, made up the rest of the party. The expedition had received approval of, and generous support from the Young Explorers' Trust. The Scott Polar Research Institute in Cambridge had assisted in the planning and in compiling the list of scientific observations which were to be made of the adaptation of plants and lower animals to the conditions to be found in the Arctic.

In spite of the worst summer in Spitsbergen for thirty years, the expedition completed the study of flora and fauna. Some members also managed to climb the highest mountain in the area, Newtontoppen (1,717 metres). They manhandled sledges containing food and equipment for five days, mainly in white-out conditions. Snowstorms buried the base camp, and ice such as that which would have sunk a trawler in Arctic seas, formed in sheets over the tents and weighed down guy lines. Sledging was done at night in order to make use of better snow conditions. Collapsing crevasse bridges caused harassment, when the whole party was negotiating a blizzard. After four weeks, the expedition returned to England safely, although two members had to be taken off the plane in wheelchairs, suffering from frost-bitten toes.

Photo by courtesy of R.D. Armstrong

R.D. Armstrong – Scenes from Armstrong camps

MUSIC

School music began with the formation of an orchestra of about half a dozen strings and two or three wind instruments, in 1877. This orchestra attempted Haydn's first Symphony. In 1880 the first "May Concert" was given and these continued successfully for twenty years. They were joined by other termly concerts. In 1894, Dr A.H. Mann, who was the organist at King's College Chapel, took control of the orchestra and unexpectedly the quality of the school players went down, partially due to the introduction of outside help. This also depleted the funds for school music. However, in 1906, the appointment of an assistant music master, who was resident in the school, soon showed effects in the rebirth of the school orchestra.

From 1918 onwards, the school choir became the back-bone of school music. The end of the Christmas term was marked by a Carol Service. 1920 saw the start of annual Bach recitals in the Chapel by the choir, with the assistance of a University orchestra. The Orpheus Club was started in 1920, with about twenty boys meeting together every Sunday evening after chapel in the two winter terms, to hear papers, and vocal, instrumental and gramophone recitals. The club is still flourishing in 2000.

During the stay in Scotland, the annual Carol Service was much appreciated by the large congregation in the West Kirk of Pitlochry. *The Mikado, Iolanthe* and *HMS Pinafore* were produced in the town Public Hall, the proceeds going to local charities and to the Leysian Mission. Meanwhile the Orpheus Club met twice a week, and the number of boys studying instruments steadily increased.

Many of the traditional features of Leysian music were continued or revived after the Pitlochry exile. The annual Bach Recital in the Chapel was modified, so that the works of J.S. Bach alternated each year with the works of other composers. From 1950, these concerts were given by the Choral Society, which was formed from the Choir and other volunteers from The Leys, together with members of the Perse School for Girls.

In 1958, it was decided to give additional annual concerts in the Dining Hall, thus making it possible for secular works to be sung by the Choral Society. Examples of works performed at these concerts are *Songs of the Sea, Carnival of the Animals, Hiawatha's Wedding Feast* and *Rio Grande*. Two groups of singers performed in the 1960s: the Glee Club and the Shepherdson Society. This Society gave several concerts, one of them including *A Short Lenten Mass* circa 1280, discovered in manuscript in the school library.

The construction of the school theatre, with provision for a music department, and the appointment of Sam Grice to assist Ken Naylor, the director of music, and to teach brass, increased the numbers learning to play instruments. It also meant that as well as orchestras, the school could include bands and brass ensembles in concerts. During the second half of the 1960s, the choir twice made recordings for Anglia Television and in 1968 made a record to commemorate a year of distinguished solo singing. During this period, the Shepherdson Society died out but was replaced by the Pepys Society

Large scale choral works, performed in co-operation with the other local schools, continued until the formation of the Sixth Form Colleges in Cambridge. With the reduction in the number of full services in the Chapel, the choir declined in numbers and importance. Its most outstanding performance was for the Centenary Service in King's College Chapel in 1975, when the treble line was strengthened by a few boys from local prep. schools.

During Richard Walker's time as Director of Music, large scale Choral performances were reintroduced, and this continued during the time of his successor, Peter Noyce, when the choirs were augmented by staff and parents of pupils of The Leys and St. Faith's. With the arrival of girls in the school in 1984, the choir went from strength to strength. Following their contribution to the Morning Service which was broadcast live on Radio 4 at the outset of the Gulf War, they were invited to sing in St. Paul's Cathedral and Westminster Abbey. In 1996, the choir made a recording called Χαιρετε and they also made a tour of Paris.

The range of music-making in the school is extensive, with over 35% of the pupils learning to play instruments. The members of that first orchestra in 1877 would be amazed at the skill and repertoire of the modern pupils. All types of music from Classical to Jazz and Heavy Metal are performed in concerts throughout the year. Rock Operas and West End Musicals have replaced the Gilbert and Sullivan productions of fifty years ago. A prize competition, started in 1993 in memory of Muriel de Vinny, has produced some outstanding solo performances.

161

"Arden of Faversham"

The School Orchestra conducted by K.N. Naylor

162

DRAMA

Plays had been performed from time to time in the Great Hall before it became the Dining Hall. Its use as the Dining Hall released space on the ground floor of School House, and that became the school theatre, with a stage with a proscenium arch at the west end. The seating consisted of oak benches until the early 1960s, when second-hand cinema seats added a great deal of comfort. Each year, a play or an opera was performed on Speech Day and the two evenings preceding it.

House drama competitions involved productions on two successive evenings, with three plays on the first, and the remaining two and the adjudication on the second. Eventually, performances of well tried one-act plays became tedious. In 1958 the adjudicator was John Barton, who was about to become Director of the Royal Shakespeare Company. During his extremely stimulating adjudication, he suggested a fresh approach to the problem of what to produce. He said that just performing the first act of a good play might whet the appetite to see more, or 'the play within the play' would be equally stimulating. The next few seasons saw the "rude mechanicals" play from *A Midsummer Night's Dream,* and the first acts of *The Cherry Orchard, Macbeth, Rope* and *Waiting for Godot* being performed in the competition.

In 1967, the building of a new theatre was completed. For several years there was a major production for Speech Day. The slightly inflexible structure of a Speech Day play and house plays was then modified to take account of two important facts. First, boys of the same age benefit from working with each other across House divisions and second, successful and committed drama work springs, like music, from regular experience throughout the year. The inter-House competition was moved to the beginning of the school year, and involved only the new Third formers. The same dramatic piece was performed successively by each of the Houses. This made comparison easier, but was rather tedious for those watching, and the competition ceased.

Stephen Siddall directed many memorable plays, some extending on apron stages to half-way down the auditorium. These included *A View from the Bridge, The Crucible, The Tempest,* and *A Midsummer Night's Dream.* Nicholas Wilde directed *A Servant of Two Masters* and Sidney Child directed *Peer Gynt.* At the same time, with the completion of the Queen's

Building, another smaller and less formal acting area was provided in the form of the Studio. Various activities including plays, dialogues and poetry readings flourished in these two venues. Although girls from local schools had previously taken parts in plays at The Leys, the admission of girls to the school on an equal footing, in 1984, brought a new dimension to the drama. The success of the rock operas and musicals mentioned in the Music section above owed much to their talents, particularly in dancing and singing.

Drama is now part of the curriculum, with courses available for both A level and GCSE examinations. Specialist drama staff enjoy the benefit of professional technical support staff, and they provide excellent entertainment throughout the year.

THE FANTASTICKS

This was a club which provided extra drama to supplement the annual school play or opera, and the House Drama competition. Sometimes it presented plays and at other times revue-style entertainment. One of its annual commitments was to visit The Leysian Mission in December and to entertain the members at their Christmas Party. Early in 1969, two members of the Fantasticks, Crispin Thomas and Howard Bird, planned an alternative form of entertainment by making a film. At the end of the Summer term they assembled a small cast and went to Byron's Pool, Grantchester where they enacted a "knock-about' play called "The War Game". It was a very simple plot, with soldiers and spies, most of whom ended in the river. Mrs Pat Houghton, wife of the Housemaster of North B, recorded the action on black and white 8mm film.

Part of the next term was spent in editing, adding sub-titles and recording background music, since the production was in the style of a silent movie. Ken Naylor, Director of Music, played sympathetic background music on the piano, and the film was ready for the scheduled visit to the Mission. However, on the appointed day it snowed so heavily that all trains to London were cancelled. Not wishing to waste the film, the producers entered it for a competition organised as part of a BBC2 programme called "Review". It was awarded third prize of £100. The first place was taken by a 35mm film made by a professional film maker and second place by a 16mm film produced by a trainee at a film school. The whole cast of the film attended the recording of the screening of the awards at Shepherds Bush. The following year saw the production of a more ambitious film, still in 8mm, but in colour, about *The Fortnightly*. Sadly, once Crispin and Howard had left the school, The Fantasticks ceased to exist.

THE OLD LEYSIAN UNION

The Old Leysians at Cambridge University in 1878 started a club known as U.L.O.C. (the initials for Cambridge Old Leysian Union backwards). Members met for breakfast in each other's rooms. The Old Leysian Union was founded on 26 April, 1882 and first met in a room at Mullen's Hotel, Ironmonger Lane, London, E.C. and then in a room above the Mansion House Station. The meetings were on the last Wednesday of every month, except July and August, at 7 pm. A frugal dinner preceded the meeting and members afterwards smoked, debated, or enjoyed a musical evening together. Annual Dinners were held in London which over 100 were attending by 1900. The subscription then was 25/- (£1.25), for which a member received copies of *The Fortnightly* and could attend the Annual Dinner and any other of the dinners without charge.

The Dinners could only be attended by Old Leysians, but the other social event of the year, the Conversazione, was an occasion where ladies and friends of the school could be entertained. This was usually held in either the Hotel Métropole or the Princes' Hall Galleries in London. To begin with, part of the entertainment was provided by the school orchestra, but eventually professional musicians were employed. At one of these, Dr Moulton was presented with his portrait, painted by Hubert Herkomer, which now hangs in the Dining Hall. At another, the Governors launched the Debt Relief Fund. The last of the Conversaziones was held in 1907.

At first the Cambridge Dinners were organised by U.L.O.C. and were held after the annual rugby match between the Old Leysians and the University. The practice of entertaining the Varsity side at the Dinner was changed when the fixture was dropped. Subsequently, the members of the school XV were guests and once there were girls in the sixth form, the guest list was adapted to include the girls' hockey side, also. In recent years, it has further included the school prefects and the Editor of *The Fortnightly*.

In 1929, a comprehensive reorganisation of the constitution was made to encompass the various branches which had been formed in different parts of the country. Some of these have since had to close down through lack of support. However, the Yorkshire and North East, Midlands and Manchester branches are still flourishing in 2000. In 1933, a Benevolent Fund was established to give support to Old Leysians, or their children who are suffering financial hardship through circumstances beyond their control. As well as keeping members in touch with each other and with what is happening at the school, the Union also financially supports the Old Leysian Rugby Club, the Golfing Society, the Rifle Club and other Leysian causes.

THE LEYSIAN MISSION

Old Leysian members of The Leys Christian Union in 1885 proposed that The Leys should found a Mission in the East End of London. The result was the establishment of the first Leysian Mission at 199, Whitecross Street, St. Luke's, London E.C. in premises requiring considerable repair.

By the end of the first year, there was a small Bible Class for men, a Sunday School for twenty children, an Evangelistic service on Sunday evenings, and a whole range of activities during the week. By 1887, the Mothers' Meeting had an attendance of over 270. The Mission was accepted by the costermongers who worked nearby. Apparently, if the Salvation Army appeared, they would be pelted with vegetables, but any outdoor service organised by the Mission would go unmolested.

It was soon obvious that larger premises were required, so a plot of land in Errol Street was purchased, and the building completed in 1890. The Mission now held a regular Sunday Morning Service as well as occasional Communion Services. The other work of the Mission developed steadily; the men's Bible Class was extended to include woman, there was a social hour and march before Evening Service, a Football Club, Christmas Club, Summer Holiday Club, Saturday Afternoon Outings Club and a Brass Band. Meanwhile the Sunday School had increased to over 500 children attending each week.

By 1899, new premises again became necessary. It was felt that the new Mission should not move away from the area or it would lose the influence it had gained. There was also an advantage in being near Wesley's Chapel. A site in the City Road with a long frontage was found for £36,400. A tender for £51,477 was accepted to build the new Mission. In it would be a large Hall to seat about 1,600, a small hall, a gymnasium, six sets of club rooms and many classrooms. As well as a flat for the Honorary Secretary, there was

The Leysian Mission, 1885-1890 – 199 Whitecross Street

The Leysian Mission, 1890-1899 – Errol Street

accommodation for Old Leysians and other young men working in London who needed accommodation and who were prepared to devote their spare time to the running of the Mission. Shops and offices on the street frontage would provide revenue. The Prince and Princess of Wales (later King George V and Queen Mary) opened the main hall, which was named the Queen Victoria Hall in 1904. The boys from The Leys and most of the masters attended, and the Cadet Corps provided the Guard of Honour.

The total cost of the building including site rose to £110,000. A substantial grant was obtained from the Twentieth Century Fund, the Metropolitan Chapel Building Fund and the Fernley Trustees. By 1907, there were twenty devotional classes a week, with a membership of 1,038 full members and 799 on trial. The number of men, women and children who entered the building each Sunday exceeded 5,000. Two complete trains were required to take the Sunday School on its annual outing to the seaside.

Both wars affected the Mission. During the First World War, the building was used as an air-raid shelter. Because of the numbers of men joining the armed forces, the Men's meeting shrank to a shadow and there were no male teachers for the Sunday School. During the Second World War, a bomb hit the extreme end of the building and the large Hall roof and the organ were destroyed by fire. About 40% of the population moved away from the area. Air-raid shelter was provided for a number of the oldest members of the Mission. Free tea was provided for hundreds of people who had taken shelter and were returning to their homes at day break.

For a few years after the war, it appeared that the devastated local areas would never be highly populated again. Contrary to earlier expectations, however, the local population grew again, being housed in huge new blocks of flats. Building licences were obtained to repair the damage caused by the bombing. £90,000 of the total £120,000 required for the repairs came from the War Damage Commission and an appeal for the remaining sum was launched. The Joseph Rank Benevolent Trust responded with the offer of up to £15,000 on a pound for each pound raised basis. The generous response from Old Leysians and friends of the Mission secured the rest.

On 6 June, 1955, Queen Elizabeth the Queen Mother reopened the large Hall and then toured the building. Very soon there were up to 70 activities, of more than 30 different types, taking place each week. The Boys' Brigade was one of the organisations which started to thrive again. In 1979

The Leysian Mission, 1899-1987 – 112 City Road

consideration was given to moving the Mission out of its premises. The building, declared at the time of its opening in 1904 to be the second largest Methodist building in London, was now showing signs of its age. Maintenance costs, and the probable necessity of meeting the Fire Safety Precautions suggested that it was time to find a new site for the Mission.

The building was sold in December 1986 for £2,200,000 and the final event took the form of a Thanksgiving Day on Sunday, 8 March 1987. At first the building at 112 City Road was used to provide shelter for the homeless, but then it was transformed into a block of luxury flats, known as Imperial Hall. Plans had been drawn up to merge the Mission with Wesley's Chapel, a little way down City Road from the existing building. The cost of providing accommodation on the Chapel site was estimated to be £1.5 million. The balance of the proceeds of the sale were paid into the Leysian Mission Fund. Amongst the fund's objects would be:

1. The maintenance of the ministry of the United Society.
2. The maintenance of the buildings on the Wesley's Chapel site.
3. The development and support of ministry amongst those experiencing deprivation in Inner London and elsewhere, thus continuing the traditions of the Mission.

The Dedication of the new Mission Centre was attended by Princess Alexandra on 29 July, 1989. It is impossible to list the names of the many Old Leysians and others who dedicated much of their lives to the Leysian Mission. However two people are remembered in the entrance to Wesley's Chapel, by a plaque bearing the simple inscription:

In memory of Keith and Ray Payne

(1910-1993)

for 52 years of loyal service

Ray Payne was one of the daughters of the Revd Harry Bisseker, the third Headmaster of The Leys, who had himself worked at the Mission from 1904 to 1910. Keith Payne was an Old Leysian. A fuller history of the Mission was written to coincide with its Centenary by Miss E.M. Pook.

THE OLD LEYSIAN RUGBY FOOTBALL CLUB

This was inaugurated in 1877 at a meeting convened by J.C. Isard and E.S Whelpton on 29 December, which was attended by some half-dozen enthusiasts. There were only a few Old Leysians at the start of 1878. Isard

Lady Renfrew, Mrs Ray Payne, Lord Renfrew, Keith Payne, Mr and Mrs. Bellis
on the occasion of the Paynes' Golden Wedding Anniversary
The group are standing in front of the portrait of Mrs. Payne's father, the Revd Harry Bisseker

raised scratch teams to play against the school twice in the Lent term. The school won one of these and the other was drawn. The remaining history of the Club is covered in Chapter 7 - *Leysian Sport.*

THE OLD LEYSIAN GOLFING SOCIETY

Old Leysian golf was started in 1901, organised by J.H.S. McArthur. One meeting every year was held, and it was found to be a most pleasant and successful institution, much appreciated by Old Leysians. Matches were played against a team of Old Millhillians in 1910 and 1912, which were both won by the Old Leysians, and again in 1923, when the Old Millhillians won.

In 1924, when the Halford-Hewitt Public School Old Boys' Golf Competition started, the Old Leysians, who were found to be the earliest of Old Boys Societies to have held Golf meetings, entered but were beaten by the Old Harrovians. An Old Leysian team has competed every year since 1928. The Old Leysians have twice been represented on the Halford-Hewitt committee, once by F.R. Brown and once by N.S. Washbourn.

The Old Leysian Golfing Society was formed in 1932, with G. H. Cobley as the first President, and its team reached the last eight of the Halford-Hewitt Competition in 1937. After the Second World War, it took a little time to get the Society on its feet again. Apart from making contact with members, there was difficulty in arranging fixtures. Food rationing made visitors unwelcome at most clubs.

The first official meeting after the war was held in October 1947. In terms of concrete achievement in representative matches against the former pupils of other schools, the years 1956 to 1962 were the most successful in the history of the Society. In 1958 the Old Leysians reached the semi-final of the Halford-Hewitt Cup and in 1962 they were in the last eight. In April 1958, when the team reached the semi-final, the headline which appeared in a Sunday newspaper was "Tomorrow's semi-finals will be between Eton and Harrow and Charterhouse and The Leys - three Goliaths and a David." T.D. Page (1920 to 1924) represented the Old Leysians forty-seven times in this tournament.

Competition for the Bernard Darwin Trophy began in 1959, with the entry confined to the sixteen schools who played in the first Halford-Hewitt tournament. The teams each consisted of six players aged fifty or over. After two appearances in the semi-finals, the Old Leysians won the trophy in

1962, beating Charterhouse in the final. Between 1963 and 1970, they reached the final once, and the semi-finals twice, and again they reached the final in 1972, losing to Radley. In 1992, the Senior Bernard Darwin Trophy, for players over sixty-five, was started and a Very Senior Darwin Trophy for over seventy-five year olds, was won for the Old Leysians in 1996 by R. K. Walker-Sloan (1930 to 1935) and E.W. Edwards (1926 to 1930).

The Grafton-Morrish Competition, another tournament for Public School Golfing Societies, was started in the late 1960s. Over one hundred such societies play in qualifying rounds throughout the country in June, with the final rounds being played in October. In 1976 the Old Leysian team qualified for the finals but was eliminated from the final sixteen by Charterhouse, who were the eventual winners. In 1984, the Old Leysians were beaten in the final by Sedburgh. In 1999, the Old Leysians won the Schools Putting Tournament at the Royal Wimbledon Golf Club.

The Society now has over twenty fixtures a year, and there is always a meeting before an Old Leysian Branch Dinner, as well as the Cambridge Dinner. A great deal of credit for the success of the Society must go to Nigel Washbourn (1951 to 1955) who has been Treasurer and Secretary for thirty five years.

THE OLD LEYSIAN CRICKET CLUB

The club was founded in 1881 and, in its early years, as well as playing matches against the school, had a short tour in the summer playing against Cambridge clubs. The records show that in some seasons they went further afield, and at one time they had a regular fixture against Kettering. In 1930 it was decided to form an Old Leysian London club, playing matches regularly throughout the season. Various Old Boys' teams, most of the Hospitals and other clubs were on the fixture list. In the 1930 season against the Honourable Artillery Company, the Old Leysians were left with 252 runs to make in order to win, which they did in under two hours. The Second World War brought the club to an end, and now the annual match against the school on Speech Day is the only fixture.

THE LYSANDER BOAT CLUB

In 1965, the Lysander Boat Club was registered with the Amateur Rowing Association. Derek Baker, the inspiration for the Club, became the first President. Membership is open to Old Leysians, masters, boys and parents, and others by invitation. The members were encouraged to enter crews for Cambridge Rowing Association events and in out-of-term events to form combined crews with present Leysians. The special purpose of the Club is to support and encourage rowing at The Leys, in particular by making capital grants towards equipment.

By 1977, the club had purchased, for the school, an eight, a coxed four and two sculling boats. Richard Armstrong succeeded Derek Baker as President in 1981. In that year an Old Leysian crew raised funds by a sponsored row to Ely and back. This money, together with more from a special appeal, enabled the club to purchase a set of oars. Soaring costs of boats have meant that the Lysander Club can no longer purchase boats for the school themselves, but through subscriptions and donations, grants have been made to the school boat club to help with the purchase of major items.

Because of the geographical problems of getting a crew together and the commitment of Old Leysians to other clubs, it has only been possible to hold an annual race against the school. In 1994, a women's race in fours was instituted against the school, but by 1998 only two had been held, both won by Lysander. In 1997, Richard Armstrong retired from the office of President and was succeeded by Charles Fraser. Richard Armstrong was created Honorary Life President.

THE OLD LEYSIAN LODGE

Following the example of the old boys of many other Public Schools, Old Leysians decided in 1922, on the suggestion of Colonel Durell, at that time Bursar of The Leys, a founder (and Deputy Master) of the Old Wellingtonian Lodge, to found a Masonic Lodge. The Lodge was to be comprised of Old Leysians, past and present Governors, Masters and Officials of the School. This was interpreted to include "...other persons who have rendered special service to or are connected with the school...."

The Cambridge Lodge Alma Mater No. 1492 sponsored the petition to found the Lodge. The 31 Founders signing the petition were: S.C. Berry, Revd H. Bisseker (the Headmaster), J.S. Cannington, Sir James Carmichael (Governor), Dr Gurney Dixon, Colonel A.J.V. Durell (Bursar), R.E. Garnett, Revd E.D. Green, W.H. Gunton, Professor H.C. Gutteridge, Colonel L.H.P. Hart, R. Hartley, T.W. Helme, Professor G. Pearce Higgins (Governor), A.

McArthur Holman, C.H. Hume-Reid, W.A. Lindsay, J.H.S. McArthur, Dr A.H. Mann (staff), W.A. Margerison, G. Northcroft, Lt.Colonel W.L. Owen, H.F.M. Peatling, J. Arthur Rank, T.B. Rowe, C. Hampton Vick, R.M. Vick, G. Russell Vick, R.W. Vick junior, J. Ewart Walker, Dr E.S. Whelpton.

The Consecration Meeting was held on 22 February, 1923, and the records of some of the joining members at the first Regular Meeting on 16 May, 1923, represent an intriguing cross section of occupations. There was an author, a civil servant, a cotton manufacturer, a dealer in precious metals, a farmer, a schoolmaster, a solicitor, two merchants and two surgeons.

From the outset, the Lodge endeavoured to hold one meeting a year at Cambridge, usually in the Isaac Newton Masonic Hall on the evening preceding the annual Rugby match between the Old Leysians and the University.

In 1936, the Annual Festival of Public School Lodges was held at The Leys. There were 412 Masons present, representing 27 Lodges. Of this total, 117 were either members of the Old Leysian Lodge or their personal guests. By the outbreak of the Second World War, the membership of the Lodge was 78. Just before the outbreak of war, the secretary of the Lodge received a letter from an Old Leysian, T.G.J. Mathias, who was not a Freemason. His letter read:

H.M.S. Gloucester
Devonport
25-11-38

Dear Mr Secretary,

 Not really having the foggiest idea what Freemasonry really stands for, and being a little mystified by Hitler's fulminations at it, I should be glad if you could send me a copy of the 'Aims and Relationships' statement.

Yours sincerely
T.G.J. Mathias
Lieut. (E) Royal Navy

There is no record as to whether Mathias received an answer. Very sadly, he died on active service in 1940.

One effect of the war was that in the Summons to meetings the words "..and uniform" were included to allow serving members of the armed forces

175

to attend correctly dressed. This addition was not removed until 1956. Meetings during the war were held at varying times and with varying meal arrangements, including no meal at all. Two members of the Lodge who were prisoners of war in Germany were sent gift parcels. To avoid retaliation, no mention of Masonic connection was made. In the archives of the Lodge there is a receipt from the fund in the name of "Mr. O.L. Lodge". If anyone responsible for security in the camps had tried to check on the background of their prisoners, they would have been misled by the fact that there was a J.S.H. Lodge at the school between 1942 and 1948.

Until 1994 the Lodge met in London, but in that year moved to its present home, Freemasons' Hall, Bateman Street, Cambridge. Regular meetings are held on the first Tuesday in March, the first Wednesday in May the third Friday in September (or the Friday of the Old Leysian weekend, if different) and the fourth Friday in November.

In 1998, the Lodge celebrated its 75th anniversary with a Garden Party at The Leys. Proceeds went to the Provincial 2002 Festival in support of the Masonic Trust for Girls and Boys, a charity which has supported pupils at the school.

CHAPTER NINE

The Leys at War

The school was only twenty-five years old when the South African (Boer) War broke out. It had not by then had an Officer Training Corps nor had many Old Leysians joined the Army. However about thirty Old Leysians fought in that war and five were killed. Their names are recorded on two bronze plaques which were originally displayed in the Great Hall. On completion of the school chapel, they were fixed to its north and south walls. There is a similar memorial recording the career of Sidney Hodge, whose life was shortened by a fatal illness contracted whilst he was a medical missionary in China.

It was perhaps as a result of the hostilities in South Africa that several Old Leysians including C. F. Hadfield, then active members of the Cambridge University Volunteers, suggested that the school should have an Officer Training Corps. The Governors asked Dr Moulton to circulate the parents to obtain their views. He wrote to 153 parents and received 81 replies, 78 of which of which were strongly in favour. The Governors then authorised him to make financial arrangements with the master who would be in charge of the new Corps, and they said they would be willing to make a grant towards the annual expenses. They also stated that they were willing to advance the money for any buildings required, although this would have to be repaid from the funds of the Corps once it was up and running. At the next Governors' meeting, the Headmaster reported that applications to join the Corps exceeded the places available. He also said that the armoury would be placed in the old Fives courts, that a site had been selected for the Morris Tube (an enclosed miniature rifle range) and that arrangements had been made about uniform whereby the boys would purchase their own trousers but the tunics would be loaned by the Corps.

He appointed J.H. Hayes (Old Leysian. and a member of staff) to be the

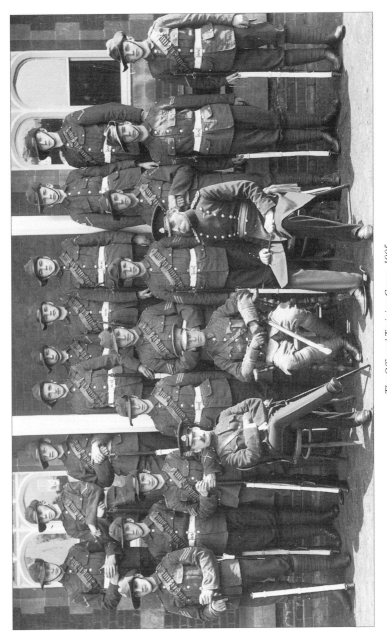

The Officers' Training Corps, 1905
(note: the style of headwear was that worn in the Boer War, only recently finished)

first commanding officer in 1900. At first, the Officer Training Corps was affiliated to the 3rd (Cambs.) Volunteer Battalion Suffolk Regiment, until 1909 when, under the Territorial scheme of the War Office, it became a contingent of the O.T.C. (Junior Division). By 1910 the establishment was raised to two companies, and J.S. Mellor (another Old Leysian, and also a member of staff) took over command of the contingent.

When, in August 1914, the declaration of war came, Captains Hayes and Mellor contacted all Old Leysians and those who were eager to enlist, with the co-operation of the Bursar, were offered accommodation and training facilities at the school. It was, of course, the school summer break and all the domestic staff were on holiday. The chef, some local cleaners and the school Sergeant soon converted School House into eating and sleeping quarters, and what claimed to be the first special training class of the war in the country assembled on 10th August. The University O.T.C. quickly followed the school's example, and provided a training course which the Leys contingent joined.

The local Royal Army Medical Corps was called upon to provide a hundred beds for cases of illness or injury, whether from the Front or occurring among the 20,000 troops then concentrated on Cambridge. The Leys was obviously an excellent and indeed the only site available at that time. Everything in the school not required for the hospital was stored compactly and methodically and the Bursar, rather than leave the premises, slept in the Art School. He did the provisioning and the Leys domestic staff cooked for the dozen or so officers and the nurse. The R.A.M.C. cooks produced food for the rest. Dormitories became wards, classrooms acted as store-rooms for spare equipment, masters' rooms were occupied by the nursing staff, and other rooms became operating and consulting rooms. The gymnasium provided barracks for orderlies, studies were used for medical stores and dispensary, and the Games Committee hut was once used as the mortuary. Another 100 beds were demanded by the War Office and not only were all the dormitories being used, but also the newly completed King's Building.

The first beds had been made available on 14 August and the first operation was carried out six days later. During the first few weeks, 171 patients were admitted to The Leys and then they were transferred to Nevile's Court, Trinity College. This was a cloister, completely open on one

179

side, with no heating. The original intention to use the school premises was rejected in favour of open air hospitals. Temporary buildings were erected on the cricket grounds of Clare and King's Colleges and these, together with Trinity, accommodated over 1,500 beds. The R.A.M.C. reinstated the school furniture, and the Autumn Term started only a few days late. Concern over the hostilities meant that the school numbers dropped somewhat. West House was closed, and its members were distributed amongst the other Houses. The Housemaster, W.H. Balgarnie, moved to B House.

The school soon settled into its usual routine. Some staff had joined the armed forces, but the majority of them were too old for active service. Where need arose, University dons helped with some teaching. Captain Mellor was directed by the War Office to continue military teaching, adding to his duties those of Military Instructor in Training Corps and Cadet Battalions in Cambridge.

Most of the boys joined the O.T.C. but it was not compulsory. By 1918 there were 198 pupils of whom 160 were in the Corps. James Hilton, who shared his father's pacifist views, wrote later in *To You, Mr. Chips*:

"The careful assessments of schoolmasters were blotted out by larger and wilder markings; a boy who had been expelled returned as a hero with medals; those whose inability to conjugate *avoir* and *être* seemed likely in 1913 to imperil a career were to conquer France's enemies better than they did her language; offenders gated for cigarette smoking in January were dropping bombs from the sky in December. It was a frantic world; and we knew it even if we did not talk about it. Slowly, inch by inch, the tide of war lapped to the gates of our seclusion."

Hilton remembered that Sunday chapel sermons, very often preached on the theme of forgiving our enemies, were followed by Mondays watching cadets practising bayonet drill on sacks on the football field. He was obsessed by this paradox and could not decide which behaviour was the more hypocritical.

Sport continued to play a large part in the life of the school. However, there were concessions to the war effort. Some boys turned out munitions punches in the workshop for the Woolwich armaments factory, and part of the field was dug up to produce potatoes and other vegetables. One curious entry in *The Fortnightly* was a call from the Games Committee for boys to collect 'conkers' to be converted into explosives. A later entry thanked everyone for their efforts but reported that the harvest had been kept at the school for too long and had rotted before it could be sent off. The swimming baths were reserved for use by the troops in the Lent term of 1915 and in the summer Belgian students seeking refuge in Cambridge were also allowed to swim. In 1916, one hockey pitch was reserved for Serbian refugees who were staying at Cheshunt College, just off Bateman Street.

There were two references in different issues of *The Fortnightly* to an Old Leysian, G.W. Gathergood, flying low over the upper quadrangle, much to the delight of the members of school who remembered him as the former captain of cricket. Gathergood survived the war and his flying experience helped him to become the test pilot for the 'Aircraft Manufacturing Company' based at Hendon Airport. During his peacetime flying career, he held twenty-three British speed records. He also won the first post-war aerial Derby.

By the end of the war 922 Old Leysians had served in the forces and 146 had been killed. Twelve of the teaching staff and twelve of the domestic staff enlisted, with two deaths in each category, including a former school Chaplain. Several of the Governing Body also gave their services, some reaching high office.

One of the sad tasks for the Headmaster, Revd Dr Barber, was to write short obituaries of those Old Leysians who were killed. These were published from time to time in the current issues of *The Fortnightly,* and as a complete collection in the 1920 edition of *The Leys Handbook.* The wording strikes us today as flowery and verging at times on the ridiculous, but at the time it reflected the feelings of most people. One death which occurred on 1 July, 1916 (the first day of the Battle of the Somme) was described as that of "the fifth Old Leysian to be killed on that glorious day". Such words could have given little comfort to grieving parents.

The walls of the school chapel are lined with memorial tablets to many of those who died, and the War Memorial on the outside of the east end of the building gives all the names. This includes that of Dr Moulton's grandson, and the sons of other members of staff. Seven families lost two sons and two families lost three. Although all deaths would have caused great sorrow, one Newfoundland family of Ayre lost two sons and a nephew who had been at the school, and another nephew who had been educated elsewhere, all on the same day, the fateful first day of the Battle of the Somme. This tragic co-incidence is recorded in at least one guide book to the Somme Battlefields.

One evening in September 1917, Lt. Harding R.F.C. was killed in an air-raid which hit his Mess. His younger brother, a Captain in the Royal Warwickshire Regiment, had been wounded in Mesopotamia and on his return to England was promoted to a position on the Air Board. He was accidentally drowned in the Thames almost at the very hour of his brother's death in France.

There were very few Old Leysians who were taken as prisoners of war. It appears that the Headmaster wrote to some of them in their captivity. E. Foster, who had been in School House, and only left in December 1916, had joined the Royal Flying Corps as a Lieutenant. He was taken prisoner and received the following letter:

Dec 13, 1917

My dear Foster,

It is no use, I fear, to wish you a merry Christmas, but such wishes as can be fulfilled we send you warmly and with love. And I fancy that your young spirit will manage to distinguish the day from others and that there will be a certain amount of gaiety even in your somewhat depressing circumstances. I hope that you are able to find some regular mental occupation otherwise I should fear that you would tend to stagnation and deterioration. Can you learn some new language or develop your mathematics or go in for a course of English literature. That sounds like your old Schoolmaster again, doesn't it? But seriously I think it is good advice. We are just drawing near to the Christmas holidays.

The Housematches have just been finished and you will be glad to hear that School won the Shield after a most equal game with B by 3 to 0. Today we have been playing with Bedford Grammar School in a demi-mist. Our ground is too grassless owing to much drilling, so we went to Pembroke's ground where it was softer under the frost. I couldn't stay to the end but when I left things were even. The Bedford boys however were "beefier". I will leave my letter open to state the result, for even now I dare say you haven't lost your interest in such results.

On Friday night the Literary Society is to give scenes from Nicholas Nickleby, profits to go to the Public Schools' Hospital. They are somewhat disturbed by the fact that Blore, who was to have been Squeers, has suddenly been called to his Cadet Unit. No doubt they will come out all right. Very probably you will amongst yourselves be doing something of the same sort to while away the time.

Mrs Barber joins me in warm good wishes. I am

Ever Your Affectionate

Head

He obviously forgot to send the result of the Bedford match! A year later, the war was over and Foster released from his prison camp.

Jan 9, 1919

My dear Foster,

How delightful to have you home again. What a time you and your Mother must have had when she saw your face again! And so the whole grim war is ended and you are through it scatheless. Your imprisonment must have been a testing time morally and physically. I hope you have come thorough it stronger and better. What you have been through has indeed made a man of you in a sense in which no ordinary lapse of years could succeed. You are still some distance under your legal majority but you won't need to wait till the law recognises your manhood, will you.

We shall be glad to see you some time when you have the opportunity of coming. I am receiving boys back for the new term. We meet earlier because influenza drove us home at the beginning of December. You will be interested to see a considerable increase since the two or three years ago when you left. We have 189 boys and East has three dormitories full. Changes are coming here as everywhere. Mr Isard has retired and is residing at the Mission. His successor Col. Durell is laying hold well. Good Herbert Brett died at the beginning of the holidays, and you may have seen in the papers that Dr Marseilles died suddenly and tragically last week. It is long in the history of the school since such ancient landmarks have been removed. But when there has been continuity for a long time such changes are likely to come all at once,

Matthews has just left as Head Prefect and Wilfrid Lowry is succeeding him in that office. Probably that will give you more sense of change than anything else.

And now you will be settling your future life. Be wise in your

183

choice, and be hardworking when you have chosen. And take care that the mutual understanding which you and your men gained of each other in your united danger and warfare helps you to be a generous and sympathetic sharer in the new relations between master and man in the future.

Mrs Barber unites with me in love to you and kindest good wishes for your Mother.

Your Affectionate Head

Dr Marseille, whose tragic death was mentioned in the letter, had joined the staff from Manchester Grammar School in 1889. He had taught French and German at both schools. He was from Alsace and his relatives had fought on opposing sides during the war. This had led to a state of depression which coupled with his wife's painful, terminal illness caused him to commit suicide in January 1919. Herbert Brett, who was also referred to, had been the Senior Butler at the school and his father was the original gardener.

One civilian death which occurred as a result of war was that of Revd Dr James Hope Moulton, son of the first Headmaster, one of the original sixteen pupils and someone who had taught at the school at one time. James was a leading expert on Zoroastrianism and had given the Hibbert Lectures on this subject in 1912. He published them the following year in a weighty volume which runs to a preface and four hundred and sixty-eight pages. It not only deals fully with history and beliefs but has evidence on almost every page of his gift of looking at things with the eyes of the people about whom he is writing, and not merely from the dispassionate view-point of a modern scholar investigating the dead past.

He had recently lost his wife when he was invited to India in 1915, primarily for the purpose of meeting and lecturing to the Parsees, descendants of the early Zoroastrians, who had now migrated to Bombay and settled there and elsewhere in India. At that time there were only about a hundred thousand Parsees in India but they were prominent in business and occupied positions in public life out of all proportion to their numbers in the total population. James received the tragic news whilst he was in India that one of his sons, Ralph, had been killed on the Somme. His own health was far from good - he overdid things as he had always done and made little allowance for the demands of a tropical climate.

He sailed from Bombay in March 1917 on the *City of Paris* and was

184

joined in Port Said by his friend Rendel Harris, who had been torpedoed on the way out to India and had got no further than Egypt. The *City of Paris* was torpedoed off Corsica and though all on board got into the boats, and most reached land safely, the boat carrying Rendel Harris and James was lost. They rowed for three days but James, who was troubled by boils and run down in health, died from exposure in the open boat on 7 April, 1917 and was buried at sea. Rendel Harris was rescued and nursed back to health.

The war over, the school returned to normal. A new Headmaster, the Revd Harry Bisseker, took up office in 1919 and gradually the school numbers grew. The War Memorial Fund was set up with several aims, including giving financial help with the education of the children of Old Leysians who had been killed during the war, the establishment of scholarships and the erection of a suitable memorial to the fallen. Eventually the War Memorial was unveiled by the Duke of York (see Chapter 10 - *Royal Visits to The Leys*).

In 1938, when the Munich Crisis seemed to threaten another war, the Chairman of the Governors of The Leys School, Lord Stamp, who happened to be head of L.M.S. railways, offered the Gleneagles Hotel in Scotland as a safe haven for the school. The offer was declined, but just in case of war and bombing, the boys of the school dug trenches six feet deep (but with no tops) at the far side of the field running along the perimeter from the squash and fives courts towards the steps down to the footpath to Latham Road. The trenches were not used, as it was discovered that there were extensive cellars under the Headmaster's House with enough room for the whole school to shelter.

In a similar manner to the efforts made during the First World War, some masters and boys worked in the school workshops after lunch, producing circular brass discs which were sent away for use by the armed forces.

On 5 June, 1940, all parents received a letter refuting the rumour that Cambridge was being evacuated. The rumour was no doubt caused by the fact that Cambridge University had decided to end its term immediately examinations were over, in order to allow undergraduates to join their Local Defence Volunteer units (Home Guard) or Home Defence Force. Dr Humphrey reassured parents that the Regional Commissioner for Civil Defence had told him that the school would be informed as soon as possible if evacuation became necessary. The Headmaster was in touch with the

Headmaster of Haileybury College and both schools had been advised that for the time being their premises were not required for extra hospital facilities, although they might be in the future.

On 14 June, the parents received another letter stating that the Governors had decided to postpone Speech Day. However, the annual Commemoration Service would be held and Mrs Humphrey would distribute the prizes afterwards. The usual long weekend break would take place, but parents were asked to refrain from seeking permission for their sons to make long journeys from Cambridge at that time.

Another letter to parents followed on 18 June advising them as to what action they might consider, but still claiming that evacuation from Cambridge was not yet called for. The end of term letter dated 17 July stated that there seemed to be no good reason for ending the term early. There had been no air raid warnings in Cambridge over the previous four weeks, and no bombs had dropped anywhere in the vicinity since the middle of June. Following the routine information about travelling arrangements and provisional dates for future terms, there was a hint of doubt over the place of assembly for the next term.

A fortnight later the Chairman of Governors, Lord Stamp, sent a circular to all parents explaining the problems discussed at the recent Governors' meeting. In it he said that the Governors approved of the views of the Headmaster expressed in his previous letter, and that they were concerned over the conditions in which members of the school would have to live and work if they were evacuated from Cambridge. Furthermore the letter explained that whereas the Ministry of Health had considered requisitioning the school as an annexe for Addenbrooke's Hospital, as a result of the ending of the campaign in France, the Governors had been informed that it would not now be necessary to do so.

On 5 September, the Headmaster wrote a very long letter to all parents, explaining that he had now received a letter from the Senior Regional Officer to the Ministry of Health, stating that the school was required at as early a date as possible. The Headmaster went on to say that although it had been suggested that the school might be able to remain in Cambridge with boys staying in Colleges or large private houses, it had not seemed a workable solution. Dr Humphrey had investigated alternative sites and only a week before had seriously considered using the Atholl Palace Hotel in Pitlochry.

The Headmaster's letter of 18 September confirmed the move to Scotland, and that the hotel staff would be in a position to have the hotel ready for the start of term on 3 October. The exile in Scotland had begun and is described in Chapter 11 - *Exile in Pitlochry*.

The Health Ministry were looking for a large hospital just far enough inland to be safe, to be able to deal with casualties after an invasion of Europe by the Allies. By taking over The Leys, which was only about 400 yards from the then Addenbrooke's Hospital, they would have a suitable building. The school annexe was not only used for military personnel, but many residents in Cambridge were also treated there for a variety of ailments. By October 1940, The Leys had space for 375 patients, the University Examinations Hall provided another 100 beds and the hospital itself 358. By the time the hospital moved out of the school buildings it had treated 19,922 in-patients there who stayed for an average of 15.5 days.

Before the school had been converted for use as a hospital, the buildings were used as a cleansing station for evacuees and their mothers from London. 3,312 were treated in a short time. The average length of stay was only 48 hours, but some needed treatment for skin disorders and stayed longer. The nursing staff of the hospital complained that this was not really part of their duties and prevented them from looking after more urgent cases.

The basement of East House was strengthened in case of air raids and converted into the operating theatre. At the same time the Sanatorium in Brookside was to be Addenbrooke's Ear, Nose and Throat department with 77 beds for patients. School House was used for both male and female patients. There are no records showing in which buildings the nursing staff lived. However, the minutes of the Board meetings of the Governors of the hospital do record that the Sisters had requested that gas fires should be fitted in their rooms as they were 'abnormally cold'. Their request was turned down, but the Matron promised to move them to warmer accommodation. In the same documents, the hospital authorities had expressed concern that difficulty with transport might cause fuel shortages, so they stored 100 tons of coal at the school for emergencies.

One sad entry in the Hospital Governors' minutes was about patients' visitors. It concerned children under the age of 12 who had broken limbs. They had to have been in the hospital for four weeks before they were permitted to receive visitors and even then they could only see them between 2.30 pm and 4 pm on Saturday afternoons.

The top floors of North A and B Houses were used for male patients, whilst the ground and first floors were used for Maternity and Gynaecological cases. Part of the banisters were removed to get the stretchers up the stairs,. After the war, no one could find the pieces to restore them, so to this day there are very odd looking gaps at the turnings on the half landings. East House, which had mainly been for orthopaedic cases, had metal banisters which could not be removed. The new Addenbrooke's Hospital orthopaedic ward had a display of photographs of East House in action with one showing a patient on a stretcher being precariously carried upstairs to one of the wards following an operation. Later, a lift was built on the end of the House where the Housemaster's house is now. This was used to get patients up to the other floors more safely.

King's Building was used to house the Radiotherapeutic Centre. When the School returned from Pitlochry, the hospital authorities asked if the Centre could still function in the school. Dr Humphrey refused, on the grounds that the boys might be upset to see the condition of some of the patients. The machines were temporarily stored and then used in a prefabricated hut, put up on the hospital site in Tennis Court Road.

After the war, Addenbrooke's decided to use the lift attached to the end of East House in their main hospital. They stored it at the school for a few weeks before transferring it to the Trumpington Street site. A few years later, the Housemaster's house was added in the place where the lift had been attached. It had been proposed in a scheme for the development of the school after the war, that a new West House should be built, as a mirror image, on the end of East. This was no longer possible. When the earlier plan had been discussed, one objection to it was that the Headmaster's family would lose their privacy, as the end of the proposed House would closely overlook some of their rooms. The Governors' minutes at that time rejected this as an argument, on the grounds that the Headmaster's house ought to be pulled down anyway, because it was so old! Since then the original Leys House has become a Grade II listed building and such vandalism is no longer permissible.

A deputy matron who was still alive a few years ago, remembered nursing Canadian soldiers in East House who had been severely injured at the Battle of Arnhem. The hospital porters were conscientious objectors, who had been all been male dancers in the Royal Ballet Company. On one occasion they were required to take a patient from one ward to another, but they could not be found. Eventually the very angry deputy matron discovered them practising ballet steps, holding on to a hospital trolley. The Leys carpenters still use one of two trolleys, which once transported bodies to the mortuary in the basement of the Science Block. This room has now become the Senior Biology Laboratory.

The Ministry of Supply used some of the Science Block as the Cambridge Training School for Laboratory Assistants. Here, women technicians were trained to analyse materials supplied on Government contracts, such as boot polish for the troops. This was to check that unscrupulous dealers were not selling substandard goods to the Government. There were also three scientists working on something secret. It must have involved the element phosphorus, since they left several jars of it behind. The Leys Chemistry department has been using it ever since and still has some left!

At the end of the war, British soldiers who had been Prisoners of War were due to come to the school for de-briefing and health checks before being returned to their regiments. One lady, who was involved with the Red Cross, was given the task of getting things ready. She was appalled at the state of the enamel mugs and plates, and also of the beds being provided for our troops (not the fault of The Leys School!) She was cycling home in a rage and rode through traffic lights showing red. Fortunately, owing to petrol rationing, there were very few cars about. Two policemen standing at the corner rebuked her for doing this. She replied that they ought to have better things to do than standing around telling cyclists off. They took her name and address and she was prosecuted. She wanted to appear in court to make a protest about the standard of equipment for the ex-prisoners of war, but her husband would not allow her to do so, and insisted that instead she should plead guilty and pay the fine.

During the Second World War, over 700 Old Leysians served in the armed forces. 87 Old Leysians and others associated with the school gave their lives, and their names are inscribed on two panels added to the Memorial to those who fell during the 1914-18 war. Once again *The Fortnightly* had recorded their deaths, together with a brief summary of their lives at school. The language of the Second World War obituaries was less flowery than that of the First.

The school also lost the Chairman of Governors, Lord Stamp, killed together with Lady Stamp and their eldest son in an air-raid in London in 1941. One Old Leysian, who was a civilian, was executed by the Japanese. The Revd Alfred Sadd was subsequently the subject of a BBC radio documentary *'Missing, Believed Immortal'*. Before the war he had been posted by the London Missionary Society to the Gilbert and Ellice Islands in the Pacific. When the non-native population was being evacuated, Alfred elected to stay and carry on his work with the islanders of Rongorongo. The Japanese occupied the Islands, and he was arrested. They spread the Union Jack before him and ordered him to walk over it. Instead he picked it up and kissed it. He was sent for trial to Tarawa, but first instructed a native pastor to take care of the manuscript of the book he had been translating into Gilbertese. The book was *Concerning the Bible* by Revd Conrad Skinner, who was Chaplain at The Leys for many years.

The morning after Sadd arrived, the Japanese decided that all Europeans should be killed They stood in a line and Alfred went out and stood in front of them and spoke some words of cheer. He removed his blindfold and faced the Japanese executioner, who beheaded him with a sword. All the Europeans were then killed in the same manner.

After the war and the subsequent abolition of National Service, a small but steady number of Leysians joined the Armed Forces. Three of them served during the Falkland Islands war, and although one, Ian Stafford, was wounded, thankfully none were killed. He described how his wound was first treated on the shore in a field hospital, and he was then transferred by helicopter to the *S.S. Uganda*, which had been requisitioned as a hospital ship. The ship would sail close to the islands in the late afternoon to pick up the wounded. The average time on the ship was 7-14 days, which normally included a second operation to clean and seal the wound. His main memories were of being in a large ward to the aft of the ship, and that the ward sister was a beautiful blond naval nurse - he was still single at the time!

During the wars which devastated the former Yugoslavia, Mark Cook, who was a Colonel of the Gurkha Rifles, found himself in 1992 commanding all British troops in the United Nations Protection Force in Croatia. He was so moved by the plight of the children in the ruins of the

Martin Bell, OBE, MP

Col. Mark Cook, OBE

shell-destroyed orphanage at Lipik that he eventually resigned his commission so that he was free to raise funds and supervise the rebuilding of their home. Sixteen months after promising the children that they would do so, he watched them return to their building, which had become a symbol of hope. From this enterprise he and his wife started a new charity, *Hope and Homes for Children*, with the aim of restoring orphanages in war stricken areas of the world. Whilst he was still a serving soldier, he had gone to Sarajevo to meet another Old Leysian, Martin Bell, who had overlapped Mark at school. Martin was reporting live on BBC television news when he was hit by shrapnel. Mark was standing next to him and was seen on British television going to the rescue. After treatment in the United Nations hospital in the basement of a nearby building to remove the larger pieces of shrapnel, Martin was taken to Zagreb and then flown back to London. He still had a piece of shrapnel inside him, but was soon reporting for the BBC in war-torn areas once again.

In 1999, secret papers released by the Public Records Office revealed that in 1963 The Leys had been earmarked to play a supporting role for the Eastern Region should a nuclear strike be aimed at Britain, causing the collapse of central government. When these papers were released, only two of the School's Governing Body of 1963 remained alive. Neither could remember that this suggestion had been discussed at meetings. However, the papers disclosed that the regional seat of Government was to be in Brooklands Avenue, a short distance from the school and The Leys' role in the Second World War must have made it an obvious choice to provide further support. Thankfully, the threat of nuclear war has diminished, and to the best of our knowledge the school buildings are no longer required by outside agencies.

CHAPTER TEN

Royal Visits to The Leys

VISIT OF H.R.H. THE DUCHESS OF ALBANY

Following the death of the first Headmaster, Dr Moulton, the Governors planned the building of a chapel in his memory. Queen Victoria's daughter-in-law, the Duchess of Albany, was invited to lay the foundation stone which is on the outside and to the left of the main entrance to the chapel. Her Royal Highness laid it on 20 June, 1905, and remarkably the chapel was completed just over twelve months later.

The Duchess had travelled to Cambridge the day before and stayed in the Master's Lodge of Trinity College. She drove to The Leys the following morning, arriving at the Headmaster's House at 11 o'clock, where she was met by a Guard of Honour from the Officer Training Corps, commanded by Capt. J.H. Hayes. The National Anthem was played by the band of the 3rd (Cambs) V.B. Suffolk Regiment. After the masters had been presented to her, Her Royal Highness proceeded to the hall where many of the 600 invited guests were assembled for Morning Service, conducted by Dr Moulton's son, the Revd J. H. Moulton.

Afterwards the school and congregation assembled outside the hall at the building site, where a platform had been erected for the Royal party. The proceedings were somewhat curtailed by a shower of rain. Fortunately there was a canopy over the Royal platform. After a short address by Sir George Hayter Chubb, Mr J.H.S. McArthur, Secretary to the Governors, presented Her Royal Highness with a casket to be placed under the foundation stone. It contained copies of the daily papers and of the Cambridge Review, together with copies of *The Fortnightly* and the Leysian Mission Magazine. The Duchess was then presented with ceremonial builders' tools for the laying of the Foundation Stone. The architect, Mr Robert Curwen, presented a trowel, the bursar, Mr J.C. Isard, a mallet, and the builder, Mr W. Saint, a

The Duchess of Albany leaves the Headmaster's House

The Duchess with the Headmaster, Dr. Barber and Sir George Hayter Chubb

plummet level. The stone was placed in position with the assistance of the Clerk of Works, Mr W.H. Hudson. In a clear voice the Duchess then said: "I declare this stone well and truly laid. In the name of the Father, and of the Son, and of the Holy Ghost, Amen."

Next Dr Barber, the Headmaster, delivered an address, after which a buffet lunch was served in a tent on the lawns. After lunch the rain had ceased and the rest of the day was fine. The guests returned to the Hall for the Prize Giving at 2.45 p.m. On ascending the platform, the Duchess was presented with a bouquet of carnations by P. Holman, the youngest of three brothers at the school. After several speeches, the prizes were presented by Her Royal Highness and special mention was made of one won by a Japanese boy, Todo, for a drawing which included perspective, a style of drawing which had not previously been used by Japanese artists.

The Duchess went to the swimming bath which she formally opened, and watched a display of life-saving and 'fancy' swimming. Tea was served on the lawns whilst the guests watched a lacrosse game. At 5.30 p.m. the guests returned to the hall, which was again crowded for a concert. Her Royal Highness listened to the earlier items and then had to leave for the railway station, which her train left at 6.37 p.m., conveying the Royal Party and many of the visitors. They arrived at Liverpool Street Station at 7.49 p.m., where the visitors respectfully bade adieu to the Duchess as she drove away from the station.

The Duchess of Albany had enjoyed her visit to The Leys so much that she said she would return as an ordinary visitor for the official opening of the chapel on 12 October, 1906, at noon. A special train brought the Royal party and other guests from London, just in time to be seated in the chapel - the Duchess and other public figures on the right and Mrs Moulton and her family on the left. There were nearly 400 in the congregation for the dedication service. At the end of the service, the Duchess and the other guests moved outside to witness the unveiling by his widow of the memorial stone to Dr Moulton. The south door by the vestry was formally unlocked by Lady Chubb, wife of the Treasurer to the Governors, Sir George Hayter Chubb, was a generous benefactor to the chapel, paying, among other things, for the east window. After the formal proceedings, lunch was served for 280 guests in the Great Hall. The Duchess's party and Mrs Moulton and her family sat on the dais, which was much larger than it is now, with the

Headmaster and the Governors. The only decoration was Dr Moulton's portrait.

After the meal there were formal speeches. The first was from Sir George Hayter Chubb, who welcomed the Duchess, Mrs. Moulton and the other guests. Lord Justice Fletcher Moulton responded on behalf of the Moulton family, and the Rt. Hon. Sir Henry Fowler expressed the indebtedness of the school to the Treasurer, Sir George Hayter Chubb, for his ability, industry and generosity. With the formal proceedings over, the Duchess left for London.

VISIT OF HIS MAJESTY KING GEORGE V

The Honorary Secretary to the Governors, J. H. S. McArthur, made a suggestion at one of their meetings that they should try to invite the King to open the new library block. A petition was sent through the Home Secretary, and finally His Majesty gave a conditional assent. The detailed arrangements for the visit to inaugurate the Library and classrooms were made by Sir George Hayter Chubb, and the King sent a letter expressing his entire satisfaction with them. On Thursday, 30 April, 1914, the King arrived by car from Newmarket. Contemporary newspaper reports spoke of his being given an enthusiastic welcome as he drove through the "poorer part of the town."

"Thousands of people lined the route from River Lane and the crowds of school children waving their small flags and eagerly trying to catch a glimpse of the Sovereign as the car passed slowly by, was a sight not soon to be forgotten. East Road is not one of the most beautiful thoroughfares of Cambridge, but the inhabitants had made it look very bright and gay with Union Jacks and a liberal display of red, white and blue bunting."

Only one newspaper mentioned that two suffragette petitions had been thrown at the King's car. One, on the way to the school, was thrown in Lensfield Road near the Roman Catholic Church. It hit the roof of the car. The other was thrown as the car returned down East Road and this time the chauffeur was hit in the face. It was obviously not anticipated that the King would be in a closed car. Both incidents happened so quickly that very few people were aware of them.

The weather was not all that might have been desired; there was a keen wind and the sky looked threatening, but the rain held off. The King arrived at the new gateway and was greeted by Sir George Hayter Chubb, the

King George V, 1914

(the wire, which lowered the top stone into place, can just be seen passing from the top centre of the picture to the marquee - see page 198)

Headmaster, the Revd Dr W.T. Barber and the Secretary to the Governors, Mr J.H.S. McArthur. The King was wearing a silk hat and frock coat, dark grey trousers , light brown gloves, dark brown spats and a red tie. He carried an umbrella and wore a bunch of violets in his button-hole. The closed oak doors of the gateway were opened and the King led the way to the upper quadrangle where he was introduced to several of the Governors. The band of the Leysian Mission played the National Anthem, and a Guard of Honour of about 50 boys of the school Officer Training Corps, commanded by Captain J. Mellor, presented arms. The King then inspected the Guard of Honour, which had been drawn up in two ranks facing a marquee in the middle of the quadrangle.

The formal inauguration of the new buildings was carried out in the marquee, where on the edge facing the gateway there was a square red-covered column reaching from the floor to the awning. On the inner side of the column was a locked panel. Sir Aston Webb presented a small gold signet ring to the King. This ring contained a tiny gold key, folded away under the stone. It opened like the blade of a knife and with this key, at the sound of a bugle, His Majesty opened the doorway in the red-covered column. At once the cords which stretched from the column to a block and tackle which held the top-stone of the gable over the arch, began to move. The stone dropped slowly and squarely into place, and the crowd gave three cheers.

King George then undertook a rapid inspection of the school. He first visited the chapel, where he admired the carvings, most of which were the work of Sir George Hayter Chubb. Before leaving, he signed the visitors' book. On his way to the hall he saw some small children at a window of the Headmaster's House and delighted them by waving. In the hall there was a large gathering of parents and guests. His Majesty was greeted by the playing of the National Anthem on the organ by Dr A.H. Mann and the hymn "Now thank we all our God" was sung by the choristers of King's College Chapel and the assembled gathering. The King listened to a short address of welcome from Sir George Hayter Chubb. Replying, he made reference to The Leys' religious influence and also the good work done in the founding of the Leysian Mission in the East End of London. He then presented a blue ribbon and seal to the Senior Prefect, C.C. Moore as a memento of the visit.

In the gymnasium, His Majesty watched some of the youngest members of the school going through a course of Swedish drill, which he remarked he regarded as far superior to older and more formal gymnastic systems. In the swimming baths he saw a 90 yard race won by P.W.C. Northcroft, whom he presented with a silver cup. The King's next visit was to the Kelvin Building (Science Department) where he found a class of boys at work on Chemistry. He recalled that chemistry was always known as "stinks" in his boyhood. He noticed that one member of the class was an Indian and the King spoke to the boy in Hindustani. He laughed when he saw another boy, by accident or design, manoeuvre a spurt of water so that it descended in a graceful curve onto the Headmaster's scarlet gown.

On his return to the gateway, he passed through North A and B Houses where he commented on the ingenious compromise of an open dormitory with cubicles which gave privacy for changing and washing. Before he left the school to return to Newmarket, he asked the Headmaster to award an extra week's holiday. His visit had lasted just one hour.

The King agreed to sit for his portrait, which was paid for by Sir George Hayter Chubb. Because of the outbreak of war, the sittings for the artist, T.H. Nowell, were postponed until 1919. His Majesty asked for the protrait to be hung in the new library. Although eighty-six years have passed, his wish has not yet been granted, and the portrait is at present hung in the Dining Hall (the old Great Hall).

VISIT OF THE CROWN PRINCE OF JAPAN
(later Emperor Hirohito)

Following a change of dynasty in Japan, the new Emperor started a policy of sending the sons of members of his court to British schools and universities. Although the school had been founded for only a few years, several Japanese boys were sent to The Leys, so that by the turn of the century there were about twenty Japanese Old Leysians. One of these became Master of Ceremonies in the Emperor's court, and another Secretary to the Prime Minister of Japan.

When Crown Prince Hirohito visited the University in 1921 to receive an Honorary Doctorate of Law, he first called at The Leys, which so many notable Japanese had attended. During a brief visit of only about ten minutes, he inspected a Guard of Honour commanded by Captain John Stirland, which paraded on the quadrangle in front of the North A and B Houses.

199

VISIT OF H.R.H. THE DUKE OF YORK
(later HIS MAJESTY KING GEORGE VI)

At the outbreak of the First World War there were approximately 1,000 Old Leysians of military age, and of these 927 served in different branches of the Services, and more than half this number joined the Forces within six months of the outbreak of hostilities. 149 Old Leysians and one former School Chaplain lost their lives. 78 of their names are recorded with their ranks and regiments on individual tablets which form a band running round the inside of the Chapel. All the dead Leysians of both Wars are now recorded on the outside of the east end of the building. After the cessation of the First World War, a fund was established which in part was used to fund the erection of the memorial. Its central feature is a sculptured figure of St. George set in a carved niche with a background of gold mosaic. The arms of England, Scotland, Wales and Ireland, together with those of The Leys are included in the design. The names of the fallen are inscribed on panels of Hoptonwood stone. At the base is a quotation from *The Pilgrim's Progress*: "My marks and scars I carry with me to be a witness for me that I have fought His battles Who will be my Rewarder."

Part of the Speech Day celebrations of 1922 included the unveiling of the memorial by the then Duke of York, later King George VI. During the morning, a service had taken place in the chapel conducted by the Revd Henry Howard. After lunch the rain had ceased, but the wind was boisterous. A large number of parents and guests, together with the boys, had assembled facing the east wall of the chapel when at 2 p.m. the Duke was met at the King George V Gateway by the Chairman of the Governors, Lord Marshall. After introductions to the Headmaster, the Revd Harry Bisseker, and several of the Governors, the Duke inspected a Guard of Honour formed by about 100 members of the school O.T.C, the band of the Cambridge University Officer Training Corps having previously played the National Anthem.

The Duke then walked to the space in front of the memorial and the Headmaster said prayers. In welcoming His Royal Highness, Lord Marshall said that Old Leysians, parents and friends had contributed over £46,000. Apart from paying for the memorial, a large part of the fund had been used to provide scholarships and other allocations had been made for a pavilion and the purchase of a sanatorium.

The Duke then released the Union Jacks which had been covering the

The Duke of York (later King George VI) unveils the War Memorial, 1922

Crown Prince (later Emperor) Hirohito inspects the Guard of Honour, 1921

memorial. In his speech he said that the record of service of Old Leysians during the war was one of which present and past members of the school might justly be proud. He went on to say:

"The passage of time has brought us to a situation which offers little or nothing heroic. Disenchantment with the new order of life, which may not have justified our expectations during those years of strife, has to some extent overtaken us. We are faced by anxieties which, in comparison with those of war, may appear sordid, yet must be faced if the Empire is to live. Let the recollection of the sacrifice of those whom we honour today bring an additional measure of generosity and patience to our dealings with each other, so that we may understand and not minimise one another's difficulties."

"Let us not forget those remote days of mutual and united sacrifice, nor fail to preserve the ideal for which those Old Leysians gave their lives. Only thus can our Empire be set on its feet, and the wounds of war, which still affect the world be gradually healed."

The buglers of the O.T.C. sounded the "Last Post" and the ceremony closed with the benediction given by the Revd Dr E.C. Pearce, Vice-Chancellor of the University of Cambridge. The Duke then entered the chapel and inspected the mural tablets presented in memory of individual Old Leysians killed in the war. After the National Anthem was sung, His Royal Highness left the school premises. The remainder of the people present went to the Great Hall, where the Speech Day celebrations continued.

VISIT OF H.R.H. THE PRINCE OF WALES
(later THE DUKE OF WINDSOR)

Papers discovered in the school archives give the background to this visit. The Prince of Wales had met several Japanese Old Leysians at a reception. They asked if he had ever visited their school and on discovering that he had not, pressed him to do so. The Governors' minutes show that they were disappointed that there was not a large project for him to open. However, the squash courts and miniature range had just been completed, and he agreed to make an informal visit to the School on 22 June, 1932 to open them. The

202

The Prince of Wales (later the Duke of Windsor)
opening the Squash Courts and Miniature Range, 1932

203

account from *The Fortnightly* of the short one hour visit best describes the occasion:

"For the visit was essentially informal despite the doubts of anyone who saw the sorely-tried members of house-platoons industriously cleaning for the third of four full-dress parades on consecutive days, or the over-worked employees of Pullars of Perth labouring to produce a pair of spotless white flannels for everyone in the School. Again, though it might seem to be a singular coincidence that when His Royal Highness arrived in view of the pitch, the best batsmen in the School should be performing against the School's best bowlers, that the batsmen in every house-game were wearing two brand-new pads instead of the usual solitary dirty one, and that a very good race was in progress soon after the Prince reached the swimming-baths, yet such fortunate coincidences merely show how things may happen when the 'powers that be' interest themselves in them."

"The Prince arrived, wearing a straw hat (to the immense delight of expectant journalists) and received a Royal Salute from the Guard of Honour drawn up on the Quad while the remainder of the School looked on and was photographed by press photographers. After inspecting the Guard of Honour, the Prince went to the Library, where the chief dignitaries of the School were presented to him, then to the baths and then to East House, where the super-polished floors nearly caused a tragedy. The party then moved on, via the pitch to the Squash Courts, which were inspected, and then officially opened, together with the New Ground (Latham Road). After taking tea in the Headmaster's garden and kindly exposing himself to the attack of innumerable cameras, he departed, having won the affection of the whole School, not least because of the commendable speed with which he inspected the Guard of Honour and the gift of three days added to the summer holidays and one to the Speech Day week-end."

For the visit in 1932, the fives courts next to the squash courts had been renovated. By the late 1950s the fives courts were rarely used for their intended purpose and instead provided storage space and bicycle shelter.

VISIT OF QUEEN SALOTE OF TONGA

The Revd James Egan Moulton, who was the brother of Dr W.F. Moulton, the first Headmaster of The Leys, had arrived in Sydney on 31 May, 1863. He was twenty-two years old and newly ordained, and was en route for Fiji where he had been posted as a Methodist missionary. He was informed that unmarried missionaries were not allowed to serve in the Islands of the Pacific because of the possibility of sexual temptation. He was engaged to be married, but his fiancée had been persuaded by her parents not to accompany him from England because they did not want her to go to 'cannibal Fiji'. Moulton wrote home begging her to join him and marry him so that his work as a missionary could proceed.

Meanwhile he needed employment. A group of Methodists led by the Revd John Manton were planning to open a school which "although the Institution will be decidedly Wesleyan in character, it shall be open to the sons of parents of all religious denominations." Manton heard of Moulton's arrival and of the fact that he had recently been teaching in England. He offered Moulton the position of the first Headmaster, with the task of getting classes started until adequate staff could be sent from England.

This only took a year and in the meantime Miss Emma Knight, his fiancée, had come to Australia and married James, so that he could now fulfil his calling to be a missionary. The Fiji vacancy had been filled, but the King of Tonga, George Tupou I, who was a committed Christian, invited James to improve education in his kingdom. James and his wife went to the Tongan islands and after three months he preached his first sermon in Tongan. He established Tipou College, which for over a century was to have the greatest influence on Tongan life and leadership. He also began the revision of the Tongan Bible, and revisited England in 1877-80. At that time Dr Moulton was completing the work on the English Revised Version of the New Testament, and James took the opportunity to consult his brother. In the end the Tongan Bible was published six months before the English Revised Version. Sir Henry Dale wrote of how during one of James's visits to The Leys, 'he delighted the resident masters at dinner with a string of 'tall' stories, dealing with alleged experiences of his own in the Pacific. At intervals, the Headmaster, would look at his 'romantic' brother with a puzzled expression and ask, "and is that really a statement of fact?" "Entirely so", was the reply. "Ah! then there is nothing more to be said." The

Revd James Egan was evidently something of a character; but he did a fine job for the Tongans. James is known in Tongan history as "Tongan Moulton". Because of the connection with the Moulton family, The Leys is usually visited by the Tongan Royal family when they come to England.

Queen Salote, when in England for the Coronation of Queen Elizabeth II, on 2 June, 1953, had a six weeks tour of England and Scotland organised for her by the British Council. She paid an informal visit to the school on 27 May, 1953. She had first visited Girton College, where she lunched with the Mistress, Miss M.L. Cartwright, and then travelled by car to the school, arriving at 2.30 p.m. Although it was an informal visit, there was a tight schedule of presentations of all the senior staff, who had been positioned in buildings which the Queen was due to visit. She was accompanied by her daughter-in-law, H.R.H The Princess Mata'Aho, the wife of the Crown Prince, Mrs. Windrum, wife of the Consul in Tonga, who was acting as Lady-in-Waiting and Mr. J.S. Neil, former British Agent in Tonga.

Because of the weather, the Headmaster, Dr Gerald Humphrey, had to make a number of changes in the intended programme. Starting in the chapel, Queen Salote heard a Bach Prelude played by one of the boys. She then visited the library, and the swimming baths where she watched some relay races and diving. The Royal visitors then went to the science block via the tuck shop. When they emerged from the science building, it was pouring with rain. Mr. G.F. Green, the Senior Biology master, fetched his impressive Humber Super Snipe to take the Queen, Princess, and Lady-in-Waiting back to the Headmaster's house. Meanwhile, the Headmaster ran via the School House (now Dale) basement, pursued by panting officials of the British Council, to receive the Queen and her party when they re-arrived at the front door of his house. Dr Humphrey wrote later that he felt that "the trying circumstances had shortened my life by about five years." (In fact he lived to see his 91st birthday!) Following tea, one of the Governors addressed the Queen on behalf of himself and his colleagues, and she left at 4.20 p.m. in the pouring rain to go to Evensong at King's College Chapel. Following the visit, the Headmaster sent the Queen a specially bound edition of Sir George Hayter Chubb's book on the school chapel.

A few days later, riding in an open carriage in the Coronation procession, Queen Salote made a lasting impression on the nation by not hiding under an umbrella despite the rain. When her grandsons were at The Leys, one of

Queen Elizabeth, the Queen Mother's first visit to the school, 1961

The Queen Mother is introduced to the Governors

The Queen Mother inspects the Guard of Honour

them, Prince Alai, explained to his Housemaster that in Tonga it would have been discourteous for the Monarch to drive through the country covered, so that she could not be seen by her loyal subjects.

FIRST VISIT OF H.R.H. QUEEN ELIZABETH, THE QUEEN MOTHER

The first major rebuilding project after the Second World War was to replace the old West House building (now itself renovated as the new School House). The original building was at first considered temporary. Following the opening of North B House in 1883, it was used as extra accommodation for masters, and West House ceased to exist. As the school numbers increased it was reopened as a boarding house, but there was a short period during the First World War when it again closed because of falling numbers.

When Mr Alan Barker was appointed as Headmaster, he started a programme of new building. The new West House was modelled on the needs of boarding houses of that time, and contained four dormitories, day-studies for the Sixth Form, a common room with an additional small quiet room for a library, and a classroom attached to the house for use as a preparation room. Queen Elizabeth, the Queen Mother accepted an invitation to perform the formal opening ceremony. Protocol at that time called for morning dress or dark suits for men, and ladies there for the occasion were expected to wear hats and gloves, even if they were not going to be presented.

Her Majesty arrived at 3 p.m. on 6 June, 1961, and drove straight to West House. She was welcomed by the Lord Lieutenant, the Chairman of Governors, Sir Henry Thirkill, and the Headmaster. The Guard of Honour under the command of Cadet Under Officer 'Paddy' Hopkirk gave the Royal Salute, whilst the band played the National Anthem. Having inspected the Guard of Honour, she moved to the front of the new building where the Governors were presented to her.

The stone which she was to unveil had been temporarily placed on the north wall of the House, so that the crowds could witness the ceremony. She mounted the dais with the Headmaster and was presented with a bouquet by his son, Adam. Following the unveiling of the plaque, she was given a tour of the House by the Housemaster, Mr Dick Bennett. After the inspection she moved towards the pavilion. Small groups of staff had been positioned at points round the route to be presented to her. A cricket match had been in

Queen Elizabeth, the Queen Mother's first visit to the school, 1961

Adam Barker, the Headmaster's son, presents the Queen Mother with a bouquet

The Queen Mother talking to Dr. Humphrey (the previous Headmaster) and his wife.

progress, which had halted ten minutes before she arrived at the school. The players, Old Leysians and the School 1st XI, were also presented to her. The captain of the Old Leysian side was F.R. Brown, the former captain of the England team. Play resumed when the Queen Mother reached a small open marquee which had been erected on the Headmaster's lawn. Here she took tea with the Headmaster, Mrs. Barker and invited boys, including the Prefects. A band played and the Glee Club sang for her entertainment. Guests and parents were given tea in a large marquee beside East House. One memorable feature of the tea was the enormous quantity of strawberries provided.

Finally Her Majesty signed the visitors' book in the Headmaster's house. She was presented with a gift of books, including a copy of the Headmaster's book on the American Civil War. After the Queen Mother had left, it was discovered that she had left her bouquet behind. Mrs Barker carefully undid it and presented a flower to every boy who had met her. Hardly had she finished when the telephone rang. It was Clarence House. "Her Majesty is most upset - she left her flowers behind - please could you send them on to her" Jean Barker said "Of course". She gathered the individual flowers together, re-assembled the bouquet as best she could, and took it to London and to Clarence House herself, with an explanatory letter. She received a charming letter saying that the Queen Mother apologised because she had guessed what had happened, "but goodness - she had enjoyed the strawberries and cream!"

SECOND VISIT OF H.R.H. QUEEN ELIZABETH, THE QUEEN MOTHER

Some time later, the Headmaster, Mr. Alan Barker and Mrs. Barker were invited to a Garden Party at Buckingham Palace. The Queen Mother spoke to them and said how much she had enjoyed her visit to The Leys when she opened West House. Alan Barker was quick to invite her to re-visit the School, and she accepted for 14 June, 1973. A new classroom block was in the process of being built, and a stone was incorporated at the base to record her second visit. She graciously permitted the building to be named Queen's Building to celebrate her day at the school. The whole atmosphere was much more relaxed than on her previous visit in 1960, when there had been long lines of chosen people for her to meet. This time she mingled with guests on the Headmaster's lawn and talked with them informally.

Queen Elizabeth, the Queen Mother's second visit to the school, 1973

Susan Lang, daughter of the Housemaster of East House presents a bouquet

The Queen Mother is introduced to Stephen Benson and Roger Royce,
members of the Old Leysian Cricket side.

211

FIRST VISIT OF H.R.H. THE DUKE OF EDINBURGH

Prince Philip's first visit to the school in 1963 was to see how his Award Scheme was flourishing in Cambridge. The Leys was chosen as the venue because he could land in a helicopter directly within the school grounds, and, as time was going to be short, he could avoid the usual formalities occasioned by a Royal Visit, which would include introductions to the Lord Lieutenant of the County, the Mayor, the Town Clerk and other dignitaries. Several meetings took place months ahead, attended by the organisers of the various activities to be inspected. It was planned that he should see work involving Civil Defence, First Aid Instruction, Police Work, Fire Fighting, Life Saving and Nursery Care. Only twenty seven minutes were allowed for the visit. Since the helicopter was going to land on the far side of the field and the Duke was to walk past the groups outside and inside West House, finally ending up at the Swimming Bath, a car was hired to save precious time by rushing him back to his helicopter. On the eve of his visit, the organiser, Mr S.C.E. Whitehead (the master in charge of the Award Scheme at The Leys), and the author walked over the route with a stop-watch, so that the Duke could be hurried along to the next area if necessary.

The Duke piloted his own helicopter and the organisers were informed that he disliked being able to see the rescue vehicles which had to attend for any such visit. The fire-tender and the ambulance, complete with the school doctor, were hidden behind the buildings of the squash courts. The Duke arrived on time and kept to the tight schedule. He first inspected the work of Civil Defence on a make-shift scaffolding tower. He then saw Leys boys practising first aid bandaging outside West House. Inside were girls from another school, learning how to bath a baby. The Police aspect of the 'Public Service' part of the Scheme involved the safety inspection of bicycles. The Duke then moved to an area now covered by the theatre, where cadets were being instructed by the Fire Brigade on how to extinguish an oil fire. Finally he went to the swimming baths to see a demonstration of life-saving. He said that he was pleased with all aspects of the Award work that he had seen, and he then left to see similar activities of the Scheme in the county, at Sawston Village College. He worried many spectators on take-off, when he seemed to skim the tall sequoia by the Pavilion and they wondered whether the rescue services might have to show themselves after all!

Prince Philip, The Duke of Edinburgh's first visit to the school

The Duke passes the Civil Defence demonstration

The Duke watches various bandaging techniques

The Duke talks to the cadets in the Fire Fighting demonstration

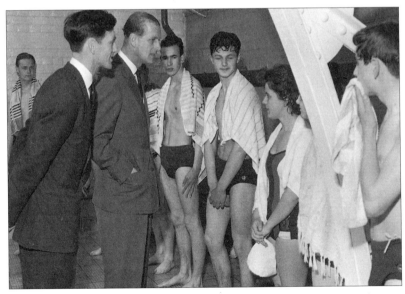

The Duke, together with Mr S.C.E. Whitehead speaks to some of the Life Saving class

214

VISIT OF KING TAUFA'AHAU TUPOU IV OF TONGA

Dr W.F. Moulton's grandson, the Revd Harold Moulton, met the Tongan Royal family at lunch in Marlborough House just before Christmas 1968. King Taufa'ahau Tupou IV, Queen Salote's son, asked him to arrange a visit to The Leys and suggested Monday, 20 January, 1969. The King and Queen and their daughter, Princess Pilolevu, arrived by car from London at 12 noon. After being welcomed by Sir Frank Lee, Chairman of Governors, and the Headmaster, the Royal party visited the Chapel and then attended a reception in the Headmaster's house where they met senior members of staff and their wives. There was a luncheon party for a few invited guests, including the Bishop of Ely. He recounted afterwards that at lunch the Queen had commented that they had seen a huge Cathedral in the locality. He naturally thought that it must be the one at Ely, although he wondered how they had seen it on the way from London to Cambridge. On talking to the chauffeur, he discovered it was Royston Parish Church. "Size is a relative thing" he remarked.

Protocol in Tonga prevents any of the King's commoner subjects from eating in the same room as the Royal family. The King's aide de camp could not therefore attend the meal which the Headmaster's wife, Mrs. Jean Barker, had prepared for the occasion, so he was given lunch by one of the Housemasters and his wife. After lunch, the Royal visitors were shown round the school, where they saw many activities in progress. They left just after 3 o'clock for tours of King's and Trinity Colleges.

Following his first visit, the King decided to send two of his sons to The Leys, Princes Alai and Aho Tukuaho. They were both put into North B House. During their time at the school between 1972 and 1977, the King made several informal visits to see them. On his first return visit, he was again introduced to members of staff and their wives. The King showed a great interest in teaching methods, especially in Mathematics and spent a long time discussing techniques of instruction with Mrs Hazel Brown (wife of Ronald Brown, Head of Physics) who was a lecturer in Mathematics at Homerton College. The King was a large man, weighing in excess of 23 stones, so his official car caused some amusement, since its registration number was 1 TON. Unusually, both doors at the top of the steps leading into North B House had to be opened, to enable the King to see his sons' accommodation. On one of his unexpected visits to see them, the King

Mrs Jean Barker with the King of Tonga

*The King discusses methods of teaching Mathematics
with Mrs. Hazel Brown and her husband Ronnie*

Photos by courtesy of Cambridge News

discovered the Headmaster's wife sunbathing in her swimming costume in her garden, much to the amusement of both of them.

The King had been a successful athlete in his youth, and was pole vault champion of his University in New Zealand. He was delighted when Alai, the elder of the two boys at The Leys, was selected to represent Cambridgeshire in the Discus event in the National Schools Athletics competition. He was in the stand when his son made his throws. Uncharacteristically, Alai made three 'no throws' and was eliminated, although he had consistently thrown beforehand further distances than that which eventually won.

THE DUCHESS OF KENT'S FIRST VISIT - THE CENTENARY CELEBRATIONS

The School had opened on 16 February, 1875. On Saturday, 14 February, 1975 the boys celebrated the Centenary of the School with a lunch which was served by the masters. That evening there was a dinner in the Dining Hall for Governors, Masters and Guests. On the following day there was a Centenary Service in King's College Chapel attended by the boys, staff and parents.

These had been internal, domestic celebrations and it was decided that a more formal event should take place in the Summer. Rumours circulated as to who the Chief Guest might be. Speculation was ended when the official announcement came that Her Royal Highness, the Duchess of Kent would attend Speech Day on 12 July, 1975 and the rest of the celebrations on that day. She entered the Marquee to a magnificent fanfare from the school brass ensemble. The fanfare, which contained strains of "On Ilkla Moor, baht 'at" reflecting the Duchess's Yorkshire background, was composed by Mr Sam Grice, assistant Director of Music. Following the speeches, the Duchess formally opened the Kent Room, the refurbished large classroom remembered by many Leysians as the room where Preparation was supervised and also early morning drill (writing "the line").

Inside the new room, she inspected a large display of school archives which had been gathered together over the previous few months by Mr John Harding, and which provided the nucleus for the present school archives. On the steps of King's Building she was presented by Miss Elizabeth Wiseman, daughter of the Housemaster of A House, with a bouquet, and by the

The Duchess of Kent, 1975 – with Sir Arthur Armitage and the Headmaster, W.A. Barker

Miss Elizabeth Wiseman presenting a bouquet to the Duchess

Photo by courtesy of Cambridge News

Chairman of Governors, Sir Arthur Armitage, with a copy of *Partnership in Excellence*, the recently published history of The Leys.

SECOND VISIT OF H.R.H. THE DUKE OF EDINBURGH

The second visit to the School of His Royal Highness, The Duke of Edinburgh, was on 12 June, 1987, to open the Rugg Centre, the Design and Technology building mainly funded by the generosity of the Bernard Sunley Charitable Foundation and built by Bernard Sunley Ltd. This brought together under one roof several components of the school curriculum - art, computing, electronics, metal work, woodwork, photography, pottery and printing. It also provided a well equipped kitchen in which some courses on cookery are run. On this occasion, the Prince was travelling by car, because he had visited the Joseph Needham Institute in Cambridge before arriving at The Leys.

This time his schedule was not so tight, and he had ample time to see the work of all departments and talk to the students and staff. Whilst he was in the workshops, he diverted from the planned itinerary and took Mr Edward George (Old Leysian and one of the staff) into a store and closed the door. Prince Philip wanted to know if Mr George felt that the architects and builders had provided what the school needed, and Mr George was able to reassure him that they had. After his tour of the building, Prince Philip unveiled a plaque on the outside, in front of members of Sir Percy Rugg's family and representatives of the Bernard Sunley Group.

Sir Percy Rugg, an Old Leysian and a former Leader of the Greater London Council, had been Chairman of the Appeal when the Design Centre was planned. He had been a member of the Sunley Trust, and they had agreed to give some money to the Appeal when he first approached them. They then decided that, in view of the high esteem in which they held Sir Percy, they would pay for and construct the entire building, providing the school would name it after him. Sir Percy laid the foundation stone and was kept in touch with progress on the building, but sadly died two days before its completion. After the unveiling ceremony, The Duke of Edinburgh went to the theatre, where he was to speak to invited guests and parents. After a speech of welcome from the Chairman of Governors, Professor Colin Renfrew (later Lord Renfrew), the Duke gave a spontaneous address, linking the Joseph Needham Institute which he had previously visited that day, with

Sir Percy Rugg laying the Foundation Stone of the Design Technology Building, 1985

The Duke of Edinburgh at the opening ceremony of the Rugg Centre, 1987
with Lady Rugg and Lord Renfrew, Chairman of the Governors

Prince Philip in the Pottery department with Mrs. Angela Mellor

In the Camfield Press with Mr. Harold Wiseman

Prince Philip in the Art Department with Mr. John Dillistone

the new Design Centre. Finally, the Duke signed the Visitors' Book in the foyer of the theatre, and then left the school grounds by car. The invited guests had lunch in a marquee on the Upper Quad.

THE SECOND VISIT OF H.R.H. THE DUCHESS OF KENT

Following the completion of the Sports Hall, Her Royal Highness The Duchess of Kent accepted an invitation to open the new building on Friday, 15 September, 1995. She and her husband have had strong sporting associations during their lives, typified by their attendance at Wimbledon every year, and therefore she seemed an appropriate person to perform the ceremony. She arrived on a wet morning in a helicopter of the Queen's Flight. After being welcomed by the Chairman of the Governors, Dr John Long, the Headmaster and Mrs Barrett, she met the joint Senior Prefects, Ciaran O'Keeffe and Thomas Biddle. More formal presentations followed of Governors, Staff, and members of the various Development Campaign committees who had helped to raise the funds for the building. About one hundred guests then sat down to a lunch provided by the school kitchens.

After lunch, the Headmaster made a short speech of welcome to the Duchess and the other guests. He also announced that the opening would go ahead outside as planned. There were some worried guests as the rain continued to fall. The Duchess was then driven across the field to the Sports Hall, where she talked to the various groups of students she found using the facilities of the new building. Meanwhile the rain had ceased, and the school and guests assembled round the dais which had been erected just outside the Sports Hall. After speeches by the Headmaster and the Chairman of Governors, Her Royal Highness replied, pointing out how lucky the school was to have such a facility. She then unveiled a plaque to commemorate her visit. Gail and Robert, the children of the Housemaster of North B House, Martin Brown, then presented her with a bouquet. By the scheduled time of her departure, the rain had settled in. However, instead of rejoining her helicopter immediately, she walked along the long line of pupils who had been forming a guard of honour, carrying her umbrella and talking to each one. Those watching were reminded of the care and attention she always gave to the ball boys and girls at Wimbledon presentations.

The Duchess of Kent is introduced to the Senior Prefect, Tom Biddle

The Duchess says farewell to pupils in the rain

Gail and Robert Brown making a presentation to the Duchess

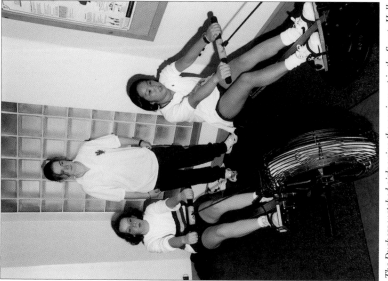

The Duchess watched girls using the equipment in the Sports Hall

225

CHAPTER ELEVEN

Exile in Pitlochry

At the outbreak of war, there seemed to be no urgency to evacuate the pupils of The Leys; indeed schoolchildren from London were being evacuated to Cambridge. Trenches were dug at the far side of the school field for daytime shelter from air raids, and cellars under the Headmaster's house, which could house up to 250 people, were adapted for night-time use. The enormous number of windows in the school caused some problems when it became necessary, and indeed a legal requirement, to black them out. Eventually the idea was hit upon of painting the windows with blue distemper and shading the lights.

However, on 12 June, 1940, the Headmaster received a letter from the Regional Commissioner for Civil Defence, warning him that the school premises might be required as additional hospital accommodation, and that therefore the availability of alternative premises for The Leys should investigated. At the same time, Lord Haw Haw (William Joyce, the propagandist for the Germans) had claimed that Cambridge was one of six prime bombing targets, because of the very high number of R.A.F. personnel training in the area. The Governors gave the Headmaster authority to plan for evacuation of the school, and after several sites had been visited, the Atholl Palace Hotel in Pitlochry, Scotland was selected. The hotel had accommodation for 208 guests with 42 bathrooms and central heating throughout. The Governors leased the whole estate, including a nine hole golf course which was turned into three rugby pitches after removing the bunkers. The hotel's own history reports that "if, during the First World War, the Atholl Palace and Pitlochry were pleased, and even charmed, to play host to the refined young ladies of the Queen Margaret Girls' School, the effect of the "invasion" during World War Two was far more robust".

The boys and staff had left for the summer holidays with an assurance from the most responsible sources that the school would be able to continue to occupy the Cambridge buildings when they returned. Just over a fortnight later, that assurance had been cancelled and the Headmaster had been asked to put the school at the disposal of the Ministry of Health.

About a dozen boys whose homes were reasonably near the school, and a few masters who were free, joined in the necessary work to gather together furniture and books ready for the move to the North. An old car piled high with desks and pulling a trailer filled with even more desks, was used to gather those surplus to requirements and to store them in the scout huts until the end of hostilities.

Three boys spent long hours collecting books which had been left in studies and common rooms by their owners, who had assumed they would be returning to Cambridge for the Christmas term. The library was emptied and the books prepared for transport to Scotland. Glassware and chemicals had to be made safe, before they too could be put on the removal lorries. The first few nights of the preparations were spent sleeping in the dormitories. The sirens regularly drove the working party to take shelter and eventually they slept in the cellars under the Headmaster's House. On the last Sunday in Cambridge, a service was held in the school chapel, conducted by the Revd Harry Bisseker, for those who had worked so hard in the previous days to prepare for the move to the North.

One member of that party, Mr Donald Hughes, wrote later:
"The chapter which we have to write will be momentous. Some members of the School have never seen the group of buildings which have meant The Leys to all Leysians until this term. As time goes on their number must increase and there may be many of us who cannot help feeling that something has been left in Cambridgeshire which can never be brought to Scotland. But this is not really true. The Leys is not local: anything that we have of value has nothing to do with bricks and mortar. If our traditions are to survive at all they will survive leaving the environment in which they were made. How is a school to be valued if not by the kindliness and character of those who belong to it? It may well be that, as we seek to build, in a new environment, on invisible foundations which we have brought from the old, we shall build better than we have done before: It may be that when time comes for us to return, we shall be enriched through the new ways in which we have been made to walk."

At the Atholl Palace, a small advance party of two, together with the hotel staff, prepared the rooms with sufficient beds. The management had been unwilling for the school to move in before 1 October, so the summer holiday had to be slightly extended. A member of staff tackled the intricacies of the railway timetables to produce travelling arrangements for each individual. When the school assembled, they found the hotel had been transformed. Lounges and bedrooms had been turned into classrooms and filled with desks transported from Cambridge. The sun lounge on the south side of the hotel was enclosed by a temporary brick wall almost 100 feet long, and provided two well-lit rooms. The vast quantities of equipment which had been transported from Cambridge were soon distributed between them, providing laboratories for Physics and Chemistry. Engineering equipment from The Leys, which consisted of six lathes, a drill, a milling machine and oxy-acetylene welding equipment, was installed in another ground floor room. The ball-room became the assembly hall, and three thousand library books were arranged in order on shelves. The layout of the hotel wings lent itself to maintaining the separate House structure, and the nine-hole golf course had already acquired rugby goal posts.

Young members of staff were lost to the forces. Cyril Lewis was made Commanding Officer of the Cambridge University Air Squadron, whilst others were to see action in various war zones. W.H. Balgarnie came out of retirement to teach classics in Maurice Howard's place and Dr F. Sandbach came to teach German in the place of his son, Wilfrid. For the first time, the Masters' Common Room had to change its name, as women replaced some of those called-up for military service. Miss Muriel de Vinny was the only member of the administrative and clerical staff to move with the school from Cambridge to Pitlochry.

New sporting rivals were found. Rugby was the sport the least handicapped by the move to Scotland. Out of twenty-five 1st XV matches played during four seasons, twenty of them were played against schools, including Glenalmond and Strathallen Schools, and Glasgow, Dollar, Merchiston and Perth Academies. However, Hockey seasons were affected both by the lack of pitches and the weather. The 1942 season was lost completely because of snow, but many boys put it to good use by tobogganing down the steep hotel drive. It was so cold that the fountain froze into a gigantic icicle.

The Atholl Palace Hotel, Pitlochry

Tobogganning down the drive, Winter, 1942

Cricket was played on a series of artificial pitches of varying speed and bounce, or on natural wickets of generally admirable texture but which suffered from the dampening effects of Scottish mist. The home pitch, carved out of the golf course, was originally composed of concrete slabs covered by matting and later by felt and matting. The open-air pool was rarely warmer than 60°F and therefore was only used for about three weeks in the year. *The Fortnightly* frequently reported that swimmers had to share the pool with maturing frogs.

The ledger detailing the food purchased during the Pitlochry stay reveals interesting supplements to the normal school diet, during food rationing. Over ten per cent of the monthly purchases of meat were venison, which cost nearly half as much again as beef per pound. Large numbers of rabbits, and a few hares and chickens supplemented the meat rations. As well as a great many cod, haddock and sardines, there was always some salmon and even the occasional crayfish. Perhaps these last items only found their way on to the staff dining tables. The egg ration was increased from the official one per person per week, owing to a Ministry ruling that eggs from farms above 3000 feet were exempt from war-time regulations. In 1940 large numbers of grapefruit and bananas were still available. These disappeared from the monthly purchases of fruit and vegetables the next year. However, oranges appear in the 1944 lists. Another hint of luxury living was the purchase of eleven bundles of asparagus.

One aspect of The Leys' impact on the local community was recorded in a booklet published by the hotel to celebrate "A Century of Service". It said that some boys described their time at the Atholl Palace as 'the happiest days of their lives', but that:

> "Not all the local Landowners were quite so happy. This arose from an unfortunate misunderstanding over the ownership of their trout, salmon, hares, pheasants, rabbits – indeed, anything edible or saleable. Maybe the Headmaster should have been more curious about the sudden upsurge of interest in the breeding habits of ferrets. Perhaps he should have grasped the significance of the vast amount of night lines, snares, purse nets, and even catapult elastic that reached the school through mail order. As it was, certain boys' relentless pursuit of all forms of wildlife made the Highland Raiders of history seem a mild and half-hearted bunch."

"The poachers were as well organised as the Mafia, just as ruthless, and pioneers of Military Intelligence. During the war all Keepers and Ghillies were members of the Home Guard, and with uncanny foresight, the pupils timed their expeditions to coincide with the nights that the Home Guard held manoeuvres somewhere on the other side of Perthshire."

"One retired Ghillie recalls that not only did the boys poach his salmon, but on one occasion chopped up a boathouse to provide fuel on which to grill the feast. The evidence against them was the Atholl Palace cutlery they left behind once they had eaten."

"But it was not simple greed that motivated the poachers; many were learning valuable lessons in trade and business practice that, no doubt, helped their careers in later life. Fresh food was in short supply, and a thriving trade was developed with several local butchers, in addition to the private deals that were arranged."

It was revealed that some enterprising Leysians were catching rabbits and sending them by train to their parents to supplement their rations, when one boy received a letter from home which said "Many thanks for the rabbits which arrived this morning. We were very glad to have them as un-rationed food is hard to find in Cambridge. Further supplies welcome".

The poaching came to the notice of the Headmaster, Dr Humphrey, when a local gamekeeper complained that his hut in the woods had been entered, and some of his traps were missing. The culprits were offered the choice of being dealt with by the magistrates' court or being beaten by the Headmaster. They chose the latter.

One Leysian found that, during a check for smoking materials, he was the only one of his group to be caught with cigarettes in his room. He claimed that he was not a smoker, but had been purchasing them for his father because there was a shortage in England. His excuse was not accepted. The same boy celebrated his 18th birthday with a party in his room. He unwisely decided to leave the 'empties' outside the door of his Housemaster, Robert Morris. As he bent down, he dropped them all. The door was opened by his Housemaster who invited him in. The boy claimed to be the only person to get 'six of the best' on his 18th birthday.

The army cadets found that there were advantages in being in Scotland for field day exercises. There was actual cover for platoon exercises in Scotland, unlike the flat featureless fenlands of Cambridgeshire. The school also combined with local cadets to form a worthwhile Air Training Section. Older members of the school joined the Home Guard and trained with local units. Scotland was the perfect country for Scouting. Its thick woods provided good ground for tracking and camouflage, its mountains were excellent for climbing and signalling practice, and its valleys and streams were suitable for camping and bridge-building.

There were, however, two fatal accidents which were due to the mountainous conditions. The first was described in a letter circulated to all parents by J.E. Mellor, who was acting for the Headmaster during his absence:

20 March 1941

In view of the tragic accident which occurred yesterday, resulting in the death of two of our senior boys, Donald Simms and Stanley Fitch, I feel it important to inform all parents without the loss of time.

The Rovers and Scouts were engaged in scouting exercises under the experienced supervision of scoutmasters and assistant scoutmasters. The ground on which they were working was in the wooded area adjoining the Bruar Stream, but precise instructions were given to boys to avoid the river and its banks. Beside the river there runs a regular public footpath used by the numerous visitors who frequent this beauty spot. The river is far below the path at the bottom of a deep gorge. It would seem that these two boys, who were working as a pair, went some yards beyond the path and down the bank, where they slipped on a mossy boulder, and fell into the stream at the bottom of the gorge. Dr Newton, the School Medical Officer, states that, in his opinion, both boys were stunned immediately and could have experienced no pain. The accident itself was not witnessed, but the sound of it was heard and at once investigated. The bodies were in such a position that for some hours they could not be recovered.

It is not possible to express the grief felt by the whole school, and the deep sympathy which goes out to the families of the two boys.

J.E. Mellor

233

The other fatality involved Miss Joan Targett, aged 25, who was killed in an accident at the Tummell Falls on 22 September, 1944. She had joined the school as Junior Cook in January 1939 and had only just been promoted to the position of Head Cook at the start of the Christmas Term in 1944. There was a further very serious accident, though not a fatal one, when Donald Hughes, one of the masters, who was later to become Headmaster of Rydal, lost the sight of an eye on a Home Guard exercise.

Performances of Gilbert and Sullivan operas, including *The Mikado, Iolanthe and H.M.S. Pinafore*, were produced with the help of several local residents, in the Pitlochry Public Hall. Several other entertainments were given in the form of public concerts or plays, and by these means sums of money were raised for the Leysian Mission and also for local Pitlochry charities. The Literary and Debating Society was relatively unaffected by its move to Pitlochry, other than that annual dinners could not be held. The topic for the first debate in Scotland was "That this House hails as long overdue the retirement of Mr. Neville Chamberlain from public affairs". The reports of the debate show a very good understanding of the current political situation. It is perhaps surprising that the motion was defeated by 22 votes to 12.

Much of the entertainment seems to have consisted of films. *The Fortnightly* in November 1940 reported:

> "We have been going to the cinema, both in the hotel and in the town. Three Ministry of Information films were much enjoyed, and there has been a devoted attendance at the silent films on Saturday nights. The two special matinees arranged for us at the local cinema, however, have undoubtedly been most popular of all."

As early as December 1943, the Governors had raised the question of de-requisitioning the Leys estate, following the end of war. A great deal of correspondence had taken place on the subject, and whilst accepting that the national interest must always be supreme, they felt that they must bear in mind the interest of the school, ready for the time when the crisis was over. T.C. Wyatt, the Bursar of Christ's College, was a Governor and had been acting on behalf of the School in Cambridge. In a letter to the Chairman of the Governors, Sir Norman Birkett, Wyatt reported several matters in connection with the position of Addenbrooke's Hospital at that time:

> "There was a new X-ray therapy department for the treatment of cancer which had been sited in the King's Building and, as this

was the unit for the entire region of East Anglia, its establishment had to remain confidential."

Addenbrooke's had 300 beds in its main hospital, 400 in The Leys and 100 in the University Examinations School. At the time of the letter there was a waiting list of 600 patients and with the knowledge that following the invasion of Europe there could be increased pressure on bed space, the necessity for retaining The Leys was obvious. Eventually, many of the Canadian casualties from Arnhem were treated in the School and the medical inspection of many British Prisoners of War following their release also took place there.

A doctor on the Addenbrooke's staff was quoted as saying "you don't seriously think we are going to be turned out of the premises for a school"! A spokesman for the Ministry of Works had said "from what I hear confidentially, the Governors will need their biggest guns if they are hoping to get the Leys buildings back". Of course, the Governors did not expect to be able to re-occupy the buildings yet, but they were preparing for the action which would be needed when hostilities finished.

At the Governors' Meeting on 16 June, 1945, it was reported that the Minister of Health intended to release The Leys in early November. The Headmaster, Dr Humphrey, expressed his disappointment that the school would not be able to return for the start of the Autumn term. Because of the increased number of pupils at the school, additional classroom space would have to be rented in Pitlochry. All his plans were now based on being able to return to Cambridge in January 1946.

Addenbrooke's left the site in November 1945 and a working party of boys who had been at The Leys in Pitlochry was formed under the leadership of Mr Cyril Lewis, who had been demobilised from his position of Commanding Officer of the University Flying Corps. They started to tackle the task of turning a hospital back into a school. Its members moved chairs, tables, beds and hundreds of desks back into place; they unpacked books and moved pillows and blankets. One person's memory was of moving fifty desks from the Scout Hut which was on the site of the present Sports Hall, across the field and up countless winding stairs to the top of School House (now Granta). Fortunately, many Old Leysians had volunteered to help with the mammoth task of moving back.

In Pitlochry there was a rear guard, just as busily engaged with the task of turning a school back into an hotel. This was the responsibility of Mr Buchanan, the Housemaster of East House, with a dozen or so helpers. Corridors were stacked with furniture, inventories checked and hotel rooms refurnished. Inevitably, after five years of occupation by school boys, there were breakages and damage. The dilapidations bill paid to the hotel by the School was £9,402.15s.0d. Similarly, back in Cambridge, the Ministry of Works paid the School £1,700 for damage to the buildings. A service of thanksgiving was held on the first Sunday of the January term in the school Chapel, attended by members of the school and many Old Boys who had returned from the war.

A whole generation of boys had never known Cambridge as the location of their school. Pitlochry has a special place in their memories. In 1996, 107 Old Boys of The Leys School and their partners, former members of staff and guests, celebrated at the Atholl Palace Hotel the 50th anniversary of the return of the school to Cambridge. There was a weekend of celebrations in Pitlochry. Not only was the entire hotel occupied, but extra space in other hotels was taken to accommodate all the visitors. Inevitably, they were all in their mid-sixties to seventies, and yet Ben-y-Vrackie, the local mountain on the summit of which there is a Leys memorial cairn, was reclimbed by many at the reunion, to a height of 2,757 feet! The Headmaster at the time of the reunion, the Revd Dr John Barrett, reached the top first since he was the youngest participant. There was a reunion Dinner on the Saturday evening, and the next morning the visitors swelled the local congregation at the West Kirk, the church where the School had worshipped during its stay in Pitlochry.

On 11 September, 1999 a plaque was unveiled in the Information Technology wing of the school library by Gordon Cook, who was President of the Old Leysian Union at the time. It commemorated the fact that some Old Leysians spent the war at Pitlochry, and that many of them had contributed to the refurbishment of the room.

CHAPTER TWELVE

Men of Words

During the past 125 years, many Old Leysians have written books and articles, academic papers and reference works. It is impossible to list them all here, but their titles are recorded in successive editions of *The Leys Handbook and Directory.* This chapter deals with some of those who made their living by writing or by the spoken word.

Archibald Marshall (West House 1884) was only at the school for one term, during which he qualified for admission to Cambridge. However, he kept in touch with The Leys until his death in 1934. He spent some time in Australia and America before entering Trinity College, Cambridge in 1890. He graduated in 1894 and started writing novels. Some were based on his experiences; e.g. *Peter Binney, Undergraduate,* and *The Claimants* (which drew on both his knowledge of Australia and Cambridge University). He was the *Daily Mail* Special Correspondent in Europe, Australia and Canada in 1908 until 1910. In 1922, Yale University awarded him a Doctorate of Literature. By the time he died he had had over thirty five novels published.

Gilbert Thomas (North B House 1906-1908) left the school to enter a publishing firm, Chapman and Hall, where he joined the editorial staff. He became well known through his volumes of published poetry. *The Voice of Peace,* published in 1914, contained many verses which expressed his pacifist opinions. Conscription came into force in March, 1916. It was the sincere wish of the Asquith Government that the Conscience Clause, offering various degrees of exemption to meet the different claims of "objectors", should be made effective.

Thomas in his *Autobiography* describes graphically the lead up to his imprisonment. After his appeal for total exemption from war service, to a tribunal in Leicester, was turned down, he was arrested by the civil authorities and handed over to the military. Here a new Army Order meant that all men in military barracks who refused to obey orders on conscientious grounds would be court-martialled and sentenced to civil imprisonment. Thomas was committed to Wormwood Scrubs Prison for six months hard labour. Following this, he was transferred to Knutsford, near Manchester, in the old Cheshire County Gaol. Here, he and some five to six hundred other conscientious objectors spent the rest of the war in semi-internment. Many books have been written about the First World War, covering life in the front line, the executions of deserters, the many battles, and life for the relatives back home. Thomas's book is one of the few which describes in detail the treatment of pacifists during that period.

When the war ended, he had technically been in the Army through his court-martial. He was amused to receive his discharge papers which stated that he had served with the Essex Regiment and that his conduct had been "good, except for disobedience". He returned to publishing and contributed to many literary magazines. He was a book reviewer, reading on average five hundred titles a year. However he did admit that he had to skip many pages to reach that total. During his lifetime he published eight collections of verse, six collections of essays, three biographies, including ones on John Masefield and William Cowper, and a story of a model railway.

In his autobiography, *The Making of a European,* Eric Whelpton (North B House 1909-1912) described his first days at the school:

> "From the first evening that I spent at The Leys, I realised that I was to live for the next three years in a kind of prison, an impression that was reinforced by the long and dreary Sunday that followed. We celebrated the Sabbath by rising half an hour later, a pleasant concession that was completely wiped out by the fact that between early morning chapel and 11 o'clock service we had a scripture lesson given us by a master who was obviously an agnostic. Then, sandwiched between two periods of silence in which we wrote letters or read supposedly improving books in Great Hall, there was an evening service, followed later on by prayers."

Later he described how he and some friends would cycle to Grantchester and have tea at the Orchard, where new bread and butter with jam and cake would cost one shilling (5p in today's money). On very warm days they swam in Byron's pool, which is two or three miles upstream from the school, also in Grantchester.

James in the cutting room of a Hollywood Studio

James Hilton

His career at Oxford was broken by the outbreak of war, in which he served as a Captain in the Royal Berkshire Regiment. On his return to Oxford, he met Dorothy Sayers, who became his secretary in the early 1920s. An article in the *Sunday Times* later in his life claimed that Eric was probably the model for the character Lord Peter Wimsey in many of Sayers' detective novels, and that he might have been the father of her illegitimate child. Whelpton accepted the first suggestion but strongly denied the second.

In 1922 he went to Florence to found and direct the *Italian Mail,* an English language paper, and for the next four years he was able to watch the birth and development of the Fascist state. Forced out by the excessive nationalism of the fascists, he returned to England to become Head of the Modern Side of King's College School, Wimbledon. In 1942 he joined the Intelligence Corps and fought in Tripoli. He followed the advance into Tunis and, later on, into Sicily. He was finally seconded to Political Intelligence in the Foreign Office. After the war, he became a prolific travel writer. As well as several books, including *A Concise History of Italy*, he wrote a travel column for the *Daily Telegraph,* illustrated by his wife.

James Hilton (School House 1915-1918) is probably the best known of all Old Leysian authors. His novel, *Good-bye, Mr. Chips!,* is considered by many to be the best depiction of all time of a dedicated schoolmaster. James was born in 1900. His father was Headmaster of a North London elementary school. James developed a great interest in railways and collected cards of engines. He also had a model railway. At the age of eleven he kept a diary, one of the Boots 'Three days to a page' type. On most days, as well as recording what he had done, there would be one line recording some world news - perhaps the assassination of a Japanese prime minister or a terrible train crash somewhere in the world. He was already showing an ability to record events.

James went to school in North London, first to the local elementary and then the grammar school. In June 1914, he won a scholarship to Haileybury College. However, when his father, who had always been a pacifist, discovered from the school prospectus that it possessed both a rifle-range and an Officers' Training Corps, James was withdrawn from the entry list.

It was at this time also, in the first year of the war, that James became interested in Russian affairs, especially since one of his uncles, who sent him letters describing the country, was manager of a flour mill in Russia. James began to learn the language and applied for a job in a Russian Bank in London, which he nearly got. Had he done so, he might have been sent to Russia and been there during the Revolution. These events, in any case, greatly influenced his later writings. They had an even greater impact on his uncle, who was expelled from Russia and was penniless for some time. However, prosperity returned to him, and he became Mayor of Blackpool in 1951.

When Hilton was fifteen, his father again considered the idea of sending James to a public school but, since he could not decide which school, he allowed his son to choose it for himself. The boy toured England alone, travelling on trains from York to Cheltenham, from Brighton to Sherborne, interviewing Headmasters. Only a few refused to see him. James wrote later, when describing this period of his life, that he considered that it would be a good thing if headmasters cared more about the impressions they made on the boys and less about the impressions they made on the parents. Eventually he spent a week-end in Cambridge and was impressed by both the University and town atmosphere, and by his reception by Dr Barber, the Headmaster of The Leys School. He chose this to be his school, despite its having a rifle range and an Officers' Training Corps. Relying upon the fact that his father was both forgetful and unobservant, he got himself entered for the school and joined it half-way through the summer term of 1915.

In James' autobiographical chapter in *To you, Mr Chips,* he recalls that he was not a typical schoolboy and that, as he was happy at The Leys, this shows that there was a degree of tolerance at the school. Although it was war-time, he was not forced to join the almost compulsory Officers' Training Corps. There was a certain degree of hypocrisy, typical at the time. Hilton remembered that Sunday Chapel sermons, very often preached on the theme of "forgiving our enemies", were followed by Mondays watching cadets practising bayonet drill on sacks on the football field. James was obsessed by this paradox.

He was, like many other schoolchildren during a war, very much influenced by war stories and several of his short stories, published in *The Fortnightly,* reflect his preoccupation with war, both in the trenches and at home. When he was sixteen, in the summer holidays, he had witnessed a Zeppelin raid over London. He turned his experience into a short story which appeared in the school magazine less than three weeks after the event.

Another story, *The Bayonet,* told of a night spent in a shell crater by a British and a German soldier.

Many contemporaries of Hilton at school spoke of the thrill of being in class with James, who was often asked to read out his essays to the rest of the Sixth Form. They commented on his quietness, and the only aspect of him marking him out of the ordinary was that he kept a large fish in one of the baths in the House basement and would take it out whenever anyone wished to have a bath. He would sometimes go to Evensong at King's College Chapel, and often cycle to Grantchester in the summer on half holidays for tea at the Orchard tea-rooms. On one occasion he cycled to his home in Epping Forest and back, to see his girlfriend, without the knowledge of his Housemaster.

A few of his early papers remained in the possession of his cousins, Rowland and Elizabeth Hill, who are now dead. Among these was a short novelette he had written in a school exercise book. It was a romance about a boy and girl who met whilst cycling in Epping Forest and how they fell in love. Also in the collection was a short diary he had started to keep when he was sixteen. At one point it said "No letter arrived today", and then "No letter arrived again today". He then described how the Headmaster's sermon that Sunday had helped him get over what seemed to be the end of a friendship. He went on to say that he would write down how he had met his girl friend. The events were very similar to those in the story, but were often transposed. For example, a puncture which he suffered in the story, had in real life happened to her.

Hilton's time at school finished in July 1918. He and his friends had their lives overshadowed by the war and thoughts of active service. They knew that if the war lasted long enough they would have to take part in it, however contrary that might be to the high ideals they had been taught. The imminence of tragedy hardly worried them. It sharpened the joys of school life and cushioned them against its trivial hardships. In Hilton's case it focused his memory. He wrote:

"The careful assessments of schoolmasters were blotted out by larger and wilder markings; a boy who had been expelled returned as a hero with medals; those whose inability to conjugate avoir and être seemed likely in 1913 to imperil a career were to conquer France's enemies better than they did her language; offenders

242

gated for cigarette smoking in January were dropping bombs from the sky in December. It was a frantic world; and we knew it even if we did not talk about it. Slowly, inch by inch, the tide of war lapped to the gates of our seclusion."

Hilton won a scholarship to Christ's College. At that period of the war, men could take up residence at Cambridge provided they joined the University Officer Training Squadron, doing 6 - 8 weeks intensive training before starting their studies. In the event, the war finished in November and he was able to continue his studies uninterrupted. He did so well that the College gave him a scholarship to do research for a fourth year. He lived in College for the first three years, but for his fourth year he moved to lodgings in Victoria Street, off Christ's Pieces, in rooms with a veranda, which is still visible. Whilst at school, he had started writing a novel which he finished at college. The novel *Catherine Herself* is about the Svengali-type relationship between a woman pianist and her teacher. In one episode, she gives a concert in the Guildhall, Cambridge and the description of the town, and of the streets which were destroyed to build the Lion Yard shopping centre and car park is very evocative. It has been suggested that the novel was autobiographical. Catherine, an egoist, is Hilton's other self; he always had an ambition to be a concert pianist and the character of the piano teacher was based on James' father.

On leaving Cambridge, he embarked on a career as a free-lance journalist, writing chiefly for *The Manchester Guardian*. His first work for that paper was a copy of the last story he had written for the school magazine, with just six words changed. It had also been published in Christ's College Magazine, with a different six words altered. It was the story of an illiterate Russian peasant who had been caught up in the war, fighting against Germany. When the Revolution had broken out, he had deserted like many others, to return home. However he was lost and could not remember the name of his obscure village. It ends with his death as he is knocked down by a train, and his fleeting happiness when he thinks he has reached home.

This theme was expanded later into a chapter of a novel he wrote in 1933 called *Knight Without Armour*, which was later turned into a film starring Marlene Dietrich and Ronald Coleman. It was also referred to in another of his novels, *Random Harvest*. His letters from his uncle in Russia had given him a graphic picture of a country he had never visited.

Hilton's family were quite concerned for him in the early days of his career. He was by no means financially secure. As well as being a regular contributor to *The Manchester Guardian*, he reviewed fiction for *The Daily Telegraph*. Meanwhile, he published a new novel about every two years. He even wrote, under a pseudonym, a detective novel called *Murder at School* which was set in a school called Oakington. It sounded very like The Leys of his time, and the character of the detective was based on Hilton himself.

At last came success in 1931 with *And Now Good-Bye*. In 1933 there followed *Lost Horizon*, the story of a remote corner of Tibet where time stands still. By 1935, sales of this novel had reached 110,000, which in those days was a considerable number. It was made into a very successful film in 1937 starring Robert Coleman, and a less successful musical version in the early 1970s. For this novel Hilton was awarded the Hawthornden Prize in 1933. As a result of this award, he was offered a direct commission for a short story to be published in *The British Weekly* for the Christmas edition. He said he would think about it, and went for a bicycle ride in Epping Forest. He returned with an idea, and four days later had completed *Good-Bye Mr. Chips*. The editors were thrilled with and yet embarrassed by the result, as it ran to 17,500 words instead of the 3,000 word short story they commissioned. Their solution to the problem was to publish it as an inset supplement. It appeared on 7 December, 1933, and was illustrated by Bip Pares.

The book was sold to an American magazine, the *Atlantic Monthly*, who decided to publish it in spite of their usual rule not to use anything that had previously appeared in print. It was so successful that it was published in hard-back form in the United States, and then appeared in England in that form for the first time in October 1934. At that time, an American lady sent a copy to a rather nice English schoolmaster she had met in the United States. She was amused to read in his letter of thanks that this schoolmaster had just been appointed to the post of Headmaster of The Leys, the school which had provided the background for the novel. Little did she know when she bought the book, that soon she would be the wife of that Headmaster, Dr Gerald Humphrey, and living in The Leys School.

The cover of the first edition, published by Hodder and Stoughton, distinctly shows the King's Building gates of the school. For some time there was argument as to the identity of the model for Mr. Chips. Hilton had based

James and Greer Garson during the filming of "Mrs. Miniver"

James in his study.   Note the Oscar on the extreme right of his desk

his character, Mr Chipping, on a master at The Leys, W. H. Balgarnie, who had retired to live in 6 Brookside. This was where he was living when he was visited by Hilton, who like many former pupils, called upon him when he visited Cambridge. (See Chapter 4 - *They served them all their days*).

Through the success of both *Lost Horizon* and *Good-Bye Mr Chips*, Hilton was invited to go to Hollywood as a script writer, and to bring his wife with him. This presented him with a slight problem as, perhaps a little ahead of their time, his living-in partner was not married to him. Alice Brown was a secretary working at Bush House, part of the BBC. They went to Eastbourne and were married in the Registry Office there to avoid publicity in London, as he was by now becoming a public figure. He was then able to go to Hollywood, where he became the highest paid scenario writer of his time.

They travelled to America by boat, and were met by the Press at the Docks. Both were interviewed and made a broadcast. James gave a lecture at Yale. Then they travelled across to Los Angeles and Hollywood, where again they were given a tremendous reception. Dinner invitations flooded in and they soon numbered Fred MacMurray and his wife, and Paulette Goddard (who was married to Charlie Chaplin at that time) amongst their friends. Other names mentioned in letters home were Leslie Howard, Basil Rathbone and Joan Crawford. They would have supper one evening with the British Consul, the next with the vice-consul and his wife, then with Frederick March and his wife. The glittering parties and the sudden change in life-style from that of a part-time journalist and a BBC secretary proved to be disastrous to their marriage. James went to Mexico to file for a divorce, and Alice returned to England. James married a red-headed starlet called Galina Kopinack, but this does not seem to have been a successful marriage either. It had broken up before the out-break of war, and it ended in divorce in 1947. Galina estimated at the time that James was earning £12,000 a year. She sued him for £200 a month.

James won an Oscar for the screen play of *Mrs Miniver*. Greer Garson also won an Oscar for Best Actress with her performance in the title rôle. As well as *Mrs. Miniver*, he wrote the screen plays of *Camille, Foreign Correspondent, The Tuttles of Tahiti*, and *Forever and a Day*. Several of James' own books were also screened, including *Knight Without Armour* starring Marlene Detrich, *The Story of Dr Wassell, We are not Alone,*

246

Random Harvest and *Rage in Heaven. Good-Bye, Mr Chips* won an Oscar for Robert Donat, but, surprisingly, Hilton did not work on the screen play of his own novel.

He continued to write. *Morning Journey* written in 1951, is set in Hollywood and depicts the tensions caused by the production of films and the relationships between directors, actresses and script writers. *Nothing So Strange,* written in 1948, is also set in America and the Hollywood area of California. The plot deals with the scientific conflict eventually leading to the dropping of the atomic bomb on Hiroshima.

By 1950, he was becoming disillusioned with the pressure of the Hollywood style of life. He wrote to his family that he wished he could go back to writing novels at his own pace. He was a modest and retiring man, for all his success. He came to Cambridge in 1951 and visited the school. His family have photographs of him outside the school dining room. He sat and watched the First eleven playing cricket, but he made no attempt to tell anyone who he was.

Hilton died of cancer of the liver in 1954. He spent the last six weeks of his life in hospital and Alice, his first wife, was at his bedside during the last three weeks. *The Times* carried daily bulletins about his health in the last few days of his life.

He left an estate worth £89,280, which was a considerable amount in 1954. The equivalent today would be around a million pounds. He left £8,928 each to his secretary and to Alice, £178 a month to his father for the duration of his life, and the rest of the estate to Elizabeth Hill, his cousin and lifelong friend. Galina, his second wife, was refused any share of the estate by a judge, who ruled that James and Alice's Mexican divorce was not legal and therefore that James and Galina had never been married in the eyes of the USA courts.

Hilton is not a fashionable writer nowadays, but before the war his novels were critically acclaimed and widely read. They appeared in translation in many languages and *Good-bye Mr Chips* is now a text book in Japan.

Malcolm Lowry (West House 1923-1927) was born on 28 July, 1909, the youngest of four sons. His father was an accountant to a cotton broking firm called Bustons. He had gradually advanced his position, and after several house moves had finally settled in the Wirral. Malcolm had three brothers, Wilfrid (who eventually played Rugby for England), Stuart and Russell.

They all went to Caldicott Preparatory School in Hitchin and then The Leys. He and his brother, Russell, both said that their mother was cold, uncaring and self-centred and that they had more affection for their nanny, Bey.

At Caldicott, Malcolm was befriended by the school captain (nicknamed 'Chilblains'), James Furniss. James and his family later were immortalised as the Taskersons in *Under the Volcano*. In 1923, Malcolm went to The Leys and was placed in West House, as his three brothers had been before him (first one in 1909) under W.H. Balgarnie.

Malcolm was a bookworm, although he did play some sport. With the encouragement of both Balgarnie and F.W. Ives, another English master, he started to write for *The Fortnightly* under the pen name CAMEL, derived from his full name Clarence Malcolm Lowry. Muriel Bradbrook, in her biography of Lowry, dismisses his school writings as being of no literary importance. There were two short stories: *A Rainy Night* which portrays the inhuman indifference of a traveller to a dying man, and *Satan in a Barrel* which shows the Faustian end of Judge Jeffreys.

At school, Malcolm, whose nickname was 'Lobs' (Lobster) because of his red face when he became angry, became a close friend of Michael Rennie, who was to become a film star, and Roland Hill, who later wrote music and was a producer for the BBC. Roland and Malcolm published some sheet music whilst still at school. The three were slight misfits and no doubt sought consolation in each other's company. Malcom had a girl friend, Carol Brown, whilst he was at school, and many of his letters to her are reproduced in a book of his collected letters recently (1998) published by Professor Sherrill Grace of the University of British Columbia. Most of his collected papers are to be found in the library of that University.

He certainly started drinking heavily whilst at school, and by the time he got to Cambridge University he had become an alcoholic. Gordon Bowker in *Pursued by Furies* summed up Lowry as a:

"Twice married, eternally constipated, accident-prone, self-exiled, syphilophobe who sustained a marginal existence as an alcoholic in London, Paris, New York and Mexico and who lived in the remote obscurity of British Columbia for fourteen years at his father's expense". He should have returned to school to prepare for the Cambridge College Entrance Examination. Instead, he caused a sensation by signing on as a deck hand on a tramp steamer to Shanghai and Yokohama. His local Liverpool newspapers gave the story 'front page' treatment. The experiences he had are recorded in the semi-autobiographical novel *Ultramarine*.

On return to England, he had to have extensive coaching for the Latin papers in the Previous Examination (colloquially known as 'Little-go'), which fulfilled the minimum requirements for entry to the University of Cambridge. He was eventually successful and was accepted into St. Catharine's College where his tutor was Tom Henn. He and a fellow freshman, Fitte, spent a lot of time together and Malcolm was utterly shattered when Fitte gassed himself in his college room. He is reputed to have spent most of his three years drinking in the bar which used to be in the basement of the Victoria Cinema, and his examination results were poor. It is fairly certain that he eventually got his degree on the strength of his novel *Ultramarine*.

He wrote to an author, Conrad Aitkin, and they became good friends. Aitkin acted as a sort of guardian, with Malcolm's father's blessing and financial support. They spent some time in Paris and Spain and, in Granada, Malcolm met Jan Gabrial, whom he married in France. They went to Hollywood, where Jan was secretary to James Stewart, Olivia De Havilland and Carol Landis. In 1936 they visited Mexico - arriving on All Souls Day - The Day of the Dead. Mexico was to have a great influence on Lowry and on his major work, *Under the Volcano*.

He and Jan returned to the USA and Malcolm underwent treatment for his alcoholism which was straining their relationship. In Hollywood he met Margerie Bonner, who had been a teenage silent movie actress. He divorced Jan and married Margerie.

They moved to Canada and rented a shack on Dollerton Creek. Malcolm wrote and drank. After a disastrous fire which burnt down the shack, Margerie managed to rescue one copy of the manuscript of *Under the Volcano*. Malcolm's time in Dollerton is now commemorated by an enormous boulder with a plaque on it, and a trail down the creek. Finally he and Margerie returned to England and settled in Ripe, in Sussex.

His death was a mystery. After an argument with Malcolm, Margerie took refuge with the next-door-neighbour for the night. The next morning she returned to find him dead. Whether he had died by suffocating on his own vomit after another bout of drinking, or whether he had died from an overdose of pills, was never resolved.

It was only after his death that he became well-known. Some literary critics have suggested that *Under the Volcano* is the best novel of the twentieth century. It was eventually made into a film by the producer John Houston and starred Albert Finney as the alcoholic ex-diplomat, spending the last day of his life in Mexico during the festival of The Day of the Dead.

Lowry had destroyed many of his writings, but after his death, his widow published everything she could find. Several biographies of him have been written, including one in French and another in German. Two full-length television documentaries have also been made about him, one by a Canadian film company, who shot some of the scenes in The Leys in the late 1960s.

Another well-known Leysian author is J.G. Ballard (North B House 1946-1949). Ballard was born in Shanghai in 1930, and was interned in Lunghua Civilian Assembly Centre with his parents, by the Japanese from 1942-1945. The events he witnessed during this period were to be the basis of his novel, *Empire of the Sun*. In his internment camp was an Old Leysian, the Revd George Osborn. Osborn had organised some classes for the young members of the camp and was influential in Ballard's coming to The Leys after the war. His experiences in the camp had matured him and he found the adolescent behaviour of his contemporaries at school rather beneath him. When interviewed on television after the publication of *Empire of the Sun*, he said that food at The Leys after the war was worse than that in the Lunghua camp. He entered King's College, Cambridge to read medicine, but left after two years. He then worked as a copy writer and Covent Garden porter, before going to Canada with the RAF.

His first short story was published in 1956 in *New Worlds* and he took a full-time job, first on a technical journal and then as assistant editor of a scientific journal. In 1961, he wrote his first novel, *The Drowned World*. By 1991 he had written over twenty novels, many of them with a science-fiction theme. Although well known as an author, he became acclaimed with *Empire of the Sun*, which won several literary prizes and was turned into a very successful film. Another of his novels, *Crash*, was also turned into a film, but it received a mixed reception and was banned in some cities in England.

Sir Alastair Burnet (School 42-46) became a nationally known face on television in the 1970s and 80s as the main presenter and editor of ITV news. He had had a distinguished career in journalism. After graduating from

The house in Ripe where Malcolm Lowry died

Lowry's simple headstone in Ripe Churchyard

Worcester College, Oxford, he became a leader writer for the *Glasgow Herald* and then *The Economist*. He next became Political Editor for the Independent Television News service before returning to *The Economist* as Editor. He then became Editor of the *Daily Express*, and finally he became a newscaster on I.T.N.

Similarly, Martin Bell (East 52-56) had a distinguished career in television. He graduated from King's College, Cambridge, with a double first in English in 1962. He joined BBC TV News East Anglia and later became their Diplomatic Correspondent in Washington. He was to become well-known as a war reporter and was particularly notable for wearing a white jacket, in various war-zones in the 1990s. As mentioned in chapter 9 - *The Leys at War*, he was seen in millions of British homes reporting on the war in Sarajevo when he was hit by shrapnel. He wrote of his experiences of reporting in the face of danger in *In Harm's Way* in 1995. He eventually relinquished his career as a journalist when he became the Independent Member of Parliament for Tatton in 1997.

Both Christopher Hitchens (North B 62-66), his brother, Peter (W 65-67) and Jonathan Sale (North A 57-62) are regular contributors to a number of journals and magazines, both national and international. D.A.Q. Cregan (S 45-50) is a prolific playwright. He has written many radio and television plays in the past fifteen years, as well as several stage plays. He has also written pantomimes for the Theatre Royal, Stratford East, London.

Granta House Kitchen, 1984

Granta House Common Room, 1984

Dale House Study

Granta House Study

CHAPTER THIRTEEN

"Let us now praise famous men"

At the Centenary Commemoration Service in King's College Chapel, Cambridge, on 16 February, 1975, Revd H. K. Moulton, grandson of the first Headmaster, read the Introduction to the worship. On the same date in 2000, during the service for the 125th anniversary, in Great St. Mary's Church, Revd S. J. Burgess, the School Chaplain, read the same Introduction. Part of the passage went as follows:

"Under God's guidance has come a succession of scholars, doctors, government servants, lawyers; of soldiers, businessmen and athletes; of artists, musicians and writers; and of quiet men of character and faith who have given themselves for the benefit of the whole community both in this country and overseas".

All school histories contain material about former pupils of whom they are proud. In the last 125 years there have been many notable Old Leysians. John Stirland, the member of staff who is mentioned in chapter 3, did considerable research for an article which appeared in *The Fortnightly* in 1975 entitled *'Shining Lights'*. There is an envelope in the school archives containing over a hundred pieces of paper on which he had made notes about Old Leysians who "had made their contributions to the professional and commercial life not only of this country but of most parts of the globe". Since the publication of his article, another 3000 Leysians have passed through the school. This chapter uses some of John Stirland's article and expands the material about some of those he included and some who have left the school since he wrote it.

Their dates at school are given in brackets.

SCHOLARSHIP

The first Headmaster's son, James Hope Moulton (S 1875-82), was the earliest Old Leysian, and also the first Non-conformist at either Oxford or Cambridge, to be elected to a Fellowship, which was at King's College, Cambridge in 1888. He was a University lecturer and at the same time held the position of lecturer to Newnham and Girton Colleges. In 1908 he became Professor of Hellenistic Greek at Manchester University. His two outstanding works of scholarship were *Prolegomena* and *The Vocabulary of the Greek Testament*. He received several Doctorates: of Divinity from Edinburgh University, as had his father had before him, of Literature from London University, and of Theology from the University of Berlin. He became an authority on Zoroastrianism and it was this that had caused him to visit India in 1917. His tragic death from exposure in the Mediterranean after being torpedoed, is described in Chapter 8 - *The Leys at War.*

J.H. Clapham (A 1887-1892) became the first Professor of Economic History at Cambridge University. He, too, was elected to a Fellowship at King's College, Cambridge, and he held a University lectureship in History and Economics. In 1902 he became Professor of Economics at The Yorkshire College, which later became Leeds University. He held his chair at Cambridge University between 1928 and 1938. Among his many international distinctions, he was awarded Honorary Doctorates of Literature at Leeds and Harvard Universities. He received a knighthood in 1943. It was his name that was given to the history society at the school.

W.F. Reddaway (W 1889-1891) was another Old Leysian who became a Fellow of King's College, Cambridge. He was an authority on Slavonic Studies. From 1907-1924 he was Censor (Head of House) of Fitzwilliam House, now College, Cambridge. H. Mattingly (W 1896-1903) became a Fellow of Gonville and Caius College, Cambridge and then the assistant Curator of the department of Printed Books and of the department of Coins and Medals of the British Museum, and was honoured throughout Europe for his numismatic studies. H.C. Gutteridge (S 1889-1895) was a Fellow of Trinity Hall, Cambridge and Professor of Comparative Law at the University.

A.J. Wiles (A 66-70) is the Eugene Higgins Professor of Mathematics at Princeton University, USA. He became internationally known in the mid-1990s for his solution of Fermat's Last Theorem, a problem which had

256

puzzled mathematicians for two centuries. He was awarded the King Faisal International Prize for Science, appointed an OBE and also given an Honorary Doctorate of Science at Oxford University for his work.

SCIENCE AND ENGINEERING

Notable among more recent Old Leysian professors is R.J. Mair (A 1963-1967) who holds a chair in the Department of Engineering, Cambridge University. Previously his father had held a chair in the same department. However, whereas his father was the Francis Mond Professor in Aeronautical Engineering, Robert is the Professor of Geotechnical (Soil mechanics) Engineering. He used to tell his father, "my feet are firmly on or in the ground, whereas your head is in the clouds".

Donald Bailey (B 1916-1919) had proposed an idea of a bridge made of flat panels before the Second World War, but the proposal had been shelved for economic reasons. However, in 1940, the Military Engineering Establishment at Christchurch, Hampshire, was given permission to proceed, and a pilot model was ready for testing in 1941. The first production bridges were in service by December of the same year. Over 600 firms worked on the production of the bridge. Field Marshall Montgomery wrote in a letter:

"Bailey bridging made an immense contribution towards final victory in World War II. As far as my own operations were concerned with the Eight Army in Italy and with the 21st Army in NW Europe, I could never have maintained the speed and tempo of forward movement without large supplies of Bailey bridging."

Bailey was knighted for his contribution to the army's victory in Europe. Even today, second hand stocks of the bridge are being used to provide temporary access throughout the country, whilst more permanent bridges are being constructed.

There can be little doubt that Sir Henry Dale (S 1891-1894) was the most notable of the scientists The Leys has produced. Twenty-four universities in this country and abroad awarded him honorary doctorates. More than a column in *Who's Who* was needed to record all the honours, prizes and medals he gained. When the honours boards lined the walls of the Dining Hall, boys would pass the time spent waiting for their meal to be served by counting how many times his name appeared. Sixteen was the general

Distinguished Guests at the occasion of the 90th birthday of Sir Henry Dale, 1968
from left to right: Sir John Cockcroft, Lord Todd, Sir Frank Lee, Dr Gerald Humphrey, Sir Henry Thirkill, Sir Henry Dale, Lord Stamp, Lord Hayter, Mr Alan Barker, Lord Adrian

consensus. Sadly those boards were moved, first to the King's Building stairway, and now they are in store in the old squash courts behind West House. Dale was awarded the Nobel Prize for Medicine in 1936 and was made a member of the Order of Merit in 1944. The school held a dinner in his honour on the occasion of his 90th birthday. The members of the Common Room were delighted when they were invited to join the distinguished guests who attended the dinner. Sir Henry had taught for a short while at the school, following his graduation from Trinity College, Cambridge. He had learnt his science in the converted coach house behind the Headmaster's House, which was the first laboratory. He returned in 1958 to open the new biology laboratory in the Kelvin building, which had been paid for by the Industrial Fund. This Government Fund was set up to improve science facilities in schools following the Second World War. It was fitting that many of the demonstrations arranged by the boys at the opening included comparisons between the heart, liver, kidneys and other organs of common animals, since Sir Henry was such an eminent physiologist.

Sir Joseph Barcroft (A 1888-1892), following a distinguished undergraduate career at King's College, Cambridge, was appointed to a Fellowship at King's in 1899. Like Sir Henry Dale, he taught at the school for a short time before becoming a distinguished physiologist. In 1915, he was appointed Poison Gas Investigator by the Government. During his career he was awarded several honorary doctorates by other universities and he eventually became Professor of Physiology at Cambridge in 1926.

F.A. Bainbridge (S 1888-1893) was Professor of Physiology at Durham University from 1911 to 1916 and London University 1916 to 1921. D.W. Winnicott (B 1910-1914) was an internationally respected child psychiatrist. The list of Old Leysians in medicine and surgery included in the Occupational Analysis at the back of every Directory is substantial and includes many specialists.

THE LAW

The legal profession has always attracted Leysians, and some have risen to high positions. Sir George Raymond Hinchcliffe (S 1913-1918), A.K. Hollings (A 1932-1935), N.M. Butter (S 1948-1951) and Lord Peter Oliver (S 1934-1938) were High Court Judges, and Lord Oliver was a Justice of Appeal. Sir Godfrey Russell Vick (W 1906-1910), Arnold Russell Vick (W

1946-1952), A.S. Trapnell (S 1926-1931), R.E. Dummett (S & A 1888-1891) and D.A.L. Smout (A 1937-1941) were Circuit Judges. D.F.C. Clayton (W 1943-1947) was Chief Naval Judge Advocate and E. G. Moelwyn-Hughes (A 1950-1956) is the Vice Judge Advocate General, at the time of writing. Several Old Leysians have been Recorders and many have had distinguished careers as Barristers.

G.R. Glendinning (S 1927-1932) rose to the position of Chief Constable, first of Perth and Kinross County (1950-63) and then of Wiltshire (1963-1979)

THE CHURCH

Two Headmasters, Dr Moulton and Dr Barber, have held the position of President of the Methodist Conference. H. Clare Lees (A 1884-1889) became Archbishop of Melbourne, Australia and J.W. Hunkin (S 1904-1909), Bishop of Truro. W.A.L. Elmslie (S 1899-1904) was Principal of Westminster College, Cambridge (Presbyterian Church) and Michael Skinner (S 1932-1938) was Principal of Wesley House, Cambridge, which is a Methodist Theological College.

Following the visit of David Hill, then a renowned missionary, in the early days of the school, many Leysians became either medical or ordained missionaries. Possibly the most distinguished of these was S. R. Hodge (S 1875-1880). At the end of his time as a pupil, he remained at the school and Dr Moulton prepared him for ordination. He then went to medical school and on qualifying, was posted to the Wesleyan Mission House, Hankow, China where he was surgeon-in-charge. Sadly he died in 1907 from an infection caught in the hospital. There is a bronze memorial tablet to him inside the chapel on the south wall.

Another more recent Old Leysian missionary was George Robson Osborn (B 1918-1924). On leaving school, he went to King's College, Cambridge where he read Classics. When he graduated he moved to Wesley House where he read Theology and trained for the Methodist ministry. Part of the obituary notice which appeared in King's College, Cambridge Annual Report dated October 1980 said:

"Following ordination he sailed to China where he worked first in Peking and then he taught in the Wesley Middle School, Wuchang. Following the attack on Pearl Harbour in 1941 he became one of two thousand people interned by the Japanese at Lunghua near Shanghai. Two hundred of these were children[1] of school age. George Osborn was the obvious choice to be the Headmaster of an improvised school. "Lunghua Academy", as it proudly called itself, consisted of a near-derelict building with broken windows, ersatz benches, tables and blackboards, and almost no books or stationery. It was in an otherwise forbidden area of the camp, and the children had to be lined up and counted daily by the Japanese guards before the gate was unlocked. But the Headmaster was described as "resourcefulness itself, with a quite unbeatable spirit, almost enjoying deprivations because of the challenge they presented". Immediately after the war "Lunghua Academy", almost to a man, were deemed to have attained matriculation standard by the Cambridge Local Examinations Board.

In 1946 he returned to Wuchang but in 1948 the approach of the communist armies made it advisable to send his family home to England. Eventually his presence became an embarrassment to his Chinese friends and he left China for the last time in 1951."

He became Secretary of the Methodist Education Committee in 1951 until his retirement in 1970 and was a Governor of The Leys from 1951 to 1976.

[1] including James Ballard (see Chapter 12 - *Men of Words*) who was to base his novel *Empire of the Sun* on his experiences in that camp.

THE ARMED SERVICES

Not many Leysians have made the Forces their career. Since the end of the Second World War, one or two each year have joined the Army, Navy, Air Force or the Marines. Some of these have seen active service. A number have reached Colonel or equivalent rank. The highest ranking officer was Lieutenant-General Herbert Lumsden (B 1910-1911). He served in the First World War in the Royal Artillery as a Second Lieutenant and was awarded the Military Cross. Later he transferred to the 12th Royal Lancers, an armoured car unit, which he later commanded. He had been awarded the D.S.O. for his work with the British Expeditionary Forces in the early fighting in Europe, just after the Belgian Army had had to surrender.

In 1941 he took over command of an armoured brigade in the Middle East. He was awarded a bar to his D.S.O. for his part in the El Alamein fighting and was slightly injured. Winston Churchill said his Corps "struck like a thunderbolt". Lumsden showed the same dash with his tanks as he had with his horse when riding in the Grand National. He left his command of corps, to become Churchill's special representative with General MacArthur in the Far East. Although only 45 years old at the time, he made a great success of it and was made a Companion of the Order of the Bath. He was killed by a shell whilst he was on the bridge of an American warship in the Pacific.

Brigadier Greenacre (W 1913-1916) served as Equerry to the Prince of Wales and also during the brief time that he was King Edward VIII.

DIPLOMACY

Old Leysians have held positions in various Embassies and High Commissions throughout the world. It is only recently, however, that two have risen to the office of Ambassador. A.C. Thorpe (A 1955-1960) was Ambassador in Tokyo from 1991 to 95, Manila from 1995 to 98 and is now Ambassador in Mexico. T.N. Young (W 1957-1961) was Ambassador in Azerbaijan from 1993 to 97 and is now High Commissioner in Zambia.

THE ARTS AND MUSIC

The school has produced several well-known musicians. P. Dickinson (S 1945-1953) was the first Professor of Music at Keele University. He appeared in a television programme about himself and his compositions in the early 1990s. R.G. Weddle (B 1955-1959) was organist and Master of the Choristers at Coventry Cathedral between 1972 and 1977. After a short period as Director of Music at Edinburgh Academy, he moved to France, where he set up a school to teach choral music. The French have no tradition of the singing that is so commonly performed in English churches and cathedrals. A.E. Floyd (S 1890-1893) was organist at St. Paul's Cathedral, Melbourne, Australia for many years.

T.C. Yealland (A 1967-1971) is a singer who has won prizes in Germany for his lieder songs and A.C. Lane (A 1969-1974) performs under the stage name of Andrew Forbes-Lane with the English National Opera, Kent Opera and also at Glyndebourne.

The Leys has produced few professional actors. Michael Rennie (W 1924-1926) appeared in several films and television programmes, perhaps being remembered best as Harry Lime in *The Third Man*. Richard Heffer (S 1959-1964) appeared in the films *Dr Faustus, Waterloo* and *Women in Love*. He has also appeared on the West End stage and in small parts in television drama following his success in *Colditz* and *Rabies*.

Lord Rank (B 1901-1906), better known as J. Arthur Rank, the founder of the cinema and entertainment empire, had started his career in the family flour milling business. He was also a Sunday School teacher who felt the need for better visual aids for his classes. He founded a company called *Religious Films* to meet this need and then discovered the commercial value of the cinema. He began to make entertainment films in his studios and next he built a chain of cinemas to show these films. Later he diversified into other branches of the leisure industry.

H.S. (Jim) Ede (A 1909-1912) was a patron of painting and sculpture who converted four slum cottages at Kettle's Yard in Cambridge into a museum. He opened the doors of his home every afternoon to visitors and even lent paintings from amongst those he did not have room to hang, to many Cambridge people, including undergraduates. In 1926 he first saw the work of Gaudier-Brzeska, a sculptor who had been killed in the First World War. After the death of Sophie, the widow of Brzeska, he purchased most of her husband's work and wrote *Savage Messiah*, a biography of the artist, which established Brzeska's reputation. In 1966, Ede transferred the ownership of Kettle's Yard and its contents to Cambridge University and helped them to endow and build an extension to the house and an exhibition gallery.

Authors and journalists are covered in the Chapter 12 - *Men of Words* and similarly, international sportsmen in Chapter 7 - *Leysian Sport*. The names of county players and university blues in various sports are recorded in the successive editions of *The Leys Handbook and Directory*.

North B House Dormitory showing the 'Horse Boxes'

CHAPTER FOURTEEN

Boys will be boys

Life for the modern pupil is very different from that of an early Leysian. It is difficult to imagine the school with no electricity, no central heating, no radio, television or telephone. Important events were recorded in *The Fortnightly,* but that magazine gave only a few insights into every day life in the Houses. In an effort to fill the gap, Old Leysians still living, who had been in North B House before the Second World War, were asked in 1975 to send in their recollections of how they spent their time out of the classroom. There were none alive who had been at the school before 1900, but the replies received covered almost a continuous period from 1901 up to 1939.

The dormitories in all the houses had contained structures known as 'horse-boxes'. These were small wooden enclosures at the head of each bed, to give the owner a small degree of privacy whilst changing and washing. Each cubicle contained a washbowl and jug, a soap dish and toothbrush holder and a chamber-pot. All had the pre-1914 school crest on them. There are a few examples of each of these in the school archives. The chamber-pot had a secondary use as a curling stone, until the detriment rate for breakages against the iron bedsteads became too high. There was a reported incident when the boys awoke to find all North B House's pots arranged in the letter 'B' with soap dishes to represent the quotation marks, on the upper quad. Sadly, over a hundred chamber pots were thrown away in the 1960s when a store room had to be emptied below what is now Dale House. Only three are now in existence. There was no running water in the dormitories and only one night-lavatory on each of the two landings for a total of about forty boys in the house.

In each house there was a resident caretaker and his wife. The boys would be woken by a bell rung by the caretaker. His wife, assisted by one or two maids, would carry hot water from the taps on the landings to each boy's cubicle, so that he could wash. After breakfast, the maids would clean out the cubicles, empty the chamber pots and make the beds. The maids were called 'Bombs' by the boys. It was some time before the author discovered that this was short for 'Abominations', a sad reflection on the class structure within the school before 1930. The caretaker would have cleaned all the boys' shoes already, before waking the House. However, the boys were expected to clean their rugby boots and were also responsible for getting their dirty clothes into the laundry baskets. The caretaker and his wife issued drinks of cocoa from their quarters in the basement before bed-time each night.

Eventually the boys had to draw their own hot-water from a tap outside the dormitory door. One boy from the 1920 period remembered being told by the four or five seniors in his dormitory to fetch them some hot water from the tap on the landing. There has never been fagging at The Leys, and so he refused. To punish his defiance they made him report to the dormitory after breakfast for a week. Here he was forced to swallow a different dose of laxative each day. They were liquid paraffin, Angiers Emulsion, Gregory powders, and Andrews Liver Salts. He said it did him no particular harm, but actually cured a natural tendency to constipation. In fact, since there was an inadequate number of lavatories in the school, most boys returned from home with the family's favourite laxative; hence the varied assortment he was given.

The four boarding Houses, at the time of the First World War, were still lit by gas lights. Each pendant consisted of a horizontal cross with four burners at the ends of the arms. Toluene was added to the coal gas at the gas works, to give a flame which provided more illumination. However, during the war, toluene was needed to manufacture Trinitro-toluene (TNT) for use in explosives. Boys of this era recalled how difficult it was to read or do prep by the pale blue flickering light of gas without the added toluene. Normally the burners had gas mantles, which improved the lighting, but dormitory ragging, involving the hurling of slippers, inevitably resulted in some of the delicate mantles being broken. Even with electric light in the 1970s, the lamp shades were not immune from breakage caused by flying slippers!

When first built, each House contained a few studies for the Prefects. The lower parts of the walls would be draped by lengths of cretonne brought from home and the upper parts were decorated with team photographs.

266

School House Study, pre 1939

There would be a cane arm chair to sit on, a shelf or two for books, and a gas ring on which to heat kettles and saucepans. The sub-prefects had to be content with a 'study-bathroom'. There were about four bathrooms, in most cases in the basement of the House. Drawing boards borrowed from the Art School were placed over the baths to turn them into tables. Material was draped around the baths to disguise their primary function, and deck chairs and cushions served as furniture. Three or four boys would use these as rooms where they could relax, and at week-ends entertain their friends to meals of baked beans, toasted muffins, buns, scones, cakes and tinned fruit and jellies. Should a member of the House require a bath, normally the occupants would leave the room for a while, but sometimes the bather would allow them to stay so that he could join in whatever feast they were having.

In 1914, George Scott Page, Theo Nicholson, Christopher Thomson and James Whitehead formed a 'dining club'. They were served their meal through a hatch in the wall by a junior, Joseph Esmail, dressed up in a sort of livery, with fake silver buttons made by covering the ordinary ones on his jacket with silver paper. They had menus, which were works of art in themselves. Some of these have survived to the present day, and show an ambitious range of food. A report by School Inspectors in 1919 criticised the use of bathrooms as impromptu studies, and the practice ceased. For years after leaving school, the group of friends would meet and take the current Housemaster of North B out to dinner. The basement studies officially had access only to a communal gas ring at the end of the corridor. Some study owners had their own Primus stoves and some even confessed to running an illegal gas stove off the room lighting. The risk of fire they ran is frightening to contemplate.

Each House contained a Common Room, which doubled up during the day time as a classroom. In the early days, furniture was scarce and far from comfortable. Wicker-work arm chairs were a luxury reserved for the School and House Prefects. The juniors would have to perch on the wooden desks.

The lavatories were a place of refuge for Gilbert Thomas who wrote in his *Autobiography*:

"No provision was made for play or hobbies as distinct from the dull grind of sport; nor was there any hole or corner where I could be sure of half-an-hour's privacy for the reflection I equally needed. Yes, there was just one place; and many afternoons did I spend, with a book or newspaper, or even with my own thoughts, safely bolted within a lavatory! The coming and going of boys to the adjoining closets, the incessant sound of chain-pulling and flushing, the discomfort and draughtiness, did not make this an ideal hermitage; but it was better than none."

"Once I sought refuge in the empty School Hall, which was "out of bounds" except for normal purposes during working hours. There I was happily composing an essay for my own amusement when J.C. Isard, the much smiled at but much loved Bursar, appeared. On his begging to know my business, I confessed the truth. Ironically, yet very genially, he asked me to remember him when I became the Poet Laureate."

Thomas did not become Poet Laureate; however he did become a journalist and book reviewer and had several books of his poetry published. One book he had published just after he was imprisoned during the First World War as a conscientious objector. One chapter of this book, *Autobiography,* deals with his experiences in prison, which he did not seem to find as traumatic as his time at The Leys.

During the war-time, ices sold at the tuck shop were water ices and these were not altogether satisfying. A boy called Denholm bought an ice cream freezer. There was always spare milk in the house left over from "elevenses" or tea. The remaining ingredients needed were a block of ice, sugar and some custard powder. Denholm's partner in the venture, Pratt Boorman, had the task of breaking bounds every Saturday afternoon by leaving by the side gate of The Leys and crossing over the fen, or by the "outer gate" by Belvoir Terrace, and cycling to pick up a block of ice from the fishmongers.

The two boys soon discovered how popular the ices were and indeed they had too many friends to be able to supply them all. They started to charge 3d. (about 1p) for an egg-cup full of ice cream. It was a most beneficial speculation, which kept them in pocket money for the rest of the week. The custard was made on Saturday night and frozen between lunch and the letter-writing period on Sunday afternoons, and they were always sold out.

After the First World War, the school was given a large field gun, a souvenir of the hostilities. It stood on the piece of ground at the north-east corner of the school grounds where the North B Housemaster's house was eventually built. At the end of each summer term, the members of North B House used to push the gun on to the centre of the quad, pointing it at the chapel. In 1926, a bar was cemented through the tail, but that was cut through and the usual procedure followed. The gun was then exiled to the garden of the Sanatorium, which was in those days in Brookside.

In 1927, the doors in the basement of the House were unscrewed from their hinges, and at about 2 a.m., the majority of the boys (except Prefects) crossed the road. They then unscrewed the garden gates to the Sanatorium, sat a number of boys on the barrel to raise the tail, and pushed the gun across the road, through the King's building gateway and into its traditional position. As a result of this escapade, all the boys of the House were compelled to write out *Hamlet* during the holidays as a punishment. It left some of them hating the play for the rest of their lives.

Male institutions throughout the world seem to follow initiation customs. There were two which have been mentioned by many Old Leysians in their accounts of their school days. One is that new boys were made to stand on a table and sing a song to the assembled House. Occasionally, if the audience did not consider the performance was good enough, the unfortunate new boy would have his face blackened with a burnt cork. Sometimes this was done just before supper so that the victim had no time to wash his face before having to go into supper or chapel. His humiliation was therefore all the worse, since the whole of the school could see what had happened to him. The new boy singing tradition was still in action when the author joined West House as House Tutor in 1957, but the face blackening was no longer being carried out.

The other initiation ordeal which new boys had to face was that they were made to crawl under the row of beds in the long dormitories. As they emerged from under each bed they would be hit by pillows wielded by the rest of the boys in the room. Great relief was felt in the 1960s when dormitories were sub-divided into smaller units and modern beds arrived which were lower, making it impossible to crawl under them. The author was reassured by pupils very recently that no such ceremonies exist to-day.

To many readers these ceremonies seem like bullying. Both Gilbert Thomas and James Hilton (see Chapter 12 - *Men of Words*) wrote that during their schooldays they were not aware of any bullying. When the subject was discussed recently with an Old Leysian, he felt that there are several degrees of oppression of one pupil by another. There is verbal teasing on a single occasion, but this can very often lead to repetition by an individual or by a group, and can cause much unhappiness. Physical bullying leads to even greater unhappiness. It has been unfortunate in the past that minor but unkind teasing has, by "tradition" taken place on a victim's birthday, which should be a particularly happy day, not one to dread.

No school can claim to be absolutely free from bullying. From what one reads in the press, it seems universal. However, part of the recent national legislation in 'The Children's Act', requires that schools should designate 'independent listeners', not connected with the school, whom worried children can approach for help. This is done at The Leys, as at all schools, and must be an improvement on "the good old days".

In the early years of the school's history, security in the Houses was principally aimed at keeping the boys in. All the windows had bars and the doors were locked by either the caretaker or the Housemaster at a published time. The resourceful members of B House had scraped the mortar from some of the seating of one of the basement window's bars. They were then able to swivel the bars and climb out of the house. Several boys wrote to the author about these escapades, but none elaborated as to what they did once they were out of the House. In modern times, security aims to keep strangers out of the house, since a number of thefts have occurred when members of the public were simply able to walk into boarding houses at will. Each front door has a touch button combination lock fitted to it.

Until 1929, the whole school did their prep in the Great Hall, supervised by a junior master. Inexperienced masters, especially new ones, could become a target for practical jokes. One which the author was told about occurred when the gallery of the Hall still contained an organ. An explanation of the mechanism of an organ is needed for anyone who does not understand how such an instrument produces its sound. Air is pumped to the instrument, but no sound occurs until one of the stops on the keyboard is opened to allow the air to pass to a certain set of pipes. One evening, some boys turned the organ on and wedged down one key, which was capable of producing a very strident note. A length of fishing line was attached to a suitable stop and fed down into the body of the hall. Prep started, and suddenly the silence was shattered by the piercing sound of the organ, which had been activated by the tugging of the fishing line. It had been pulled very hard in order to snap the line, which then recoiled into the organ loft, thus concealing the identity of the those responsible. The unfortunate supervising master took a long while to fathom the mechanism so that he could stop the noise.

As mentioned earlier, school food was supplemented by food in the Houses, from tuck boxes and the Tuck Shop itself. Until the introduction of self-service in the Dining Room in 1983, the boys ate formally in House groups within the Dining Room. At first, food was served by young waiters who would carry up to six plates at a time to the tables. Later the professional waiters were replaced by junior members of each house who, in teams of four, were paid a few shillings for a week's work. They ate after the rest of the school and on the whole enjoyed the task, since it meant that they could have larger helpings of their favourite food. Eventually some would take the place of others on the rôta who were less enthusiastic, and almost became professional waiters themselves.

It could, however, hold some terror for young boys who, especially at meals when staff were not present, would be threatened with 'lines' if they did not get a particular prefect a second helping of egg and chips before the rest of the House had been served. During the Headmastership of Alan Barker, the Governors removed the weekly wage on the grounds that the 'waiter' was serving his community. Instead they gave what would have been the term's total wages to the House, to help to pay for newspapers and other small luxuries.

The refurbishment of the kitchens, together with the adaptation of the dining hall to allow for self-service, meant that waiting ceased and the amount of wastage was reduced since, in theory, boys and girls would only take what they wanted rather than being served an enormous plateful of food which they did not fancy. The changes also allowed for a choice of menu, in the hope of satisfying everyone. There has been a positive response to any criticisms about the food, and innovations have produced attractive new menus under the direction of Howard Dickinson, the catering manager.

There are a number of stories about less satisfactory meals in the past. At one meal, in the mid-1960s, North B House turned up for lunch as usual, since attendance at all meals was then compulsory, but only four out of sixty-five members of the House accepted the food that was offered to them.

The Headmaster, Alan Barker, noticed the concern of the Lady Superintendent, and he summoned the Housemaster to find out why his boys appeared to be staging a food strike. It transpired that all the boys not now eating had been up most of the night with upset stomachs, whilst the four who were not affected had refused the shepherd's pie served at supper the previous day. Because no other House was affected, the kitchen staff at first ruled out food poisoning, but the school doctor called in the local health inspectors. On investigation, it turned out that the method of preparing that particular dish was suspect, but luckily it was only one tray, the one which was served to North B, that had been contaminated. The boys' behaviour was exonerated and the preparation of shepherd's pie was from that time onwards carefully monitored.

This was a small incident, compared with an occurrence in 1923. One morning as the school came into breakfast, the whole hall stank of bad fish. Each boy had been served two mackerel on a plate. Without any visible conferring, the Top Table got up and filed out, carrying the mackerel. They were immediately followed in order by boys from the other tables. In perfect order, they marched to the Bursar's office, then in North A House, deposited their stinking fish on his desk, and marched back to the Dining Hall, where Grace was said, and they were dismissed. The Bursar found 520 fish on his desk when he arrived for work. No comment was ever made and no disciplinary action was ever taken, but there was a noticeable improvement in the food from that time.

Sometimes time conjures up erroneous stories in the minds of former pupils. The author's attention was drawn to an autobiography by an Old Leysian, Reginald Hine, *The Recollections of an Uncommon Attorney*. These were mainly his recollections of having been a solicitor, but in a chapter about his school days, he claimed that there had been a riot in the dining hall which was so bad that the police were called and the Riot Act read. However, when a copy of this book was eventually traced to the library of the Department of Education at the University of Cambridge, in the margin, in W.H. Balgarnie's unmistakable handwriting, was a comment that this passage was nonsense and there had been no such occurrence.

Fire-extinguishers seem to have held a fascination for the boys ever since the beginning of the school. One issue of *The Fortnightly*, published soon after the opening of North B House in 1883, reported:

"Considerable excitement was occasioned about a week ago by the rumour that there had been a slight outbreak of fire in North B. However the fire buckets nobly justified their existence and some energetic would-be firemen threw enough water about the passage where the fire was to have put out fifty such fires as it proved to be. Finally when it was all over, the Senior Prefect arrived breathless and exhausted on the scene, having carried a "Fire Queen" on his back from School House. It is worthy of mention the extincteur belonging to 'B' had been emptied by someone who shall be nameless, presumably for a joke - and it had not been refilled"

As a result of this incident, Mr Isard, the Bursar, founded a school fire-fighting force manned by representatives from each House. By all accounts the first practice was a disaster and their services do not seem to have been called upon at any later date.

Over the years, misuse of extinguishers must have cost the school thousands of pounds in replacement bills. Another event, again in B House, in 1979, occurred after break one morning. An unknown member of the House had smoked an illegal cigarette in the laundry room and dropped his stub-end on a small pile of freshly laundered items. A sub-prefect, visiting the room, saw the small wisps of smoke arising from a pair of underpants. He aimed the fire-extinguisher at the seat of the potential fire. It so happened that dry powder extinguishers had been provided in this area of the House. All the clean washing was covered with the powder and had to be returned to the laundry. If the sub-prefect had thrown the underpants out of the window, it would have saved a lot of mess and expense. However, later in life, prompt action by the same person, as a police cadet, saved the lives of two children in a burning car, when he smashed the window with his truncheon. He was awarded a medal for his bravery.

A fire in the basement of King's Building was caused when two boys were servicing cooking stoves for Duke of Edinburgh's Award Scheme expeditions. A petrol spillage caught fire and soon spread along the corridor. The fire brigade came quickly and tried to enter the school grounds through the iron gates at the front of King's Building, only to get stuck. There was considerable confusion with the traffic on Trumpington Road, as the appliance had to back out and then get in through the open entrance by the Deer Park. After they had successfully put out the fire, it was discovered that there was considerable damage in the basement to the electrical wiring of the building.

In 1972, the staff were having dinner in the Masters' Common Room. After a while they smelt burning and investigated in the Art School above. An aggrieved student had set light to waste paper in a dustbin. The flames had reached the roof of the room and the beams were on fire. Prompt action by the masters and the speedy arrival of the Fire Brigade saved the building, but not before considerable damage had been done to the wooden ceiling of the room. The Art School has now been incorporated into the Staff Common Room, and the dining table is over the spot where the fire had been started.

In the years before radio and television, boys had to make their own recreation. Table tennis was played on a long table in the common room with a low board or row of books for a net. A variation was table soccer played with coins. This must have been a forerunner of Subbuteo, combined with tiddly-winks. The more serious student could play chess, and when Kellett was the Housemaster, he would pit his skills against several of the younger boys, in simultaneous games.

The North Houses played 3-a-side hockey on a small square of ground where the study extensions now stand. Those wishing for a more energetic activity would play 'outer golf', where they counted the number of strokes of a hockey stick that were taken to drive a ball all the way round the outer perimeter of the school grounds. There was a short period when 'diablo' was all the craze. This was a double ended top which was spun on a string held between two rods. The aim was to throw it in the air whilst it was still spinning and catch it onto the string on the way down. The columns of *The Fortnightly* in 1907 said that many members of the school were fed up with the pastime and hoped that it would soon lose its appeal.

During a Biology practical in the late 1950s, each boy was set the task of removing the mouthparts of a cockroach and mounting them on a microscope slide. This was a very delicate procedure, so the master in charge was not surprised when one boy came up to ask for a fresh specimen. It was still alive and needed to be dropped into a jar of ether to be killed very quickly, before being dissected. Instead, the astonished master watched the boy return to his place with the cockroach, put it in his mouth and swallow it, and hold out his hand to his neighbour for the settlement of a bet of half-a-crown (12½p) that he would not do so.

If a sixth-form pupil is consistently underachieving, he or she may be required to attend a session known as the "Star Chamber". This is held in the Headmaster's study, and attended by his or her Housemaster or mistress, tutor and subject teachers. It is therefore impossible for the pupil to play one teacher off against the other whilst attempting to find excuses for a poor overall performance.

On one such occasion in the late 1980s, the interview had just started when the telephone rang. The boy was immediately required in the Science Building, where his 5ft. long pet python had escaped from its cage and was lying across a doorway, preventing anyone getting through the door. The "Star Chamber" broke up in disorder and never reconvened to discuss that particular boy.

Staff cars have always been a target for schoolboy pranks. Harold Rose used to drive a Ford Popular in the 1950s, and always parked it next to the Science Building. He was amazed, and somewhat angry, to find that it had been lifted and placed half-way up the flight of steps into the building.

One evening in 1980, two boys were returning late in the evening after an illicit trip to a local public house. One of them was in desperate need of relief, when he came upon his Housemaster's car. He unscrewed the petrol cap and urinated into the tank. The pair were very embarrassed to see the car having to be towed out of the school the next morning, because the engine could not be persuaded to run on such a mixture.

In 1988, the House Tutor of East woke up one morning to find his Fiat 500, which was a very small car, parked in the hallway of the building. Eventually the resident staff became so concerned about what might happen to their vehicles at the end of term, that many took to parking their cars overnight at the homes of colleagues who lived off the campus but nearby.

CHAPTER FIFTEEN

Curriculum and Scholarship

With only sixteen pupils, whose ages ranged from 11 to 17, it was difficult for Dr Moulton to organise the classes. A programme in Classics, both Latin and Greek, Mathematics, Science, English and Religious Knowledge was started and it must have stretched the Headmaster and his one assistant, Arthur Vinter, to the full to be able to cope with such a mixture of ages and abilities. The school numbers rose rapidly to 54 in January 1876 and 84 by January 1877, and at the same time a small number of extra masters joined the staff.

In his report to the Life Donors in June 1877, Dr Moulton commented that the boys who had entered during the last year had, as a rule, been younger, and that the school had received comparatively few boys who "were backward in attainments for their age". Promotion to higher classes only came with academic success. He had, at that time, not decided to set an Entrance Examination and his remarks led one to believe that there must have been a number of pupils who were struggling to cope with their academic subjects. The numbers in the school were not yet sufficiently large for the development of the curriculum that he would have liked. He wished to divide the classes into Classical and Modern sides and also "to make provision for boys in whose case a thorough study of Natural Science is requisite".

In the first few years, the Headmaster invited external examiners to test the boys in all subjects except Religious Knowledge, which he himself tested. In 1878 he commented that in the higher classes there had been a marked advance in the quality of work. In 1879, the examiner in Classics and English, W.G. Rushbrooke, who was the senior classics master at the City of London School at the time, was so concerned about the age range and ability in the school, that he published a table in his report showing the distribution by age of boys in each form. The table is below:

No. of Boys over Years of Age	19	18	17	16	15	14	13	12	11
In the Upper V [8]	2	3	1		1	1			
In the Lower V [11]			2	4	3	2			
In the Upper IV [10]			2	5	2	1			
In the Lower IV [20]		1	4	8	2	3	1	1	
In the Upper III [20]			1	1	7	3	7	1	
In the Lower III [15]				4	2	3	4	2	
In the II Form [13]				1	1	5	4	2	
In the I Form [3]							1	1	1
Total No. of Boys [100]	2	4	10	23	18	18	17	7	1

In his comments, he was particularly surprised that, of the twenty-three boys between 16 and 17, some were to be found in every class except the highest and the lowest. Also he was surprised that the top class contained two pupils over 19 being taught with one just over 14, and one just over 15. In his detailed report, class by class, of the Latin examination, he often recorded that the younger boys in the classes performed the best. He seemed better pleased with the results in Greek. He also commented on the improvement in parsing in English, as compared with the previous year. The report gave an insight in to the work being covered by various classes. *As You Like It*, *Hamlet* and *Othello* were the Shakespeare plays being studied, together with Chaucer's *Prologue* and the Elizabethan period of English Literature. He said of Arthur Avery that "his English papers were of a very high class, and would have done him credit at any College Examination".

The Mathematics Report similarly details aspects of the syllabus. Three of the top class had done the work for the first BA Examination of London University. This seemed to involve work on Conic Sections, Higher Algebra and Trigonometry as well as quite a number of books of Euclid. Science in 1879 seemed to consist of Experimental Physics for the top class, with Elementary Physics and Astronomy for the lower classes.

By the next year, 1880, the Headmaster was able to report that five boys had entered for the Higher School Certificate of the Oxford and Cambridge Schools Examination Board. All five candidates, J.H. Moulton, T.

Darlington, J.C. Ingle, J. Southall and L. Smith gained certificates. Moulton obtained distinctions in Latin, Greek, English and Scripture and Darlington in French and Scripture. The use of external examiners had continued for the rest of the school, who by now were examined in French and German, as well as in those subjects previously set. The Science examination had been extended to cover Botany, Physiology and Chemistry as well as Physics. There was also a report on Music which included piano playing, singing and orchestral music. There was a slight criticism that the master did not have sufficient control over practising because the practice rooms were too far apart. The symphony chosen, Beethoven's in C Minor, was considered by the examiner to be too advanced a work. He advised that easier works of Haydn and Mozart should be attempted.

Dr Moulton still looked for an increase of numbers to enable the organisation of the school to "offer a fuller and careful provision for each of the distinct classes of boys passing through the School; those destined for a business life, those who proceed directly to scientific examinations in the University of London, and those who, designed for various professions, were preparing for residence in the Universities" (presumably Oxford and Cambridge). Already in 1880, two Old Leysians had graduated from Cambridge and three more were in residence.

The early forms, listed in *The Leysian Directory*, started in 1881 to differentiate between the classical and modern sides of the curriculum. Dr Moulton had wanted to make this distinction for some time. He pointed out that whereas there was very little difference in the time spent on Mathematics and English between the two sides of the school, he was going to allot more time to Modern Languages and Science (at the expense of Latin Composition) in the case of those who were preparing for business. He also promised that he would introduce special classes which would provide a knowledge of business methods for those who were likely to enter into a mercantile career.

Another of the Headmaster's hopes for the future was for a fund to provide scholarships. This need was echoed in the report of the external examiner in 1881 who commented:

"I am glad to think that the school, though still somewhat overweighted with older boys, is so to a diminishing degree; and if, as I have heard – for the rumour of generous deeds flies quickly

– there is some prospect of the speedy establishment of entrance scholarships, to enable promising boys less fortunately placed by the circumstances of their birth to become pupils here, then I have no doubt that a great and a most valuable additional stimulus will have been given to those whom I may call the natural tenants of this beautiful school."

Those sentiments have been once more realised at the end of the twentieth century by a very generous donation to enable some pupils nominated by the Leysian Mission to be educated free at the school from 1998 onwards.

The suggestion of the external examiner in 1881 that scholarships should be set up, brought an immediate response from two Governors, Atkinson and Harvey, who offered to endow one scholarship each per annum, worth £50, tenable for three years. The candidate had to be under the age of fifteen at the time of sitting the papers, and the examination would be held in two parts:

The Preliminary Examination

1. One of the Gospels (in English) to be chosen by the Candidate.
2. English Grammar.
3. Latin. Translation of easy passages by the help of a Dictionary, with questions in Grammar.
4. Mathematics. Arithmetic: Algebra to Simple Equations: Euclid, Books I, II.

The candidate having satisfied the examiners that he was capable of attempting the real examination, was then faced with the following syllabus:

The Scholarship Paper

1. Latin. Translation: Prose Composition: Grammar. Any candidate is at liberty to offer Verse Composition.
2. Greek. Translation: easy prose composition: Grammar.
3. French or German. Translation: Composition: Grammar.
4. Mathematics. Algebra: Euclid: Plane Trigonometry
5. Statics and Dynamics.

At first only a few attempted to gain scholarships and sometimes, if the performance had not been worthy, only part of the £50 was allowed.

There are some examples of work books in the archives which belonged to James Gedye in 1878. One was a copper plate handwriting exercise book,

and half its weight of small coal. There are
three stages in reaction which may be
represented by these equations.

$$Na_2SO_4 + C_2 = Na_2S + 2CO_2$$
$$CaCO_3 + C = CaO + 2CO$$
$$Na_2S + CaO + CO_2 = CaS + Na_2CO_3$$

These equations show that Sodium Sulphide
is first formed then Lime & these two
with a portion of the Carbonic Acid Gas
formed react upon one another & produce
the Na_2CO_3 as shown in the equations.
It is however mixed with Sodium Sulpide
which gives it a black colour and hence
it is called black ash. To obtain the Sodium
Carbonate from this it is heated with water
which dissolves out the Na_2CO_3. The salt
itself is obtained by evaporating this
solution and is then called "Soda Ash".
Silicate of Soda generally known as soluble
glass is used for imparting a fire-proof character to
wood. It is formed by dissolving sand in fused
Carbonate of Soda. The equation of the action is as follows

$$Na_2CO_3 + SiO_2 = Na_2SiO_3 + CO_2$$
(Sodic Carbonate) + (Sand) = (Sodic Silicate) + (Carbonic Acid)

An extract from the Chemistry notebook of J.L. Gedye, 1877 another notes on Shakespeare plays. It is not possible to determine whether the notes were his own or had been dictated. His Chemistry and Physics books showed that the syllabuses being followed were very advanced. When the Physics book was shown to the Head of Physics recently, he agreed that some parts were beyond those topics studied for A level in the year 2000. Therefore the above scholarship papers may not have been all that daunting to boys of the 1880s.

In 1893, Dr Moulton reported proudly to the Governors that all three candidates entered for the Scholarship Examination at Trinity College, Cambridge had won awards. He went on to say that this number had only been equalled by Dulwich College, and that this school contained three times as many boys as The Leys. The 1898 prospectus, published just after Moulton's death, lists the number of Cambridge Fellowships and Scholarships held by Old Leysians. There were four holding Major Scholarships at Trinity College simultaneously, and four boys had won entrance Exhibitions in History to King's and Gonville and Caius Colleges.

· The same prospectus contained the following passage:

"The school is divided into Classical and Modern sides. It is often found that boys who are looking forward to a business life lose interest in classical studies, and waste time which might as well be spent on such subjects as commercial geography and history, special arithmetic, exchanges, mercantile documents and terminology in our own and other languages, political economy, and the elements of commercial law; topics which not only appeal to the practical mind, but serve to bridge over the transition from the class-room to the counting-house. Education of this kind is extensively given in Germany and other continental countries, and has been introduced into this School."

It was possible to learn shorthand as an extra subject at a charge of one guinea (£1.05) per term. At the same time, carpentry was half a guinea, metal work, piano, singing or practical chemistry lessons were charged at two guineas, and lessons learning to play stringed instruments cost three guineas.

The 1917 Prospectus now contained details of Old Leysian scholastic successes. In thirty seven years, nine Fellowships and eighty seven Scholarships had been won at various Cambridge colleges. There were no reports of boys going to Oxford, but there had been some distinguished performances at London University. Remarkably, there were several instances of boys whilst still at school obtaining BSc and BA degrees at London University. The same document gives greater detail than the 1898 prospectus as to what the Classical and Modern side studied. All boys up to the age of 15 or 16 covered the ordinary (sic) school subjects. The boys on the Classical side spent several periods a week on Latin and Greek, whereas the Modern side covered modern languages. The distinction was not a sharp one, since boys in all forms took some Latin and French and all covered elementary science. It was possible to take German instead of Greek.

In the upper school, those who intended to enter a University took up mathematics, science and ancient or modern languages or history. Those who were going into business took a course in French and German, although Spanish or Russian could be taken by arrangement. They also studied mathematics, modern history, book keeping and elementary economics, Typewriting lessons now joined shorthand as an optional extra.

By 1923, three more Fellowships had been gained and over fifty three more Cambridge College Scholarships had been won in the six year period. Similar successes as before were reported at London University. The War Memorial Fund, which was established after the First World War, was to increase the number of Scholarships and Exhibitions available. At the same time, the Governors had established Leaving Scholarships and Exhibitions which were tenable for three years, and would assist Old Leysians at University. The curriculum was practically the same as it was in 1917.

By 1948, the lowest forms, the Lower and Upper Fourth would have studied Scripture, English History and Literature, Mathematics, Science, French, Geography and Drawing, and either Latin or German. The Lower and Upper Fifth (Years 10 and 11) were now in three divisions; Language, Modern and Mathematical sides. In the Upper Fifth, the boys took the School Certificate Examination of the Oxford and Cambridge Schools Examination Board. Success in this examination would gain them exemption from Responsions at Oxford, the Previous Examination at Cambridge, the Matriculation Examination of London and other Universities, and the preliminary examinations required in various professions. Successful candidates would pass into the Sixth form and prepare to take the Higher Certificate examinations by studying two or three special subjects. For the first time in this prospectus mention is made of Scholarships being won at Oxford University.

Sweeping changes in examinations occurred in 1950. School and Higher Certificate examinations were replaced by the General Certificate of Education at Ordinary and Advanced Level. Because it was now possible to obtain a certificate with a pass in one subject only, it was not necessary to teach to syllabuses of one examination board only. Teachers could choose a course which they considered suited them and the candidates best. At The Leys, some departments started to use the papers of the University of Cambridge Local Examinations Syndicate (UCLES). Eventually up to five boards at any one time were being used, with the consequent problems of administering the individual examinations. The introduction of modular examinations has meant that papers are being sat nearly all the year round.

Following the abolition of School Certificate, there was room for minor adaptations of the former curriculum. Most boys took Scripture, English Language and Literature, Latin, French, Elementary Mathematics and General Science. If their ability in Mathematics was above average, they would take Additional Mathematics and they could also take Greek **or** German instead of History **and** Geography. For a short period, Spanish was offered but was not very popular, and was soon dropped from the options available. It has recently been reinstated in the curriculum. During the 1960s and 70s, various minor changes to the options in the Ordinary level subjects occurred, including the possibility of studying the single subject sciences, Biology, Chemistry and Physics.

In 1987, Ordinary level examinations were replaced by the General Certificate of Secondary Education examinations (GCSE) which also embraced candidates who would have taken the Certificate of Secondary Education (CSE). Since the CSE examination had been aimed at candidates of a weaker academic level, the new GCSE offered a greater number of grades, with A, B and C being considered equivalent to an O level pass. In many subjects the new examination required project work to be done before papers were taken at the end of the year. More changes in the pattern of sixth form examinations in England are envisaged in 2000.

One result of the numbers increasing in the school in the mid-1960s, was that a more flexible choice of Advanced level subjects could be offered. It was also during this period that the numbers of Open Scholarships and

Exhibitions to Oxford and Cambridge Colleges rose steadily. What was a record number of eight Awards in 1963, was surpassed with eleven in 1971. The total achieved after the Second World War up to the abolition of the University of Cambridge Colleges' Entrance Examinations after 1985 was 114 and with a total of 378 Awards from 1880 to 1985, the average was over 3.6 per year.

Leysians when choosing between Oxford and Cambridge, have mainly opted for Cambridge. They are tempted to stay in familiar surroundings, and in the days before admissions to the various Colleges were so co-ordinated or so highly competitive as they are today, a letter of introduction to a Master or Senior Tutor could play a large part in securing a place. The Leys masters knew more such influential people at Cambridge than at Oxford. In the 1950s there were always about fifty Old Leysians at Colleges in Cambridge.

Over the years since then there have been gradual, and finally more sweeping changes. By the 1970s the Colleges were co-operating with each other by all requiring their candidates to sit the same Colleges' Entrance Examinations in November of each year. Both places and Awards were given on the basis of results in these examinations. Candidates from Independent Schools, and those from Direct Grant schools largely took the examinations in the term **after** they had completed their 'A' levels. Candidates from schools which were completely state maintained were often unable to offord the luxury of a "seventh term" in the sixth form, even if their schools were prepared to offer one, so they had to take the examination in the previous year, two terms **before** 'A' levels. This was perceived to be a considerable handicap to them.

There was a great deal of Press and public pressure on the Universities to deal with this anomaly. Cambridge decided to abolish the Entrance Examination after the one taken in 1985, so that for the first time for entry in 1987, all offers of places were based on 'A' level results and performance at interviews. Successful candidates who had not yet taken 'A' levels were given "conditional offers". They were asked to achieve specific grades in the 'A' levels, and if they did so, their places were confirmed. An additional examination was introduced, called Sixth Term Examination Papers (STEP), and some Colleges also set grades in this as part of the conditions for pre-'A' level candidates. Others set grades in 'S' (Special) papers instead of STEP.

During the same period, the number of women both at Oxford and at Cambridge rose steadily, as one after another of the former men's Colleges started to admit women also. Whereas in 1971, 13% of the undergraduate places at Cambridge University as a whole went to women, by 1999, women accounted for 46% of the undergraduate places. Until The Leys started to take girls, this meant that proportionately less places were available to its pupils. Similar changes took place at Oxford, although the Entrance Examination was not abolished until ten years after the one at Cambridge.

The academic prowess of a school used to be measured by the number of Entrance Awards gained at these Universities, but these Awards disappeared with the Entrance Examinations, so other criteria must now be used. The steadily rising number of candidates from maintained schools succeeding in getting into Cambridge, has led to fears in the Independent Schools that their pupils are being discriminated against. Coupled with the greater number of Higher Education Institutions available to them, and the more varied and interesting courses offered by these institutions, able Sixth Formers no longer assume that they must proceed either to Cambridge or to Oxford. They are looking much more widely to find the course that suits them best.

In the 1990s, League Tables based on school examination results have been seen by many as the way to judge the worth of a school. Not surprisingly, they have been dominated by the more selective schools, and schools like The Leys which have had a fairly broad ability range have not apparently compared very favourably. The current Headmaster has, with others, argued strongly that it should be 'value-added' that should be the real measure of a school's success. In recent years, the Government's insistence that results are published for an age group, rather than a year group, irrespective of whether they sat any examination, has further complicated the situation. Dr Barrett has regularly written to the Press to complain at the unfairness of this, and to argue that it is important that schools should be free to allow some pupils to take examinations early and others late, if that is appropriate, and they should not be penalised for doing so.

The effect of all this has been to make The Leys even more determined to do the very best it can for each pupil, whatever his or her ability.

CHAPTER SIXTEEN

From the Four Corners of the Earth

Sir William McArthur was the son of an Irish Wesleyan minister who set up an export business with his brother, Alexander, in Australia at the time of the gold rush in that country. He became extremely wealthy and was a great benefactor to Wesleyan Methodist causes. Sir William, who had no sons, realised that his eldest nephew had already gone to an Anglican school. He had five or six more young relatives still to be educated and he wished to find a suitable first class school, with a Methodist background, for these boys. It was he who intervened at a Methodist Conference committee on higher education and effectively killed off the scheme for the school to be started at Twickenham, sealing Cambridge and the Leys Estate as the site of the proposed new school.

There was a rumour that the school was founded for the sons of rich Yorkshire sheep farmers. The first edition of *The Directory* in 1884, shows that out of the first 361 Old Leysians, ninety-three were from Yorkshire, Lancashire and Northumberland. There was still a large Yorkshire contingent in the school in 1957. When a new, young member of staff asked some of the boys how he could get to Bradford easily at the end of term, he was informed of the usual practice. The Senior Prefect would ring up the station master at Hitchin, who would stop the 'non-stop' London to Doncaster train at Hitchin the next morning. Boys wishing to get home to Yorkshire caught the Cambridge to Hitchin train which reached there in time to connect with the Doncaster train. The platform at Hitchin was crowded and the train filled with Leys boys, most of whom had to stand all the way to Doncaster, but it was worth it to get home by the quickest, if slightly irregular, route.

Later the number of Yorkshire Leysians dwindled, and a parent organised a Wallace Arnold coach to co-ordinate travel to and from Yorkshire at the beginning and end of term. Eventually the roads to the North were so much improved and the numbers from Yorkshire had dropped to such an extent that the coach was no longer worth while.

The Leys seems to have become recognised beyond the shores of England very early in its existence. It is quite remarkable that pupils were soon coming from Japan. In the mid-1880s, there had been a change of dynasties in that country. The Shoguns had been deposed, and the new Emperor looked to the West for education and enlightenment and set in motion a programme whereby the sons of leading members of his Court were sent to Universities and Public Schools in England. It seems that one undergraduate at Cambridge University sent home news of a new school in Cambridge. Twelve Japanese attended the school before 1900, most of whom took Cambridge degrees after leaving. Many of them rose to be members of the Japanese Court.

Among the distinguished Japanese Old Leysians were Barons Fujimura, Kondo and Masuda, Count Kawamira, Marquis Nabeshima, Viscount Yamanouchi, and Counts Ogasawara and Todo. Count Soyeshima became Lord-in-Waiting to the Crown Prince in 1895 and Master of Ceremonies at the Emperor's Palace in 1896. Count Hirosawa was secretary to the Japanese Premier.

There was a Japanese Society at Cambridge University in the latter part of the 19th century. The minutes of one period show that there were only two undergraduate members, whilst the remaining ones were at The Leys. It is also recorded that Dr Moulton addressed one of their meetings. Because the Japanese would have had little knowledge of English before they came to the school, many of them were over twenty years old whilst there, and Count Todo was twenty four when he left school in 1907. In September of that year he married a widow in London. This caused a scandal in Japan since he was betrothed to a princess of the Royal family. The marriage was dissolved and he returned to Japan, where he did marry, but not one of the princesses.

Between 1892 and 1908, there were seven brothers named Beckett at The Leys, who came from South Africa. They may have heard of The Leys through the sporting record of the three Richards brothers, Joseph (1876-77), William (1884-85) and Alfred (1884-85), who came to The Leys from Capetown, and when they returned had a great influence on both Rugby and Cricket in South Africa (see Chapter 7 - *Leysian Sport*). By 1920 there had been thirty five South African boys at The Leys. A similar number had come from Canada.

When Jews were being threatened in Germany in 1935, the Society of Friends appointed a Germany Emergency Committee. On 27 February, 1935 the committee approached Dr Humphrey, the Headmaster, to see if The Leys would offer places to the sons of German refugees. The Headmaster willingly accepted some, but restricted the number 'because of the denominational nature of the school'. The first of these was Harry Reuter, who joined the school in the Summer term of 1935. He had a distinguished career, becoming Professor of Mathematics at Durham University between 1959 and 1965 and then Professor of Mathematics at Imperial College of Science and Technology between 1965 and 1983.

Another of these refugees, E.O. Brieger (who later changed his name to Blake) read a short paper to the Essay Club in January 1942, describing the internment he had experienced whilst he should have been at The Leys. One day, in 1940 when he was in the Lower Sixth, he was arrested as an alien. In his paper he stressed the bewilderment he had felt at being suddenly snatched from the even tenor of his life at school. The authorities who arrested him were evidently not expecting to have to deal with the large numbers of interned Germans. They had to spend one night in a chilly building which they discovered afterwards was a Wall's ice-cream storage shed, and until they arrived at Huyton, all the places in which they stayed were obviously prepared at very short notice.

At last he arrived in the Isle of Man, and the internees began to organise themselves a little, both for business and for pleasure He described several notable figures in the camp, and the dullness and discomfort of life. The lack of any privacy was the worst trial of all. After a short spell in the Isle of Man, he was taken across to Canada, where the Canadians were expecting to have to accommodate prisoners of war. The misunderstanding annoyed the internees and they held meetings to express their anger. They were particularly upset when the authorities tried to segregate the Jews from the Gentiles, an action which might have simplified feeding arrangements, but which had nothing else to recommend it.

They could go out under guard and do forestry work, a service for which they were paid one shilling a day. During this time his friends and relatives had been trying to procure his release, especially since he had an uncle living in Ontario. After some time he heard that he was to return to England but that he was still to be interned. Great was his joy when, on arriving at Liverpool, he heard his name read out among a list of those who were to be freed. He returned to school after eight months away from it, with a story of bad organisation, inefficiency and officiousness, and with little humour to relieve it. He changed his name from Brieger to Blake, and served in the British forces as a Captain in the Queen's Royal Regiment. After the war he read History at St. John's College, Cambridge. He spent his career lecturing in History at Southampton University.

As well as Breiger, two other Leysians, H.J. Goldschmidt and W.L. Luetkens, also suffered internment. Quite recently, Goldschmidt told me that he would always remember the day he was interned, 1 May, 1940, which was his sixteenth birthday. He was walking past the Dining Hall when he saw two policemen and he sensed quite rightly, that they had come to arrest him. He was taken first to Bury St. Edmunds and then Liverpool, before being sent to the Isle of Man. It was from here that he was deported with the others to Camp T, Internment Operations, Army Base, Canada. The correspondence in the boys' files indicates that efforts were made to get their release into Canadian homes to continue their education. Several organisations had earlier tried to locate them, as their families had had no news of their whereabouts since they had been arrested. In Canada they were treated as Prisoners of War and allowed to send out one letter and one postcard a month, and to receive the same quantity of mail back.

Eventually they were released and allowed to return to England. Luetkens took up his place at Brasenose College, Oxford, and the other two joined The Leys in Pitlochry. It appears that all young aliens living in the Eastern Counties were arrested and interned in 1940. Whereas the Home Office had reassured the parents and the school that the three Leysians could expect an early release, the Prisoner of War Department of the War Office had already sent them to Canada. Goldschmidt eventually qualified as a doctor, but when he applied for medical posts his first six applications were turned down. He changed his name to Goldsmith and received five offers of posts from his next six applications.

Another victim of oppression was Peter Kaldor. He had had to flee Hungary in 1956, at the time of the Russian invasion of that country. He was a talented musician, but knew little English. In his first few weeks at the school, he could be heard playing his trumpet in the music department, expressing his sorrow and anger at having to leave his home. During his year at The Leys, he won the Mann Memorial prize for Music and then went to the Royal College of Music. At one time he played first trumpet in the Sadler's Wells Orchestra and subsequently for the Philomusica of London and the Bournemouth Symphony Orchestra. He also became head of Instrumental Music for the Borough of Hounslow. Similarly, the school has accepted pupils from war-torn Vietnam and from what were formerly parts of Yugoslavia.

Michael Wilcockson, whilst in the Third Form in 1972, carried out a survey of the home addresses of all the boys in the school. Fourteen years later, when he had joined the staff of The Leys, he repeated the exercise. He commented, in the resulting article in *The Fortnightly* in 1986, on how the traditionally high numbers of pupils from the north of England at The Leys had dropped from 73 to 14. He went on to say that the later figures showed also that the tenuous western connection had almost disappeared. However, there was a significant increase in pupils from eastern and southern counties.

For purposes of comparison, the survey was repeated in 1999 (see Table 1). The figures show that in that year only two pupils were from Yorkshire. The overseas pupils in the Autumn term 1999 came from forty different countries, ranging from the traditional far eastern countries which now included China, Taiwan, Korea and Thailand, to several of the former Communist block countries such as Russia and Poland. The numbers coming from China are forecast to rise in the next few years. There were several European countries represented, with Germany providing the largest number, which was fifteen. However, some of those only attended the school for one term, or one year.

Since the table is used to make comparisons with Michael Wilcockson's early statistics, the figures for 1999 do not show the pupils who come from other counties in England, such as Bedfordshire, Oxfordshire and Sussex, nor the two pupils from Scotland.

The increased number from Cambridgeshire in 1999 is due to the creation of a new category of pupil: "day" as opposed to "home boarder". In the late 1990s there was a considerable demand from parents for a shorter school day which would make it feasibile to live further from the school, and still

Table 1: Number of pupils by County and Country

Northern:	1972	1986	1999
Cumbria	2	0	0
Durham	5	0	0
Yorkshire	35	13	3
Lancashire	15	1	0
Cheshire	6	0	2
Midlands:			
Derbyshire	4	0	0
Lincolnshire	10	4	1
Warwickshire	8	0	0
Northamptonshire	6	2	0
Eastern:			
Cambridgeshire	103	155	212
Norfolk	23	14	6
Suffolk	18	26	11
Essex	15	21	44
Southern:			
Hertfordshire	29	32	29
London	10	20	28
Surrey	12	5	0
Buckinghamshire	6	8	2
Western:			
Gloucestershire	5	0	0
Wiltshire	4	1	0
Devonshire	3	0	0
World-wide:			
Malaysia	14	11	6
Singapore	10	3	2
Hong Kong	1	8	8
Totals:			
Pupils from Gt. Britain	352	338	379
Pupils from abroad	62	55	121
Numbers in School	414	393	500

not be a boarder. North B House was converted into accommodation solely for day pupils, who could go home before supper and do their prep at home. This, and the provision of education for the 11-13 range, both boarding and day, has meant that the school numbers reached 500. The five-year plan, set out by the Governors in 1999, allowed for a maximum of 550 pupils which might be achieved three or four years into the new millennium. This number could be accommodated in the existing buildings although there might need to be some enlargement of classrooms. In Table 2, the figures for countries providing more than five pupils in any of the years show an interesting movement during the years just before the millennium. Signs can be seen of the effects of the economic slump in the Far East.

Table 2: Overseas Pupils

	1996/1997	1997/1998	1998/1999	1999/2000
Germany	14	16	17	15
Russia	13	14	14	14
USA		7	9	6
Nigeria	7	8	8	11
China		7	7	7
British Hong Kong	24	21	9	8
Japan	9	5	4	6
Malaysia	6	6	12	7
Singapore	7	7	3	2
Korea		6	5	
Taiwan				5
% Overseas Pupils	28%	28%	29%	24%

Organ in the Great Hall Gallery (see the story on page 271)

CHAPTER SEVENTEEN

Towards One Foundation

Any successful independent school needs to have feeder junior schools to ensure continuity of numbers. Some have their own preparatory schools attached to them. The Governors of The Leys School, having seen the school grow and become soundly established, decided to encourage the foundation of a preparatory school. In 1902 they suggested to J.H. Jenkins, who at the time was assistant Housemaster in North B, that he should start such a school. J.H.S. McArthur, who was by then Secretary to the Governors, offered to join him as a business partner.

Jenkins and his fiancée, Theodora Caldicott Ingram, had already purchased a property in Hitchin on the railway line between Cambridge and King's Cross. Brockton House was set in two acres of land and it seemed an ideal setting for the proposed school. When married in 1903, Jenkins and his wife moved into the house and decided to give the school his wife's second name, so it became Caldicott School. The school opened officially in January 1904 with eight boys. Mrs Jenkins had been a teacher and had decided from the beginning that there should be three forms, so the classes were very small, even when three more boys joined in the following term.

A programme of building was begun which provided classrooms, a gymnasium and a chapel. Since The Leys was a Methodist foundation, so was Caldicott. The school was soon recognised as successful, both academically and on the sports field. Jenkins was a classical scholar and this, together with his strong sense of discipline, had given the school a fine reputation. The First World War brought problems, however, particularly for Mrs. Jenkins, who was responsible for feeding the boys during this time of food shortages. Jenkins sold the school in 1919 to F.V. Bindon, whose approach to running it was less orthodox. In consequence the school's reputation fell and the numbers declined.

Dining Hall - Caldicott School

Chapel - Caldicott School

When Bindon retired through ill-health in 1927, his successor, ~~George~~ *Gordon* Wood, was a cousin of Jenkins, the first Headmaster. He soon improved the standards and the school regained its former standing in the town. In 1936 Wood offered a partnership to one of his staff, Jack Shewell Cooper, who accepted providing that the school moved to a bigger site. An estate of seventeen acres was found at Farnham Royal, Buckinghamshire, and the move was successfully made. However, the formal association with The Leys was lost, since the school was now so far from Cambridge. It still flourishes today as a boys' school of over 140 boarders and 100 day boys.

St. Faith's had started as a preparatory school shortly after Fellows of Cambridge Colleges were for the first time allowed to marry. R.S. Goodchild started "a preparatory school for the sons of gentlemen" in a wooden hut in the grounds of 1 Belvoir Terrace. F.M. White, in *St.Faith's - a Short History*, found that it was difficult to be certain of the exact date of the opening of the school, although he settled for 1884 after much research. The name, St. Faith's, first appeared with the move to the present Trumpington Road address, when School House was built. According to one pupil of that time, the school was named after Goodchild's wife, Faith, although there was some speculation that it might have been after their daughter, who was also called Faith. She taught English to the junior forms. Gwen Raverat, in her autobiography *Period Piece* records that her brother, Charles Darwin, grandson of the author of *The Origin of the Species*, went "fairly young to Goody's (St. Faith's)", so it would seem that the school had a nickname derived from the name of the first Headmaster. Many of the pupils of those early days were to rise to high academic office. Four, including Charles Darwin (Christ's), became Masters of Cambridge Colleges. The others were: G.A. Chase, Selwyn, E.M. Tillyard, Jesus and J.A. Venn, Queens'.

Goodchild retired in 1909 and sold the school to H. Lower, who was the son of the Rector of Fowlmere. The school continued to flourish during the war years, and was run on the same lines as under Goodchild, with the owner taking on a full teaching load with assistance from his wife and daughter. Lower was a classics graduate from Oxford and taught Latin and Greek well. He also took the Maths classes, though it is reported less well. He was in the habit of going abroad during the Easter holidays and returning with a collection of post cards, which he showed the boys, using an epidiascope, during lectures in the Christmas term. Lower's daughter taught French throughout the school, and his cousin, Mr. Fulford, was Senior Master. He was described as a "cricketer, musician, lecturer, producer, stage-manager and carpenter". Lower introduced the concept of the extended day, with extra fees payable for preparation, tea and dinner. St. Faith's in the late 1990s offers breakfast for pupils and parents, but with no boarders, dinner is not an option.

From the memory of one pupil when Lower was Headmaster, the sanitation was primitive and consisted of three or four earth closets. One notable sportsman of this era was W.G.R.M. Laurie, who became an Olympic oarsman. Duleepsinhji had also been at the school during this time. Already an excellent cricketer, he eventually got a Cambridge Blue for cricket and played for India. He was not allowed to play for the school eleven however, as he was over prep school age, and was at St. Faith's to follow a course to prepare him for his Public school and Cambridge. In 1927, Lower retired and the school came into the ownership of W.G. Butler who had been a Housemaster at Christ's Hospital.

Butler kept meticulous records, and from his arrival at the school there are complete records of pupils. He broadened the classroom studies with a wide range of lectures from a list of distinguished speakers. Extramural activities grew with his son, C.G. Butler, leading many expeditions of the Field Club and the Meteorological Society to record the patterns of weather. One notable account was of Sports Day, 1929, when 2¼ inches of rain fell from 6 pm until midnight. The sporting events finished at 6 pm and because of the deluge many parents were forced to shelter at the school. Butler also introduced the 'Staff Entertainment' and the annual fireworks party.

The days of schools being owned by the Headmaster were drawing to a close. By 1938 few schoolmasters were able to raise enough capital to buy the premises and the goodwill of schools. The Leys had lost touch with Caldicott and required another feeder school.

At the suggestion of The Leys Headmaster, Dr Humphrey, the Governors bought St. Faith's School. One of the great advantages to both schools was the proximity of the two sites. W.G. Butler remained as the salaried Head, and continued to run the school on exactly the same lines as before. This amalgamation into the Leys Foundation enabled the school to purchase Firwood, the house next to St. Faith's, in September 1938. The Leys made part of its Latham Road sports field and also the swimming bath available for use by St. Faith's.

It was thought that there might be an interchange of teaching staff between the two schools, and also access to the laboratories and Art School for St. Faith's. However, it was soon discovered that teaching 7 to 13 year olds is very different from teaching 14 to 19 year olds. It is reported that The Leys staff, in particular, found teaching the younger boys uncongenial. Just as the school was settling to a new stable structure, war broke out and Cambridge was declared a potential danger area.

In the same way in which The Leys took over an hotel in Scotland, Mr Butler took 16 boarders to the Golden Lion Hotel in Ashburton, Devon. Mr. H.B.C. English, who had just retired as Headmaster of Ardvreck School in Crieff, was persuaded to become Headmaster of the day boys, who stayed in the Trumpington Road premises. English's daughter, Margaret, later became the secretary to the Bursar of The Leys, and finally became the Assistant Bursar. Firwood was not available for St. Faith's to use, because it had been requisitioned by the Navy. The autumn term 1940 started with 23 boarders in Ashburton and 50 day boys in Cambridge.

The boarders seem to have integrated into the life of Ashburton, and enjoyed picnics, church fêtes and swimming. In Cambridge, Mr English taught the boys himself with the help of Mr. Madge, Mr Michael and Miss Michael. Despite the disturbance by air-raids, and rationing of materials, the school flourished. By the summer of 1945, there were 37 boarders in Ashburton and 114 day-boys in Cambridge. During the hostilities eight Old Fidelians were killed. The school is particularly proud of one of them, Flying Officer L.T. Manser, who was posthumously awarded the Victoria Cross. A photograph of him, together with a copy of the citation, hangs in the new Ashburton Hall. The official citation from the London Gazette of 23 October, 1942, reported his heroic deed:

"Flying Officer Manser was captain and first pilot of a Manchester aircraft which took part in the mass raid on Cologne on the night of 30th May, 1942. As the aircraft was approaching its objective, it was caught by searchlights and subjected to intense and accurate anti-aircraft fire. Flying Officer Manser held on his dangerous course and bombed the target from a height of seven thousand feet, then set course for base. The Manchester had been

The Golden Lion, Ashburton

damaged and was still under heavy fire. Flying Officer Manser took evasive action, turning and descending to under a thousand feet. It was of no avail. The searchlights and flak followed him until the outskirts of the city were passed. The aircraft was hit repeatedly and the rear gunner was wounded, the front cabin filled with smoke, the port engine was overheating badly. The pilot and crew could all have escaped safely by parachute. Nevertheless Flying Officer Manser disregarding the obvious hazards, persisted in his attempts to save the aircraft and crew falling into enemy hands. He took the aircraft up to two thousand feet then the port engine burst into flames. It was ten minutes before the fire was mastered but then the engine went out of action for good. Part of one wing was burnt and the air speed of the aircraft dangerously low. Despite all the efforts of pilot and crew the Manchester began to lose height. At the critical moment Flying Officer Manser once more disdained the alternative of parachuting to safety with his crew. Instead, with grim determination he set a new course for the nearest base, accepting for himself the prospect of almost certain death in a firm resolve to carry on to the end. Soon the aircraft became extremely difficult to handle and when a crash was inevitable, he ordered the crew to bail out. A sergeant handed him a parachute but he waved it away, telling the non-commissioned officer to jump at once as he could hold the aircraft steady for a few seconds more. While the crew were descending to safety they saw the aircraft still carrying their captain plunge to earth and burst into flames. In pressing home this attack in the face of strong opposition, and striving against heavy odds to bring back his aircraft and crew and finally when in extreme peril thinking only of the safety of his comrades, Flying Officer Manser displayed determination and valour of the highest order."

Manser's was no vain sacrifice. Within a matter of weeks his entire crew, with the exception of the navigator, who was injured in his parachute fall, were back in England, having been passed through the underground escape route system through Brussels, Paris and the Pyrenees to Gibraltar. Once in England, they were able to recount their Captain's actions and he was awarded a posthumous Victoria Cross.

During this period of the war, another Old Fidelian, Sub/Lt. W.R. Nickson, R.N.V.R., was awarded the George Medal on 3 November, 1942 "for gallantry and dauntless devotion to duty'. He had worked on mine dispersal on land and under water. There were three events recorded in the citation, off the East Anglian Coast on 14 May, 1941, off Watchett on 18 December, 1941, and at Puckpool, off Ryde Sands on 30 June to 1 July, 1942.

By September 1945, there were 49 boarders and 112 day boys back in Cambridge. Firwood had been de-requisitioned and the Governors had purchased the next two houses in Trumpington Road, Leyspring and Southfield, during the previous summer holidays, but they were still occupied by the beginning of term. Faced by all the problems of running a school well over twice the size he had had before the war, Butler appointed F.M. White as Bursar. 'Tim' White was subsequently to write a short history of St. Faith's which has provided most of the material for this chapter. In 1946 he had just been demobilised from the R.A.F. and tackled his new post with great enthusiasm. No task, from reorganising Butler's filing system to dealing with an outbreak of dysentery in the school, seems to have dismayed him. However he did receive an early shock when Butler announced that he was going to retire, largely on account of his wife's ill-health. Although as Bursar he had to deal with the applications for the post of Butler's successor, White himself was appointed to be the next Headmaster.

In August 1946, Butler retired with his wife to Ringstead in Dorset, where she died five years later. He was then ordained, and became first Rector of Overmoigne in Dorset and later Vicar of Harlow. The first task which faced White when he became Headmaster on 1 September, 1946, was to move out of Southfield, in which he and his wife had been living, into Firwood. This gave room to move some of the beds from School House into Southfield. The occupants of Leyspring, who were still there although the house had been purchased the year before, moved out as they had promised. Unfortunately squatters moved in.

By now interest in private education was growing throughout the country, and this was particularly true in Cambridge. St. Faith's entered the happy period of having waiting lists and full numbers. There was pressure from the Colleges to take more pupils, since applicants from other Universities were turning down offered appointments because of the shortage of preparatory school places for their sons. By 1959, the sons of dons made up nearly one third of the intake and accounted for half of the scholarships won since 1946.

Goodchild's school had had 63 pupils in 1898, but from then on there was a drop in numbers. It is to this that F.M. White attributes the reason for the sale to Lower, with presumably a low fee for the 'good will' of the business. The numbers then started to rise until 1924 when there were 62 pupils. After this came another drop in numbers to 28 pupils, and this was probably the reason for the sale of the school to Butler, who soon restored the numbers to over 60. However, the amalgamation with the Leys, and an injection of capital, enabled the school to expand. In 1946 the pupils numbered 160, rising through 200 in 1966 to 300 in 1979. In the 1990s, the school had reached the remarkable figure of 500, with waiting lists into the new Millennium.

The present Headmaster, Richard Dyson, was educated at Queen Elizabeth's Grammar School, Wakefield and Nottingham University, where he captained the cricket side. His first teaching post in 1963 was at Highgate Junior School. Bertie Bellis, later to be Headmaster of The Leys, was on the staff of the senior school, and at that time Richard taught one of the Bertie's sons. In 1977 he became Headmaster of Wellingborough Junior School, where he stayed until appointed to St. Faith's in 1989.

In the early 1990s, both preparatory and senior schools throughout the country were experiencing a drop in demand for boarding places. With only 34 boarders in the academic year 1993-4 and registrations for that Autumn only in the teens, it was decided to close Leyspring and rearrange the accommodation so that a pre-Prep department could be opened. The Governors decided that the remaining numbers of boarders would be gradually reduced, so the total in Firwood and Southfield declined over the next two years. Eventually the remaining boarders were housed 'en famille' with staff in Firwood, for a few months.

As the pre-prep department increased in popularity, there was pressure on St. Faith's to accept children aged between 4 and 5. The Headmaster of St. Faith's took the decision to relocate the entire pre-prep to Southfield, where the building could accommodate six forms. When boarding ceased completely, Firwood became a suite of rooms for Information Technology and individual need support.

The Headmaster of St. Faith's School, Richard Dyson

The Duke of Edinburgh is welcomed by some of the younger pupils

Photo by courtesy of Jet Photographic - The Cambridge Studio

Co-education started on a small scale, with four girls in 1995. Very soon the total number of pupils rose, and by 1999 it reached over 500. One unusual facility the school kitchens offer is breakfast for pupils and other members of their families, from 7.15am to 8.30am. Over 400 meals are served each week, with a different menu for each day. Not only parents, but siblings at other schools join the St. Faith's pupils for the meal. The school offers an extended day to pupils with both parents working. They can stay and be supervised in activities and doing prep. Recognising that school holidays can also cause problems for working parents, holiday activities are provided for those who require them.

Although many St. Faith's pupils move up into The Leys as their senior school, others choose to go elsewhere when they leave. The children are prepared for National Curriculum Key Stages 1 and 2 and for scholarships at a variety of senior schools. Some of the subjects for entry to The Leys are judged by continuous assessment, with consultation between the heads of departments of the two schools. Continuous assessment gives The Leys insight into the ability of St. Faith's pupils long before they would have had the results of the Common Entrance Examination for guidance. As a result of these changes, The Leys took the decision to offer places for entry at age 13 in the February, rather than after Common Entrance in June, thus bringing it into line with the other senior schools in the Cambridge area. St. Faith's has registered for Key Stages 1 and 2 tests in June 2000, and will therefore be included in the national Primary Schools League tables.

Year 3 to Year 8 Pupils also have one period of Music and Drama, Design and Technology, Information Technology and Physical Education as well as Sport each week. The facilities for specialised subjects were recently enhanced by the construction of Ashburton Hall, named after the place of war-time exile of the boarders of St. Faith's. This building was opened by H.R.H. The Duke of Edinburgh on 2 February, 1999. This added to the long list of Royal visits to the Foundation.

On entering the lobby to the Hall, where he unveiled a commemorative plaque, the Duke first met the Governors. Although not all were present, he was obviously surprised by the large number. He asked how many there were, and when he was told "about thirty one", he said that that was too many and "our good Lord managed with only twelve". After unveiling the plaque and signing the Visitors' Book, he met staff and Old Fidelians. Whilst

The Duke meets the staff of Chartwells

The Duke of Edinburgh inspects the F.O. Manser display

Photos by courtesy of Jet Photographic - The Cambridge Studio

The Duke inspects some of the exhibits

inspecting exhibits of the pupils' work, he was entertained by various musical arrangements.

To bring children into Cambridge from many outlying towns and villages, several coaches are provided. However, it is not convenient for every family to take advantage of these services. St. Faith's and The Leys are only two of a large number of schools causing traffic congestion during school terms. By comparison, traffic at peak times of the day is amazingly light during the school holidays. In quite a small area there are two large Sixth Form Colleges, the Perse Boys' and Girls' schools and their prep schools, St. Mary's School and its Junior department and King's College and St. John's College Schools. The Bursars of The Leys and St. Faith's have spent a great deal of time in recent years consulting parents on ways in which pupils can get to and from school without contributing to the traffic chaos. Experimental use of the Park and Ride system was initiated by the schools, with the opening of the Babraham Road site which completed the ring of such sites around the edge of the city. At first people were not convinced that this was a safe way, particularly for young children, to be brought to school. Any further development on the St. Faith's site will be subject to strict controls by the City Planning department, to avoid further traffic congestion.

In the summer holidays of 1999, the large classroom next to the old music room was divided into two. One half became a new print room with an upper level and the other half became a new office for the Registrar. The Bursar was relocated to a less exposed office at the rear of the building, and the Headmaster and his secretary exchanged rooms. The room now occupied by the Headmaster will be remembered by many as the one which had a metal fire escape extending over its bay window. On occasions during the Headship of Malcolm MacInnes, he would insist that children and staff use this escape route during fire drill. The final steps to the ground were very hazardous since the escape came to an end over a prickly pyrocanthus bush.

Also in July 1999, a further building expansion began, with the complete renovation of the school's kitchen and dining room. For several decades they had functioned as they did when the school was half its present size. It was not possible to complete the work for the beginning of the Autumn term, so for the whole term the school ate food prepared off-site, using disposable plates and cutlery. It was very much to the credit of the Catering Manager and her staff that breakfast and team teas all went ahead as if nothing was amiss.

CHAPTER EIGHTEEN

Odds and Ends

There are some interesting curiosities concerning the school that have not found a place in the preceding chapters, but still deserve to be recorded.

THE JOHN WESLEY ARTEFACTS

In 1950, the school was given three objects connected with John Wesley, the founder of Methodism, by an Old Leysian, L.H.R. Rigg.

One was a small wooden model, about 8" tall, of Wesley himself, carved from a piece of wood salvaged from the Great Fire of London. This has a nodding head and originally it was wearing a tri-corn hat, which was unfortunately lost. The hat was fairly heavy and made the head shake from side to side, which was supposed to convey Wesley's disapproval of the wickedness of the country during his ministry.

Next was a pair of taper holders which were used by Wesley during his wayside sermons. They are about 6" high without the tapers. Last came a small rosary used by Wesley. Rigg, in his letter to the Headmaster when presenting the objects, wrote "certain Methodists have been rather annoyed with me for daring to make such a suggestion (that Wesley had a rosary) but it must be remembered that Wesley was originally a Church of England priest and in fact never expressed any desire to leave the Church". A leading authority on rosaries from Julian's Shrine in Norwich examined the beads a few years ago and confirmed that the style was certainly that used by priests during Wesley's lifetime.

Rigg wrote that he wanted The Leys "to have these articles as I feel they are not fully appreciated by my family now but may be by the Greatest Methodist School". Rigg's mother had been given them by her sister who was married to Sebastian Wesley, a descendent of the Wesley family.

Portrait of John Wesley

Wesley's Rosary

*Statuette of Wesley made of timber
salvaged from the Great Fire of London*

Wesley's travelling candlesticks

At the time of the gift to The Leys, there were no living relatives who could clarify whether Sebastian was a descendent of Charles Wesley by direct line or from John through his adopted grandchildren. In 1751, John had married Mary Vazeille, a widow, by whom he had no children. By all accounts the marriage was not a happy one and she finally left him. However John, having no children of his own, referred in his Will to the children of the daughter of Mrs Vazeille as his grandchildren.

In the late 1970s, a stand was made for the rosary which is on display, together with the candlesticks, in the Headmaster's study,

THE ARMS AND CREST OF THE SCHOOL

When it was planned that King George V would visit the school to inaugurate the new Library Block, the Governors asked the King of Arms to approve a device used by the school since its foundation, and designed by Mrs. Moulton, the Headmaster's wife. This consisted of a gold chevron upon a blue shield; above the chevron a red rose between two silver mullets (spur-rowels); below it an open book with pages of silver edged with gold, above and on each side of the book three seven-pointed golden stars.

Mrs. Moulton, in a letter to J.C. Isard dated 3 September, 1908, wrote:

"You asked about the School coat of arms - the origin of which has naturally remained in obscurity, this being of entirely 'home manufacture'. The history is, simply, that in those early days when everything had to be made, and a good many small matters, therefore, came to me for the making, Dr Moulton asked me to design 'something simple and heraldically correct', whilst he supplied the motto. I should add that the design was submitted to a heraldic expert before it became the School crest, and approved by him - though I have by this time forgotten the meaning of my own ideas, except in the open book!"

Dr Humphrey wrote an article about this first coat of arms in the 1956 *Leys Handbook and Directory*. In it he said:

"Although by 1908 Mrs Moulton had forgotten what she meant some of the symbols to signify, the open book and the spurs (denoting stimulus as applied in its various ways by Dr Moulton and his colleagues and their successors) are appropriate for a school. (The open book appears on the Arms of the University of

311

Modern Crest

Crest pre-1914

Oxford; the book is closed on the Arms of the University of Cambridge). The stars probably symbolise aspiration - or faith and hope in higher things. The significance of the red rose is obscure. The red rose appears in triplicate on the arms of Trinity College, Cambridge. The two roses on the arms of the city of Cambridge are silver. The explanation may be that several of the founders of the school were from Lancashire."

"The original version was often copied incorrectly, the commonest mistake being a failure to distinguish between the five-pointed silver spurs and the seven-pointed golden stars. The memorial tablet in the Chapel on the North wall to J.G. Bainbridge has silver spurs with six points instead of five and golden stars with five points instead of seven. The same is true of the tablet on the opposite wall to G.P.B. Bickford-Smith, with the added defect that the red of the rose has flaked off leaving a golden rose. The example in one of the stained glass windows of the staff common room shows the spurs and stars correctly coloured and pointed though the rose is colourless - probably due to the original colour having faded."

The original arms, though heraldically correct, were drastically redesigned by Sir Farnham Burke, Norroy King of Arms and his colleagues at the College of Arms, and the official grant and assignation of the present Arms and Crest were presented on 31 March, 1914, ready for King George's visit in May.

The document, with its impressive attached three seals, hangs at the time of writing this book in the Old Gymnasium. The meaning of the shield is, in the main, clear. The red cross signifies the Christian foundation of the School, the open book and the lighted lamp are symbols of learning, and the spur rowel probably denotes stimulus. The significance of the red roses is obscure. As suggested above, the explanation may be the fact that several of the school's founders were from Lancashire. The crest which was added to the Coat of Arms consists of an esquire's helmet, which is usually borne by a corporate body, and above the helmet, a wyvern. The wyvern, the crest used by the Wesley family, was added to signify the association of The Leys with the Wesleyan Methodist Church. All Wesleyan schools throughout the world include the wyvern in their crest. Dr Moulton's original motto "In Fide Fiducia' (in faith is our trust) is included below the shield.

THE DURELL STAMP COLLECTION

In 1936, Colonel A.J.V. Durrell, who had retired the previous year as Bursar, presented to the School his specialised collection of stamps of the Orange Free State and Orange River Colony. The collection contained over 12,000 stamps in six volumes. It is rated as one of the three great collections in the world of this period of philately in this South African State. It contains mainly 1d and 2d stamps of that period, with examples of rare imperfections and overprinting during the Boer War. The albums fill a small safe in the school.

Apparently stamps of the Orange Free State were virtually abandoned by serious collectors after the Boer War. They did continue to attract the attention of a discriminating few, of whom Colonel Durell was one. In 1953, a small band of enthusiasts founded the Orange Free State Study Circle with the intention of studying the stamps, cancellations and postal history of that era, and to publish a handbook about them.

They studied five collections of the stamps. One belonged to the Queen, two had been bequeathed to the British Museum, a fourth to the University of Manchester and the fifth one was at The Leys. In their book they described the Durell Collection as one of the most important extant specialised collections of the Orange Free State and said that it had proved to be a most valuable source of reference material.

THE LMS RAILWAY POSTER

For many years, a painting by Norman Wilkinson of the King's Building was on display in the School Library. A few copies of the poster which depicted the painting still exist at the school. It had appeared in a series of railway posters entitled 'Famous Great Public Schools on the LMS line' (London, Midland and Scottish). However Cambridge at that time was on the LNER line (London and North Eastern Railway). When the series was being prepared by the artist, the Chairman of the Governors of The Leys, Lord Stamp, was also Chairman of the LMS. Dr Humphrey, the Headmaster, persuaded Lord Stamp that the school should be included in the series. In so doing, a railway curiosity was produced when it was displayed on LMS stations. Copies of the poster were sold to the boys at the school at the time

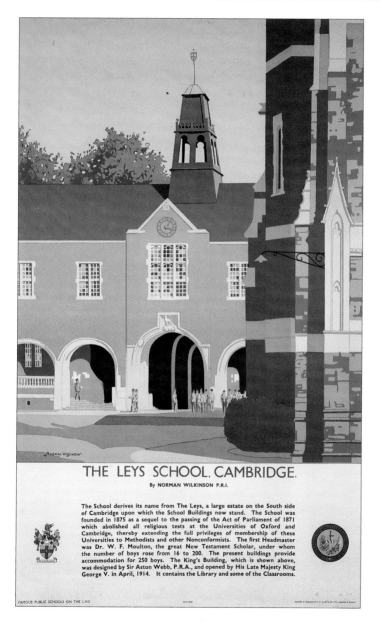

The LMS Poster

for 1/3d (about 6p) each. The school was recently offered a copy by a railway enthusiast for £175!

A great deal of trouble was taken over the description of the school which appeared under the painting on the poster, with several Governors changing the first description suggested by Dr Humphrey. Two in particular felt that the wording laid too much stress on the Methodist and religious side of the school. They went on in their letters to say that many Old Leysian parents, at that time, felt that it was a mistake to emphasise the Methodist associations of the school and to create the impression that it is a purely Methodist school. Neither would they let mention of James Hilton and *Good-bye, Mr Chips* be made, as they felt that this laid too much emphasis on one former pupil.

Other schools in the series of posters included Bedford, Berkhampsted, Fettes, Mill Hill, Oundle, Rugby, St. Paul's, Sedbergh, Stowe and Uppingham. It is interesting that well over half the description of Rugby School concerns the event when William Webb Ellis picked up the ball and ran with it, thus creating the game of Rugby. The World Rugby cup is named after him.

THE SCHOOL MUSEUM

The Museum was started in 1878 by the science master, A.H.S. Lucas. It was kept in a cupboard in the Reading Room until the Great Hall (now the Dining Hall) was built. The Museum was then moved to the largest room underneath the Hall (now the School Shop). Mr. Lucas presented the school with his collection of fossils when he left for Australia in 1882. Meanwhile, more and more objects were being donated or lent to the collection, and it was outgrowing the room.

When the new Science Block was opened in 1893, a purpose built Museum was incorporated into the building, consisting of two rooms, an upper and lower, connected by a spiral staircase. The upper room had balconies at each end, forming galleries. There was a glass case along one entire wall of the lower floor, which was filled with a display of birds and small mammals. The catalogue, published in 1908, shows that there were one hundred and ninety stuffed birds and nine small mammals in the large display case, and another sixty-four birds and mammals in individual glass cases.

The Museum in the Kelvin Building

Under the classification 'Osteology' in the catalogue are listed twenty-five animal skulls, ranging from a cat to an elephant. There was also an entry listing human remains from the Saxon burial ground at Hauxton Mill just outside Cambridge, including seven skulls, thirty vertebrae, and numerous fragments of ribs, a sternum, a complete arm and a child's left foot. Even more unusual was the skeleton of a Dodo.

There were cases with display trays of butterflies and moths, coins, and plaster casts of medallions commemorating famous people. There were even thirty-seven reduced scale plaster plaques of the Parthenon frieze. The original fossil collection had been enhanced by the addition of two more collections and forty-four pages of the catalogue were needed to list the specimens. In this section there was also an extensive range of examples of ores, some of which are used in the Chemistry department today.

Perhaps the most fascinating lists were those of objects of historical and ethnological interest. Several Old Leysians had brought back a range of objects from Australia, including manacles worn by prisoners and a proclamation issued by the Governor of Australia to the Aborigines. Other Old Leysians returning from the Boer War had brought back momentoes, including various shells, a Boer rifle and cartridges recovered from the body of a dead Boer woman.

When The Leys School Missionary Society came into being, a great number of the visiting missionaries presented articles such as a Chinese ink-slab, a compass and a wooden model of a Chinese lady's foot. One intriguing entry was "small ornament made of USA banknotes. Estimated value 10,000 dollars'. If that was its value in 1908, what would it be worth today?

Above the upper room of the Museum was another room for storage, which now houses the majority of the School archives. From this room there was access to a flat area of the roof, where an astronomical telescope could be used. The flat roof has gone and there is no official record of the museum collection being broken up. There is no doubt that much damage was caused when the contents were stored during the move to Pitlochry. When the extension was built in the space between the Kelvin building and the swimming bath in 1957, the lower and upper rooms still existed. The fossils were sold to the Cambridgeshire College of Arts and Technology (now the Cambridge campus of Anglia Polytechnic University). The coins were sold and the plaster-casts thrown away. The ores ended up in the Chemistry Department, and a few of the stuffed birds and bones in the Biology Department.

The Leys must have had one of the finest and most interesting collections of any school. Sadly, it has gone. However, there is no place in the modern curriculum for the study of such exhibits, and public opinion has turned against the display of stuffed animals.

THE SCHOOL WELL

In 1889 an artesian well was sunk 200 feet down into the Greensand layer of a water source which probably rises somewhere in Oxfordshire. When the swimming bath was constructed, the well and its pumps were enclosed in the south-western end of the building. Three pumps lifted water into the tanks, later housed in the top of the tower of the 1928 Science Building. When the demand for water dropped during the day, a smaller single pump kept the tanks topped up. The water was used to fill the swimming pool as well as for domestic purposes.

The water was tested regularly and always pronounced fit for drinking. The pipes carrying the supply around the school buildings were made of iron, and naturally over the years rusting occurred. There was often an outcry at the start of term, especially by the resident staff, when the extra pressure of water in the pipes forced dark red, rusty water out of the taps. After a few hours, clearer water flowed and peace was restored for another term.

The water was very hard and was partly softened by a zeolite bed. Analysis of the water showed that it was high in content of various salts but that the nitrate level was not yet dangerous. However, new European Union legislation would have necessitated a great deal of expenditure to ensure that the water always conformed to the much stricter standards laid down. This meant that the school had to turn to a supply provided by the City Water Board. There had always been a connection to this supply and some usage of it. However, when the school was inspected with a view to becoming a 100% consumer, the water authorities demanded that the pipework was renewed in copper from the 100mm main supply down to the 15mm pipes to the washbasins and lavatories. This was achieved in 1987, after 12 months' work. The well still exists, although the large pumps have gone back to the manufacturer in Cottenham, just outside Cambridge, as a museum piece, and a small standby pipe has been installed for some non-personal usage of the well water.

BOOK OF SPORTS

There is one copy of *The Leys School Book of Sports*, dated 1882, in the school archives. It lists comprehensive rules for playing Cricket, Rugby and Association Football, Lacrosse, Racquets, Fives and Tennis. In most cases, the rules still apply to the various sports, whether they are played in the school or nation-wide.

However, Cricket **Rule 44** states that after the delivery of FOUR balls, the umpire must call "over". **Rule 42** says "No Umpire shall be allowed to bet". The next rule allows for transgression of rule 42 to lead to the Umpire's dismissal by either side.

Some of the 60 rules of Rugby show what a different game it was then from now.

Rule 18. In the event of any player holding or running with the ball being fairly tackled, and the ball fairly held, he must cry *down,* and immediately put it down.

Rule 32. (This provided alternative methods for returning the ball to play after it had gone into touch, in a game which did not yet have line-outs for that purpose) He must either (i) bound the ball in the field of play, and then run with it, kick it, or kick it back to his own side; or (ii) throw it out at right angles to the touch line; or (iii) walk out with it at right angles to the touch-line, any distance not less than five nor more than fifteen yards, and there put it down, first declaring how far out he intends to walk.

Rule 47. This defined a "try at goal" as what is now a conversion after scoring a try. The rule was exactly the same as now.

Rule 48. This dealt with the procedure to be followed when a try had been scored between the posts. The attempt at conversion had to be taken in line with either of the upright posts and not in the centre.

Rule 49. This defined a "punt out". There was no need to try to convert the try. Instead a player on the scoring side could "make a mark on the goal line where the ball had been touched down and then punt back to his own side who could endeavour to make a fair catch, or get the ball and *run in* (score another try) or *drop goal.*

At the back of the book was a list of fines. The heaviest fine was for wearing First XV or XI colours when not entitled to wear them, or not turning up to play for those teams if selected. 5/- (25p) was the fine, which would have been a considerable sum in 1882. For similar transgressions against the Second teams, the fine was half the amount, i.e. 2/6. The list continued with a scale of smaller fines. It was 1/- for going on to the Racquet or Fives courts without india-rubber shoes. Anyone going on the Courts, on hands and knees, or with no shoes at all, would be rigorously fined. It was also an offence to walk on the cricket pitch or enter the tuck-shop on stilts. There was a strict rule about which way boys could cycle round the school and no one was allowed to cut or walk on desks. Spillages at meals were charged 3d, 6d or 1/- according to circumstances.

Index